CLEVELAND CAVALIERS A–Z

ROGER GORDON

FOREWORD BY WORLD B. FREE

SPORTS PUBLISHING

Sports Publishing books may be purchased in bulk at special discounts for sales promotion, corporate gifts, fund-raising, or educational purposes. Special editions can also be created to specifications. For details, contact the Special Sales Department, Sports Publishing, 307 West 36th Street, 11th Floor, New York, NY 10018 or sportspubbooks@skyhorsepublishing.com.

Sports Publishing® is a registered trademark of Skyhorse Publishing, Inc.®, a Delaware corporation.

Visit our website at www.sportspubbooks.com.

10 9 8 7 6 5 4 3 2 1

Library of Congress Cataloging-in-Publication Data is available on file.

Cover design by Tom Lau
Cover photo credits: Left, The Cleveland Press Collection, Michael Schwartz Library, Cleveland State University; right, AP

ISBN: 978-1-61321-997-3
Ebook ISBN: 978-1-68358-001-0

Printed in the United States of America

Table Of Contents

FOREWORD

World B. Free

I am not going to lie. I was less than thrilled when I got traded to the Cavaliers from Golden State in mid-December 1982. When I got the news, I was in shock. I was coming from a team that was struggling somewhat to a team that only wished it was in the Warriors' shoes. The Cavs had finished just 15-67 the season before. By the time I played my first game in the wine and gold, the team had won just three of 23 games in 1982–83.

Upon arriving in Cleveland, I began hearing all the horror stories about the owner, Ted Stepien. Stepien was pretty much running the franchise into the ground by way of wacky trades and other goofy moves, with players coming and going all the time, and had his eyes set on Toronto becoming the team's new home. It was a chaotic situation, to say the least. And the fans had long since become fed up with Stepien. We were playing before minuscule crowds at The Coliseum. It was a nightmare.

I knew firsthand that Cleveland was a good basketball town. I remembered, from my early years with Philadelphia, fans flocking to The Coliseum to watch very talented Cavs teams. They had guys like Austin Carr, Dick Snyder, Bingo Smith, Campy Russell, Jim Cleamons, and Jim Chones.

Times had changed, though. Boy, had they ever. When I first got to Cleveland, during a game you could dribble the basketball and hear the echo across the entire arena! Dribbling one basketball sounded like 10 basketballs dribbling at one time! When the coach would yell a play, all of the fans knew what the play was because there were about 12 people there!

However, even though I was in a lousy situation, I tried, like I always do in any aspect of my life, to turn a negative into a positive. I remember telling a reporter, "Before I leave here, this place is gonna sell out. This is the beginning of a new beginning."

The Cavaliers played much better the rest of that 1982-83 season than they had before I got there, finishing with 23 wins. With Stepien thankfully gone and under new—and much more stable—owners Gordon and George Gund, our win total jumped to 28 in 1983-84. Under new head coach George Karl, who replaced Tom Nissalke, we got off to an atrocious start, however, in 1984-85, losing 19 of our first 21 games.

I had played against George in the pros and knew he was a hard-nosed guy. It was his way or the door. We butted heads a couple of times during that terrible start. He wanted me to take fewer shots and be more of a distributor of the ball. I knew, though, that I could still roll and do what I did best, and that was shoot the ball. His way obviously wasn't working, and he realized it was killing my game, too. George and I had a meeting in his office that was very productive. We realized we needed each other to turn this thing around, and we finally found a happy medium and got on the same page. He allowed me to take my shots again, but I began involving my teammates more. I even became a decoy at times. I saw that the other players were growing, and I began to have more confidence that they'd hit their shots when I'd pass the ball to them.

We started playing much better ball. With veterans like Phil Hubbard and Johnny Davis and youngsters such as Roy Hinson, John Bagley, and Paul Thompson contributing big time, we began to come together and grow as a team. Fueled by a pair of six-game winning streaks, incredibly we put ourselves in position to earn the franchise's first postseason berth in seven years. And, on April 9, we did just that with a 114–100 victory over New Jersey in front of more than 10,000 raucous fans at The Coliseum. That attendance figure might not sound all that impressive to younger fans, but considering that we regularly played before home crowds in the 3,000–4,000 range when I first got to Cleveland, it was reason to celebrate. We finished with a 36-46 record that was good enough for the eighth and final seed in the Eastern Conference playoffs.

Our first-round opponent was top-seeded Boston, the defending NBA champion, a team that finished a league-best 63-19 and was led by future Hall of Famers Larry Bird, Kevin McHale, and Robert Parish. No one gave us a chance, but I felt we could beat the Celtics, I really did, especially after the first game up in Boston when we lost by only three points. We wound up losing the series three games to one, but, man, did we ever throw a scare into those boys from Beantown. We gave them everything we had and more. Every game was close. It just didn't go our way at the end of the three games we lost.

What made that Boston series even more special to me was the fact that, in the last two games at The Coliseum, we played before sellout crowds of nearly 21,000, bringing to reality exactly what I had told that reporter some two years earlier. It was beautiful. It was like my championship! To put it in perspective, what we accomplished in Cleveland in that 1984-85 season was an even bigger thrill for me, believe it or not, than when I was a member of the Philadelphia team eight years earlier that advanced all the way to the NBA Finals. True, I was a key cog for that Philly club, but that squad had guys like Dr. J., George

McGinnis, and Doug Collins. The Cleveland situation was more of a challenge for me. I was in my early-30s and on my last legs. After all the work I had put into basketball, building that place back up was my greatest achievement. It was something that was really needed because, although many people consider Cleveland to be a Browns town first and an Indians town second, basketball is very, very important to that city.

I was awfully proud of the LeBron James–led Cavaliers who in 2016 brought a championship to a title-starved town that deserved one like no other. There is one other thing I would like to see while I am still alive—and that is to have 21, my jersey number with the Cavs, hanging in the rafters of The Q. Even if it never happens, though, I will always have fond memories of my four years in Cleveland.

Especially that remarkable playoff run 32 years ago that brought excitement back to Cavaliers basketball after some very dark days.

PREFACE

My number one Cavs memory is when LeBron James and company defeated the Golden State Warriors in Game 7 of the NBA Finals on June 19, 2016, giving the city of Cleveland its first major professional sports championship in more than half a century. The spectacular parade and rally downtown three days later brought chills up my spine. Odds are, though, that my second-favorite Cavaliers memory will shock you. I'd put money on it.

The Miracle of Richfield? I barely missed out on all the fun, as I began following the Cavs the very next season. The near upset of Larry Bird and Boston in the 1985 playoffs? Nope. The next season's NBA Draft day that brought to town Brad Daugherty, Ron Harper, and Mark Price? Uh-uh. The Game 7 blowout of the Celtics in Bird's farewell six years later that I witnessed in person? Not. The 2003 Draft Lottery that brought to town the one and only LeBron James? His buzzer beater against the Magic six years later? Try again.

My second-most cherished Cavaliers memory came when I was 12, soon to be 13, years old, long before LeBron was even a passing thought in his mother's mind. It was a game against Bird, just a rookie then, and Boston on the night of March 22, 1980, toward the end of a season in which Cleveland finished just 37-45. The game wasn't even on TV locally, since it was back in the days when most went untelevised. I listened to Joe Tait's radio call of the Cavs' 109–105 victory—win number eight in a row—that inched them closer to a coveted playoff berth, which seemed impossible two weeks beforehand. The contest was played at a rocking Coliseum before nearly 20,000 fans. I believe, at that time, it was the most exciting Cavaliers home game since the Miracle of Richfield, even more so than the thrilling, four-overtime shocker over Magic Johnson and the Lakers some two months earlier.

The great thing about being a sports fan is that, just like in all aspects of life, everyone has an opinion. Debating who the best player is, what the best team is, who the best coach is . . . that's what it's all about.

The Cavaliers have definitely had their ups and downs throughout their 46 seasons, from their 15-win expansion year all the way to their 2015-16 championship season. *Cleveland Cavaliers A–Z* offers fans a chance to relive their favorite memories from Cavs history, plus many more, in a unique format—more than 550 items of interest, including every single player who ever suited up for the Cavs, within 26 chapters for each letter of the alphabet, plus individual, team, and attendance statistics.

It is quite possible that I am the only Cavs fan out there who has such a strong recollection of that 1980 game against the Celtics. But that's okay.

After all, to each his own.

DECADE-BY-DECADE TIMELINE

1970-71 to 1979-80

It was an inauspicious start for the Cavaliers in their inaugural season of 1970-71. Under owner Nick Mileti and head coach Bill Fitch, they lost their first 15 games, including a 141–87 thrashing by Philadelphia. Win number one came by a 105–103 score at fellow expansion team Portland. The Cavs then lost 12 more in a row to fall to an appalling 1-27. Their first win at home, the decrepit Cleveland Arena, was by a 108–106 score over their other fellow expansion club, Buffalo. The Cavs dropped to 3-37 before winning two straight games for the first time, both at home—120–107 over the Braves the day after Christmas and 114–101 over the 76ers two days later. The Cavaliers, who were led by Walt Wesley and John Johnson, finished 15-67 and in the far reaches of the Central Division basement.

The Cavs slowly and steadily progressed, for the most part, in the coming years. They improved to 23-59 in 1971-72 and 32-50 in 1972-73 but dropped to 29-53 in 1973-74, their final season at the Cleveland Arena. By the time The Coliseum, a brand new basketball palace in nearby Richfield, became their home in 1974-75, the Cavaliers' roster had some talented players on it like Jim Cleamons, Dick Snyder, Foots Walker, Austin Carr, Bingo Smith, Jim Brewer, Campy Russell, and Jim Chones.

Cleveland opened the 1974-75 season with six road games, going 3-3, including a win at defending NBA champion Boston. Unfortunately, the Cavaliers christened The Coliseum by losing badly to the same Celtics. Then they won three games in a row and went on to enjoy a solid first three months of the season, winning 22 of 40 games. They dropped eight straight to fall four games below the .500 mark before winning 10 of 13 to improve to 32-29. The playoffs were a distinct possibility. A seven-game losing streak ensued, however, before the Cavs won seven of 10 to get to 39-39 with four games left. They lost at Houston and Atlanta, then returned home for a crucial contest against New York, another team in the running for an Eastern Conference playoff berth—the biggest game in franchise history to that point. Before a then NBA-record crowd of 20,239, the Cavaliers prevailed 100–95. They needed to win their finale against the Kings three days later on a Sunday afternoon in Omaha, Nebraska, to qualify for the playoffs and close the regular season with a 41-41 record. Unfortunately, they lost 95–94 when Fred Foster's shot from the top

In a key matchup for both teams, the largest crowd ever to watch an NBA game to date—20,239—cheers the Cavs to a 100–95 victory over the Knicks, April 3, 1975. (The Cleveland Press Collection, Michael Schwartz Library, Cleveland State University)

of the key was blocked as time expired. It was a disappointing end to a season filled with hope.

With basically the same cast of characters, the Cavaliers got off to a slow start in 1975-76, losing 10 of their first 16 games. Then, on Thanksgiving Day, they acquired Akron native—and living legend—Nate Thurmond, by way of a trade with Chicago. The Cavs lost four of six games following the trade, but with Thurmond backing up Chones—giving the team a needed defensive presence underneath—they reeled off seven straight wins to improve to 15-14. When they lost to Detroit in overtime on January 7, that dropped them to 18-18, but it would be the last time they would sit at the .500 mark that season. It would be a battle between the Cavaliers and Washington for the Central Division title the rest of the way. With seven players averaging double figures in points per game, led by Chones's 15.8, the Cavs dethroned the five-time defending division champs by a single game, 49-33 to 48-34.

After receiving a first-round bye, the Cavaliers opposed the Bullets in what would turn out to be a memorable seven-game conference semifinal series, with the Cavs coming out on top. Three of their victories came in miraculous fashion—two at The Coliseum—in what would soon become known as the "Miracle of Richfield." Chones broke his right foot in a practice session two days before the start of the conference title series with Boston, ending his season. With Thurmond manning the starting center spot, the Cavaliers took the eventual NBA champions to six tough games before falling, prompting many to opine that the Cavs, not the Celtics, would have won the whole shebang had Chones been in there.

With a healthy Chones back, the Cavaliers raced out of the gates scorching hot in 1976-77, winning their first eight games. They were 16-4—their second-best record ever after 20 games—following a 98–91 overtime win at Kansas City on December 1. They leveled off somewhat and were 27-22 when Thurmond suffered a left knee injury that, for all intents and purposes, ended his career. With Elmore Smith, who had arrived by way of a trade with the Bucks three-and-a-half weeks earlier, helping out underneath, the Cavs finished 43-39, good enough for the sixth and final seed in the Eastern Conference playoff field. In a series not nearly as riveting as the one with Washington the year before, they lost to the Bullets two games to one in the opening round.

The Cavaliers started strong again in 1977–78 but dropped off and struggled to stay above the .500 mark for the majority of the season. A hot finish—nine wins in their last 10 games—resulted in another 43-39 finish and pushed them into the playoffs as the fourth seed. They were quickly vanquished in the opening round, however, by the Knicks two games to none, getting blown out at home 132–114 in Game 1 and falling 109–107 in Game 2 at Madison Square Garden on Spencer Haywood's jumper from the top of the key with two seconds remaining.

The Cavs began the 1978-79 season 4-0 but then lost 14 of their next 15 games. They heated up a little and, after a 112–108 win over the Warriors on January 7, their record stood at 17-22. That was the closest they would come to .500 for the rest of the season. They wound up 30-52 and in fifth place in the Central Division. Fitch resigned after the season.

With Stan Albeck as the new head coach, newcomers Randy Smith, Dave Robisch, and Kenny Carr on the roster, and 1978 first-round draft pick Mike Mitchell coming into his own, leading the team in scoring, the 1979-80 Cavaliers had by far the most potent offense in franchise history. Unfortunately, the team's defense was just about as bad as its offense was good.

The Cavs started poorly but improved to 19-20 by the New Year. An atrocious January and February dropped them to 27-43 in early March. An eight-game winning streak—capped off by an electrifying 109–105 triumph over Boston in a nearly sold-out Coliseum—got them within striking distance of a playoff berth. They fell just short, most likely due to a season-ending injury to Russell halfway through the schedule, splitting their final four games to finish 37-45.

1980-81 to 1989-90

With new owner Ted Stepien doing his best to ruin the franchise in every way imaginable and hothead Bill Musselman as the new head coach, the 1980-81 Cavaliers began the season 12-27 before improving enough to get to 22-32 at the All-Star break. Unfortunately they came out of the break ice cold, dropping five straight games en route to a 28-54 record. New general manager Don Delaney replaced Musselman for the final 11 games.

With empty seats behind them, Ted Stepien (left) and Bill Musselman prior to a home game with Chicago, April 7, 1982. (The Cleveland Press Collection, Michael Schwartz Library, Cleveland State University)

With Stepien (where was Delaney?) making bad, and bizarre, trades and under *four* head coaches—Delaney, Bob Kloppenburg, Chuck Daly, and Musselman again—the 1981–82 Cavaliers lost their final 19 games and finished 15-67. By this time, Stepien was known locally as "Terrible Ted," and his team was referred to by many as the "Cadavers."

With Tom Nissalke the new head coach in 1982-83, the soap opera continued as the Cavs lost their first five games for an NBA record at the time of 24 straight defeats dating back to the previous season. A month-and-a-half into the schedule, a trade that actually benefited the team brought sharpshooter World B. Free to Cleveland from Golden State. Free's long bombs were about all that Cavs fans had to cheer in a 23-59 season.

Just as he was about to finalize a deal that would land the Cavaliers in Toronto, Stepien sold the team to a local group headed by brothers Gordon and George Gund. The Cavs improved in 1983-84 but still finished just 28-54. With George Karl as the new head coach, they began the next season 2-19. However, led by Free and a surprisingly effective supporting cast, including Roy Hinson, Phil Hubbard, and John Bagley, they recovered remarkably, enough for a 36-46 record and the final seed in the conference playoffs, the team's first postseason berth in seven years. Karl's squad put up a gallant effort against Larry Bird and heavy favorite Boston in the first round, losing three games to one in an extremely competitive series.

Cleveland won just 29 games under Karl and Gene Littles in 1985-86. With former Cavalier Lenny Wilkens as the new head coach and Brad Daugherty, Ron Harper, and Mark Price on the roster by way of a remarkable NBA Draft day the previous summer, plus John "Hot Rod" Williams in the fold, the future looked bright despite a 31-51 record.

With Larry Nance's high-wire act in town in 1987-88 due to a late-season trade with Phoenix, the Cavaliers posted their first winning record, 42-40, in a decade and qualified for the playoffs. In what would turn out to be virtually a yearly ritual, they were ousted by Michael Jordan and the Bulls in the first round three games to two. The next year was even more heartbreaking. After waltzing to a franchise-best at the time 57-25 record, the Cavs again lost to the Bulls, a team they had swept all six games from during the regular season, in the first round of the playoffs. This time it was Jordan's buzzer beater—"The Shot"—on May 7 at The Coliseum that eliminated the Cavs, again in a deciding fifth game. With the flashy, and extremely athletic, Harper traded to the Clippers seven games into the 1989-90 season—a controversial move to say the least among Cavs fans—the team finished just 42-40 and again failed to advance past the opening round of the playoffs, losing three games to two yet again, this time to Philadelphia.

1990-91 to 1999-2000

The 1990-91 Cavaliers were ravaged by injuries. They were 8-7 when Price tore his left ACL, ending his season. They were 14-28 when Williams severely sprained his foot, ending his season. The Cavs wound up 33-49. The 1991-92 Cavaliers lost four of their first five games before winning 12 of their next 16 to improve to 13-8. After a loss at New Jersey, they put the pedal to the metal by reeling off 11 straight wins to improve to 24-9. They finished

John "Hot Rod" Williams drives past Larry Bird during the 1992 Eastern Conference Semifinals. (AndersonsClevelandDesign.com)

with a 57-25 record but still 10 games behind Jordan and the Central Division champion Bulls. They ousted New Jersey three games to one in the opening round of the playoffs and then in the conference semifinals eliminated Boston in seven games, dominating the Celtics 122–104 in the deciding game before a sellout crowd of 20,273 at The Coliseum. In the Eastern Conference Finals, the Cavs lost to the Bulls in six games.

The next season, the Cavaliers again started slowly, dropping five of their first eight games. They were 8-11 when they ripped off seven straight wins and 10 of 11. They were 43-27 on April 4 when they went on a 10-game winning skein en route to a 54-28 finish. They beat the Nets again in the opening round of the playoffs, but this time it took five games to do it. In the second round, they were swept in four games by the Bulls, losing the finale 103–101 in heartbreaking fashion at The Coliseum on "The Shot II"—another jumper by Jordan at the buzzer.

With Mike Fratello as the Cavaliers' new head coach in 1993-94, the team started slowly yet again and was just 7-14 a week before Christmas. A five-game winning streak culminating in overtime wins against Indiana and Charlotte, respectively, was exactly what the doctor ordered. Three straight defeats ensued, but that was just an aberration. The Cavs proceeded to win 13 of their next 19 games. A 102–95 home loss to the Knicks on February 17 left them with a 25-24 record. An 11-game winning streak upped their record to 36-24 as they primed themselves for the postseason. They wound up 47-35. Unfortunately, their first-round playoff opponent was—you guessed it—the Bulls. Even minus "M.J.," who at the time was "retired," the Cavaliers could not get over the Windy City hump, getting swept in three games, the fifth time in seven years that their season came to a close with a loss to Chicago. It was only fitting, too, that the clincher—the Cavs' final game ever at The Coliseum—came in heartbreaking fashion yet again, 95–92 in overtime.

By the time the 1994-95 season arrived, the Cavaliers had a new home in downtown Cleveland, Gund Arena. Helping veterans Price and Williams were youngsters like Terrell Brandon, Bobby Phills, Tyrone Hill, and Chris Mills. The Cavs got off to a hot start. They were 20-8 on New Year's Day. They lost 10 of their next 16 games to fall to 26-18 but then won seven of nine to get to 33-20, their high point of the season. Their win-loss record slowly went downhill, and they finished the season 43-39, still, though, good enough for a playoff berth. They were ousted in the first round by New York three games to one.

After a horrendous start to the 1995-96 season in which they lost their first seven games, the Cavaliers picked it up and, after a 92–79 home win over Denver on December 17, were 11-11. They would not fall below the .500 mark the rest of the season. In fact, they heated up even more and, after an eight-game winning streak in late January and February, found themselves with a 30-20 record. They wound up 47-35 but lost to the Knicks again in the first round of the playoffs, this time in three straight games.

The next season, the Cavs won 21 of their first 31 games but then dropped 12 of their next 16 to fall to 25-22. They played just about .500 ball the rest of the way and were battling Washington for the East's eighth and final postseason berth heading into the regular season finale at home against those same Bullets. The winner would qualify for the playoffs; the loser's season would be over. In front of a near-sellout crowd, the Cavs blew a nine-point halftime lead and lost 85–81. They finished with a 42-40 record.

With five-time All-Star Shawn Kemp aboard by way of a trade with Seattle, the 1997-98 Cavaliers began the season 4-6, but a 103–80 rout of Minnesota on November 21 was the start of a 10-game winning streak that fueled their battle for playoff positioning the rest of the season. By March 12, they had fallen to 33-30, but an overtime win against New York helped propel them to a 47-35 finish and the sixth seed in the conference. They were quickly vanquished, however, by the Pacers three games to one in the opening round of the playoffs.

In a lockout-shortened 1998-99 season, the Cavaliers stayed right in the thick of the playoff race until they lost 10 of their last 11 games to finish 22-28 and out of the postseason. Under new head coach Randy Wittman, the Cavs got off to a decent start in 1999-2000, going 11-9 in the first month-and-a-half.

Then the bottom fell out. They lost seven straight games and 10 of 11, which set the tone for the rest of the season. They wound up 32-50 and in the far reaches of the Central Division.

2000-01 to 2009-10

With Zydrunas Ilgauskas, Andre Miller, and Lamond Murray leading the way, the 2000-01 Cavaliers got off to an excellent start, winning 15 of their first 22 games. It was downhill from there, though. By January 19, they were 18-20. Wins over the Trail Blazers and Bulls returned them to the .500 mark, but it was a free fall after that in the form of a 10-game losing streak and a pair of seven-game losing skeins the rest of the way. The Cavs finished 30-52, again in the far reaches of the Central Division.

With John Lucas as the new head coach, the 2001-02 Cavaliers began poorly, losing nine of their first 11 games, hitting the 100-point mark just once. They turned it around somewhat by improving to 13-18 just after the New Year, but a 101–91 loss at Toronto was the start of a 12-game losing streak that included an embarrassing 96–64 defeat at Portland. They finished 29-53, again deep in the Central Division.

The 2002-03 Cavaliers split their first four games, including an 89–70 shocker over the defending NBA champion Lakers in the home opener. Unfortunately, that was Cleveland's high point of the season. The Cavs lost their next 15 games, hitting the century mark just once. Lucas was fired following a 95–78 defeat at Utah that dropped the team's record to an absurd 8-34. Assistant coach Keith Smart replaced Lucas. He wasn't much better, going 9-31 as the team finished 17-65, tied with the Nuggets for by far the worst record in the league.

From the ashes of that disastrous 2002-03 season came the arrival of the one and only LeBron James by way of the Cavaliers winning that spring's NBA Draft Lottery. Under new head coach Paul Silas and with a supporting cast led by Ilgauskas and Carlos Boozer, the Cavs started poorly and were 6-19 on December 17. They began to play better and by January 20 were 14-27. A trade with Portland the next day that brought to town Jeff McInnis was the real spark the team needed. The Cavs won 17 of their next 26 games to improve to 31-36. A season-ending injury to McInnis during a March 16 blowout of the Bulls was exactly what the team *didn't* need. Even with James doing his thing, Cleveland dropped 11 of its next 12 games. Three wins to end the season were not enough as the Cavaliers, who finished 35-47, wound up right behind Boston for the East's final playoff berth.

With Drew Gooden replacing the departed Boozer, the 2004-05 Cavaliers began 0-3 but, beginning with a 93-79 triumph at Atlanta, won nine of their next 10 games to improve to 9-4. By February 23, they were 31-21, and a playoff berth seemed imminent. However, six straight defeats—three of them blowouts—followed. Silas was fired on March 21, the day after a 105–98 loss to the lowly Raptors dropped the team to 34-30. Assistant coach Brendan Malone replaced Silas and went 8-10 the rest of the way, including two wins to finish the schedule, giving Cleveland its first winning season in seven years. It was bittersweet, though, as the Cavs lost out to New Jersey on a tiebreaker for the eighth and final Eastern Conference playoff berth.

Silas's pink slip was not the only organizational change that occurred in March 2005. The Gunds sold the Cavaliers to Dan Gilbert, who the following season renamed the team's home venue Quicken Loans Arena (it quickly became known as "The Q").

Under new head coach Mike Brown, the 2005-06 Cavs were Team Streak. They started 9-2 but then lost seven of their next nine games to drop to 11-9. Then they won nine of 11, lost six straight, and then won 12 of 16 before dropping eight of 12 to fall to 36-29. A 99–84 victory over Portland on March

Damon Jones hits the series-winning basket against Washington in Game 6 of an Eastern Conference first-round playoff matchup, May 5, 2006. (AndersonsClevelandDesign.com)

17 was the start of a nine-game winning streak. They wound up winning 14 of their final 17 games to finish 50-32 and in second place in the Central Division. In the first round of the playoffs, the Cavaliers defeated the Wizards, four games to two. Damon Jones nailed a 17-foot shot with 4.8 seconds to go in overtime that wound up giving the Cavs a series-clinching 114–113 victory in Game 6 at Washington. In the conference semifinals against the top-seeded Pistons, the Cavs were primed for the upset when they won three of the first five games. They fumbled their chance to clinch the series at home when they lost Game 6 84–82. Two days later they fizzled out by scoring just 61 points in dropping the deciding game at Detroit.

Unlike the previous season, the 2006-07 Cavaliers were nothing if not consistent. They never lost more than three games in a row, and that occurred just twice. They finished 50-32 again and met Washington in the opening round of the playoffs again. This time they swept the Wizards in four games. In the conference semifinals, they defeated the Nets four games to two.

Then came the rematch with Detroit, which had eliminated Cleveland in the conference semis the year before. This time it was the conference finals. The Cavs lost Games 1 and 2 at Detroit by the exact same score of 79–76. They won Games 3 and 4 at home, then returned to Detroit for Game 5. In one of the most memorable games in Cavaliers history, James played the role of Superman, even more so than usual, by almost singlehandedly leading his team to a 109–107 victory in double overtime. He scored 48 points and had nine rebounds, seven assists, and two steals. Incredibly, he scored the Cavs' final 25 points and 29 of their last 30!

Two nights later at The Q, in the first game they ever played in the month of June, the Cavaliers broke open a tight game in the fourth quarter and won going away 98–82 to advance to the franchise's first NBA Finals. Daniel Gibson scored 31 points, including 19 in the final period. He was five for five from three-point range, with three in the fourth quarter. The Cavs were quickly brought back to Earth in the Finals as they were steamrolled by San Antonio in four straight games.

The next season, the Cavaliers finished 45-37 and in second place in the Central Division. In what was becoming a yearly ritual, they faced Washington in the opening round of the playoffs. The Cavs won the first two games at home, then lost two of the next three before easily defeating the Wizards 105–88 in Game 6 at Washington to win the series. Then they faced Boston in the conference semifinals. The Celtics, who had added Ray Allen and Kevin Garnett to a roster that already had Paul Pierce, finished an NBA-best 66-16 during the regular season. The Cavs put up a noble effort. Each team won its three home games heading into the deciding Game 7 in Beantown. It turned

LeBron James reacts to a monster dunk he made against Boston during the 2008 Eastern Conference Semifinals. (AndersonsClevelandDesign.com)

out to be a classic duel between James and Pierce. James scored 45 points, Pierce scored 41, but the Celtics came out on top 97–92, ending Cleveland's season.

With Mo Williams and Delonte West aboard, the 2008-09 Cavaliers put together a season for the ages, finishing an NBA-best 66-16, the best record in franchise history. They swept the Pistons and Hawks, respectively, in the first two rounds of the playoffs. Against Orlando in the Eastern Conference Finals they split the first two games at home, losing 107–106 in Game 1 and winning

96–95 in Game 2 on James's memorable three-pointer from 25 feet at the buzzer. The Magic took Games 3 and 4 in Orlando, including a 116–114 overtime win in the latter. The Cavs won Game 5 at The Q but fell 103–90 in Game 6 at Orlando, losing the series four games to two.

With Shaquille O'Neal, Anthony Parker, and Antawn Jamison aboard, the latter who was acquired in a trade with the Wizards in February, the 2009-10 Cavaliers finished 61-21, again the best record in the league. They beat the Bulls four games to one in the opening round of the playoffs. Boston was next in the conference semifinals. The Cavs lost four games to two. The 94–85 defeat in Game 6 would be James's finale as a Cavalier—at least for a while. Less than two months later, on July 8, came "The Decision," when James announced by way of an interview with ESPN's Jim Gray that he would be leaving the Cavs to join forces with Dwyane Wade and Chris Bosh in Miami.

2010-11 to present

Life without LeBron was not exactly filled with happiness. After a respectable 7-9 start in 2010-11 under new head coach Byron Scott, the Cavaliers lost 10 in a row, beat the Knicks in overtime, then proceeded to lose their next 26 games, tying the 1976–77 Tampa Bay Buccaneers for the longest losing streak in U.S. major professional sports history, to drop to 8-45. They finished with a 19-63 record. The next season, which was shortened due to another lockout, the Cavs again began respectably, going 13-17 through the first two months. Despite the presence of Kyrie Irving and Tristan Thompson, the first and fourth overall picks, respectively, in the 2011 NBA Draft, six- and nine-game losing streaks pointed them to a 21-45 final record.

Even with Dion Waiters, the fourth overall pick in the 2012 NBA Draft, aboard, the 2012-13 Cavaliers were putrid. After splitting their first four games, it was downhill the rest of the way. They lost 16 of their last 18 games to finish 24-58. With Mike Brown back as head coach and Anthony Bennett, the top overall pick in the 2013 NBA Draft, doing essentially nothing, the 2013-14 Cavs finished 33-49.

After James helped the Heat win two NBA titles in his four years in South Florida, he announced on July 11, 2014, by way of a letter on SI.com ("The Decision II") that he would be returning to the Cavaliers in 2014-15. Joining him in Cleveland was newcomer Kevin Love, a three-time All-Star. The Cavs' brass thought the "Big Three" of James, Irving, and Love would turn the trick and bring the city of Cleveland its first major professional sports championship in more than half a century. Other key newcomers included J. R. Smith, Timofey Mozgov, and Iman Shumpert, all of whom joined the team in early January. Gritty Matthew Dellavedova, new to the team a year earlier, would also be a big contributor to the Cavs' success.

It took a while, but under new head coach David Blatt, the 2014-15 Cavaliers eventually got it together. After a six-game losing streak dropped them to 19-20 in mid-January, they won a dozen straight. They finished 53-29 in winning the Central Division. They swept the Celtics in four games in round one of the playoffs. Love, however, missed the rest of the postseason after dislocating his left shoulder in the early going of the series finale. In the conference semifinals, James's 21-foot buzzer beater in Game 4 helped the Cavs beat the Bulls in six games. They swept Atlanta in the conference finals.

The Cavaliers' opponent in the NBA Finals was Golden State, a team that won an NBA-best 67 games during the regular season and ripped through the playoffs almost as easily as the Cavs had. The Warriors had scoring machine—and league MVP—Stephen Curry plus an explosive supporting cast, including sharpshooter Klay Thompson. The Cavs lost Game 1 at Golden State 108–100 in overtime. They also lost Irving for the rest of the series to a broken left kneecap he incurred during the overtime period.

LeBron would have to do it without Love and Irving. He got off to a rousing start by scoring a game-high 39 points, grabbing 16 rebounds, and dishing out 11 assists in leading the Cavs to a 95–93 overtime victory three nights later, also on the road, to even the series at a game apiece. Led by James's superhuman performance of 40 points, 12 rebounds, eight assists, four steals, and two blocked shots, the Cavs won Game 3 at home 96–91 two nights later. James's numbers dropped dramatically in a Game 4 blowout loss, also at home. He returned to superhuman status in Game 5 on the road and Game 6 at home, but Golden State was just too good for a one-man wrecking crew. The Warriors won the championship in six games.

Irving did not return to action the next season until December 20. By that time, the Cavaliers were 17-7 and looking good. Most observers felt they were pretty much a shoo-in to represent the East in the Finals again. By January 21, they were 30-11 and battling Toronto for the conference's number one seed. That is when the team dropped a bombshell on the rest of the NBA by firing Blatt and replacing him with assistant coach Tyronn Lue. The Cavs went 27-14 the rest of the way for a 57-25 finish and the top seed in the East.

The Cavaliers swept through the Pistons and Hawks in the first two rounds of the playoffs before ousting the Raptors four games to two in the conference finals. Their opponent in the championship round? None other than Golden State in a rematch of the previous year's Finals. This time, though, the Cavs had a healthy Irving and Love. The Warriors, who won an NBA-record 73 games during the regular season, aimed to prove that their Finals triumph over

Kyrie Irving about to connect on a crucial three-point shot late in the Cavaliers' 93–89 Game 7 Finals victory over the Warriors, June 19, 2016. **(AndersonsClevelandDesign.com)**

the injury-ravaged Cavs a year earlier was not a fluke. They got off to a fine start by winning three of the first four games and looked to close out the series in Game 5 on June 13 at Oracle Arena. The Cavaliers, however, had different plans. Behind 41 points each from James and Irving—the first time in Finals history that teammates scored 40 or more points in the same game—they shocked the favored Warriors 112–97 to stay alive.

Three nights later at The Q, James hung up 41 points again, along with 11 assists and eight rebounds, in leading the Cavaliers to a 115–101 victory in a game they led 31–11 after one quarter. There would be a deciding seventh game on June 19 back at Oracle Arena. In the first close contest of the series, James and Irving led the way as the Cavs won a 93–89 thriller. James had 27 points, 11 rebounds, and 11 assists; Irving had 26 points and six rebounds. Each player hit a basket toward the end that was critical—Irving a three-pointer and James a free throw that shut the coffin door on the home team. It was the first time a team recovered from a 3–1 series deficit to win the NBA Finals. It was also the city of Cleveland's first major professional sports championship since the Browns won the NFL title all the way back in 1964.

A

ADUBATO, RICHIE

Richie Adubato was a Cavaliers assistant coach in 1993-94.

ALBECK, STAN

Stan Albeck was Cleveland's head coach in 1979-80. The team was 19-20 but then fell to 27-43 before a late hot streak got them to 35-43 and within striking distance of a playoff berth. It didn't happen, as the Cavs finished 37-45. That offseason Albeck quit.

ALEXANDER, GARY

Gary Alexander was a 6-foot-7, 240-pound power forward for the Cavaliers in 1993-94. He was signed as a free agent on March 18, 1994. In seven games with Cleveland, he averaged 2.4 points, 1.7 rebounds, .1 assists, and .4 steals per contest. He scored eight points in a 110–95 loss to the Hawks on April 13 at Atlanta. He became a free agent again on July 1, 1994, and was not re-signed.

ALLRED, LANCE

Lance Allred was a 6-foot-11, 250-pound center for the Cavaliers in 2007-08. The first legally deaf player in NBA history, Allred signed the first of two 10-day contracts on March 13, 2008, and on April 4, 2008, signed a contract for the remainder of the 2007-08 season. He played three games with Cleveland.

ALL-STAR GAME HEAD COACH

Lenny Wilkens (1988-89)
Mike Brown (2008-09)
Tyronn Lue (2015-16)

ALL-STAR GAME MVP

LeBron James (2005-06)
LeBron James (2007-08)
Kyrie Irving (2013-14)

ALL-STAR GAMES HOSTED BY THE CAVALIERS

The Cavaliers have hosted two All-Star Games—in the 1980-81 and 1996-97 seasons. The first one was on February 1, 1981, at The Coliseum in front of 20,239 fans. With the Cavs' Mike Mitchell, who replaced injured Dan Roundfield of the Atlanta Hawks, contributing 14 points, four rebounds, two assists, and a steal, the East defeated the West 123–120. The MVP was future Hall of Famer Nate "Tiny" Archibald of the East's Boston Celtics, who had nine points, nine assists, five rebounds, and three steals. Philadelphia's Julius Erving led the East with 18 points. Phoenix's Dennis Johnson and Seattle's Paul Westphal led the West with 19 points apiece.

The official logo for the 1981 All-Star Game. (*AndersonsClevelandDesign.com*)

The second All-Star Game hosted by the Cavaliers was on February 9, 1997, in front of 20,562 fans at Gund Arena. With the Cavs' Terrell Brandon scoring 10 points, dishing out eight assists, plus getting three rebounds and two steals, the East beat the West 132–120. The MVP was Glen Rice of the East's Charlotte Hornets, who scored a game-high 26 points and had a rebound, an assist, and two steals. The West's leading scorer was Golden State's Latrell Sprewell, who had 19 points. The 50 Greatest Players in NBA History were honored at halftime.

ALL-STARS

1970-71 – John Johnson
1971-72 – Butch Beard, John Johnson
1972-73 – Lenny Wilkens
1973-74 – Austin Carr
1978-79 – Campy Russell
1980-81 – Mike Mitchell
1987-88 – Brad Daugherty
1988-89 – Brad Daugherty, Larry Nance, Mark Price
1990-91 – Brad Daugherty
1991-92 – Brad Daugherty, Mark Price
1992-93 – Brad Daugherty, Larry Nance, Mark Price
1993-94 – Mark Price
1994-95 – Tyrone Hill
1995-96 – Terrell Brandon
1996-97 – Terrell Brandon
1997-98 – Shawn Kemp
2002-03 – Zydrunas Ilgauskas
2004-05 – Zydrunas Ilgauskas, LeBron James
2005-06 – LeBron James
2006-07 – LeBron James
2007-08 – LeBron James
2008-09 – LeBron James, Mo Williams
2009-10 – LeBron James
2012-13 – Kyrie Irving
2013-14 – Kyrie Irving
2014-15 – Kyrie Irving, LeBron James
2015-16 – LeBron James

AMAECHI, JOHN

John Amaechi was a 6-foot-10, 270-pound power forward for Cleveland in 1995-96. Signed as a free agent on October 5, 1995, he averaged 2.8 points, 1.9 rebounds, .3 assists, .2 steals, and .4 blocked shots per game in his one season with the Cavs. He scored 11 points in a 106–88 loss to Chicago on November 9 at Gund Arena. He was waived on July 31, 1996.

AMUNDSON, LOU

Lou Amundson was a 6-foot-9, 220-pound power forward for the Cavaliers in 2014-15. Signed as a free agent on September 26, 2014, he averaged .9 points, 1.7 rebounds, .4 assists, and .1 steals per contest in 12 games with Cleveland. He scored five points in a 106–74 victory over Orlando on November 24 at Quicken Loans Arena. He was traded to the Knicks on January 5, 2015.

ANDERSON, CLIFF

Cliff Anderson was a 6-foot-2, 200-pound shooting guard for Cleveland in 1970-71. He was signed as a free agent on October 15, 1970. In 19 games with the Cavs, he averaged 3.4 points, .7 assists, and 1.6 rebounds per contest. He scored 20 points in a 108–104 loss to the Suns on October 23 at Phoenix. He was waived on December 13, 1970.

ANDERSON, DEREK

Derek Anderson was a 6-foot-5, 194-pound small forward and shooting guard for the Cavaliers from 1997-98 to 1998-99. A first-round draft pick out of the University of Kentucky in 1997, he averaged 11.3 points, 2.8 rebounds, 3.6 assists, 1.3 steals, and .2 blocked shots per game in his two seasons with Cleveland. His best season as a Cavalier was 1997-98, when he averaged 11.7 points, 2.8 rebounds, 3.4 assists, 1.3 steals, and .2 blocked shots per contest.

Anderson scored 30 points in a 105–93 loss to the Lakers on April 3, 1998, at Gund Arena and 18 points in an 80–74 playoff defeat to Indiana on April 30, 1998, again at Gund Arena. He was traded to the Clippers on August 4, 1999.

ANDERSON, RON

Ron Anderson was a 6-foot-7, 215-pound small forward for the Cavaliers from 1984-85 to 1985-86. A second-round draft choice out of California State

University, Fresno, in 1984, he averaged 5.6 points, 2.2 rebounds, .8 assists, .2 steals, and .1 blocked shots per game in his two seasons with Cleveland. His best season as a Cavalier was 1984-85, when he averaged 5.8 points, 2.4 rebounds, .9 assists, .3 steals, and .2 blocked shots per contest. Anderson scored 27 points in a 111–101 loss to the 76ers on October 26, 1984, at Philadelphia. He was traded to Indiana on December 10, 1985.

ANDRIUSKEVICIUS, MARTYNAS

Martynas Andriuskevicius was a 7-foot-2, 240-pound center for Cleveland in 2005-06. Traded from Orlando on June 28, 2005, he averaged .7 rebounds and .3 steals per contest in six games with the Cavs. He was traded to Chicago on August 18, 2006.

APRIL

The following are five memorable Cavaliers games that were played in the month of April:

APRIL 3, 1975

In the biggest game in their brief history to that point, the Cavaliers defeated the New York Knicks 100–95 as both teams were battling for an Eastern Conference playoff berth. Before 20,239 fans at The Coliseum cheering them on, the Cavs were led by Dick Snyder's 22 points. Jim Cleamons added 19 and Bingo Smith had 18. Earl Monroe led the Knicks with 21 points.

APRIL 29, 1976

The Cavaliers defeated the Washington Bullets 87–85 in Game 7 of the Eastern Conference Semifinals before 21,564 crazed fans at The Coliseum to conclude what had been an exhilarating series. It was the Cavs' first-ever postseason. Dick Snyder drove to the basket and banked in a running, one-handed shot from five feet away to give the Cavaliers an 87–85 lead with four seconds to go. Moments later, the Bullets' Phil Chenier missed a shot from the corner as the clock hit 0:00. Hundreds of Cavaliers fans rushed the court. One of the basket stands was torn down. It was complete euphoria as the Cavs advanced to the conference finals. Snyder led Cleveland with 23 points. Chenier led Washington with 31 points.

APRIL 9, 1978

The Cavaliers concluded the regular season with a 120–117 triumph over the Kansas City Kings before 4,684 fans at Kemper Arena. The win was the Cavs' ninth in their last 10 games, which gave them a 43-39 record, the fourth seed in the Eastern Conference playoffs, and home court advantage in the opening round against New York. Leading the way for Cleveland was Campy Russell with 31 points and Austin Carr with 30. Scott Wedman led the Kings with 23 points.

APRIL 9, 1985

The Cavaliers beat the New Jersey Nets 114–100 in front of 10,185 fans at The Coliseum, clinching their first postseason berth in seven years. The Cavs recovered from a 10-point halftime deficit. World B. Free led Cleveland with 35 points. Phil Hubbard had 22. Leading the way for the Nets was Micheal Ray Richardson with 33 points.

APRIL 20, 1997

In a battle for the final Eastern Conference playoff berth—and the right to oppose the 69-13 Chicago Bulls in the first round—the Cavaliers blew a 44–35 halftime lead and lost to the Washington Bullets 85–81 in front of 20,193 fans at Gund Arena. Leading the way for Cleveland was Terrell Brandon with 28 points. Chris Webber led the Bullets with 23 points.

ARENA CAPACITIES

Please see Attendance Statistics on page 272.

ASSISTANT COACHES

Jim Lessig (1970-71)
Jimmy Rodgers (1971-72 to 1978-79)
Morris McHone (1979-80, 1984-85 to 1985-86)
Larry Creger (1980-81)
Gerald Oliver (1980-81 to 1981-82)
Gus Johnson (1981-82)
Bob Kloppenburg (1981-82)

Don Delaney (1982-83)
Gene Littles (1982-83 to 1985-86)
Ed Badger (1983-84)
Herman Kull (1985-86)
Dick Helm (1986-87 to 1992-93)
Brian Winters (1986-87 to 1992-93)
Richie Adubato (1993-94)
Ron Rothstein (1993-94 to 1998-99)
Jim Boylan (1993-94 to 1996-97, 2013-14 to present)
Sidney Lowe (1994-95 to 1998-99)
Marc Iavaroni (1997-98 to 1998-99)
Bill Blair (1999-2000)
Bob Ociepka (1999-2000 to 2000-01)
Mike Woodson (1999-2000 to 2000-01)
Keith Smart (2000-01 to 2002-03)
Jerry Eaves (2001-02 to 2002-03)
Ron Ekker (2001-02 to 2002-03)
Clifford Ray (2002-03)
Mike Bratz (2002-03, 2004-05)
Bob Donewald (2003-04)
Mark Osowski (2003-04)
Stephen Silas (2003-04 to 2004-05)
Brendan Malone (2004-05)
Wes Wilcox (2004-05)
Kenny Natt (2004-05 to 2006-07)
Hank Egan (2005-06 to 2009-10)
Melvin Hunt (2005-06 to 2009-10)
Michael Malone (2005-06 to 2009-10)
Chris Jent (2006-07 to 2010-11)
John Kuester (2007-08 to 2008-09)
Paul Pressey (2010-11 to 2012-13)
Joe Prunty (2010-11 to 2012-13)
Jamahl Mosley (2010-11 to 2013-14)
Nate Tibbetts (2011-12 to 2012-13)
Bernie Bickerstaff (2013-14)
Igor Kokoskov (2013-14)
Bret Brielmaier (2013-14 to present)
Tyronn Lue (2014-15 to 2015-16)

Larry Drew (2014-15 to present)
James Posey (2014-15 to present)
Phil Handy (2015-16 to present)
Mike Longabardi (2015-16 to present)

AVERAGE SEASON CROWDS, LARGEST TO SMALLEST

Please see Attendance Statistics on page 272.

B

BABIC, MILOS

Milos Babic was a 7-foot, 240-pound power forward for the Cavaliers in 1990-91. Traded from Phoenix on June 27, 1990, he averaged 1.6 points, .8 rebounds, .3 assists, .1 steals, and .1 blocked shots per contest in 12 games with the Cavs. He scored five points in a 120–85 defeat to Chicago on December 1 at The Coliseum. He was released on August 22, 1991.

BADGER, ED

Ed Badger was a Cavaliers assistant coach in 1983-84.

BAGLEY, JOHN

John Bagley was a 6-foot, 185-pound point guard for Cleveland from 1982-83 to 1986-87. A first-round draft pick from Boston College in 1982, he averaged 9.4 points, 6.2 assists, 2.9 rebounds, 1.3 steals, and .1 blocked shots per game in his five seasons with the Cavs. His best season as a Cavalier was 1985-86, when he averaged 11.7 points, 9.4 assists, 3.5 rebounds, 1.6 steals, and .1 blocked shots per contest.

Bagley scored 35 points in a 121–112 victory over the Bullets in Washington on February 4, 1985, and 29 points in a 120–111 loss to the Pistons at Detroit on April 1, 1983. He had 22 points in a 126–123 playoff defeat to the Celtics in Boston on April 18, 1985. He was traded to New Jersey on October 8, 1987.

BATTIE, TONY

Tony Battie was a 6-foot-11, 230-pound center for the Cavaliers in 2003-04. Traded from Boston on December 15, 2003, he averaged 5.4 points, 4.8 rebounds, .7 assists, .4 steals, and .9 blocked shots per game in his one season with Cleveland. He scored 17 points in a 99–94 triumph over Seattle on January 20 at Gund Arena. He was traded to Orlando on July 23, 2004.

BATTLE, JOHN

John Battle was a 6-foot-2, 175-pound shooting guard for the Cavaliers from 1991-92 to 1994-95. Signed as a free agent on July 17, 1991, he averaged five points, .9 assists, .8 rebounds, .3 steals, and .1 blocked shots per game in his four seasons with Cleveland. His best season as a Cavalier was 1991-92, when he averaged 5.9 points, one assist, .8 rebounds, .3 steals, and .1 blocked shots per contest.

Battle scored 26 points in a 101–90 victory over Seattle at The Coliseum on November 27, 1993. He scored 14 points in a 104–98 playoff defeat to the Celtics on May 4, 1992, also at The Coliseum. He was waived on November 1, 1995.

BEARD, BUTCH

Alfred "Butch" Beard was a 6-foot-3, 185-pound point guard for Cleveland in 1971-72 and 1975-76. He was chosen in the 1970 Expansion Draft from Atlanta. He was traded to the SuperSonics on August 23, 1972. He was re-signed on May 29, 1975, in a trade with Golden State.

In his two seasons with the Cavs, Beard averaged 13.8 points, six assists, 3.8 rebounds, .7 steals, and .1 blocked shots per game. His best season as a Cavalier was 1971-72, when he averaged 15.4 points, 6.7 assists, and 4.1 rebounds per contest. He scored 30 points in a 115–110 win over the Hawks on December 23, 1971, at the Cleveland Arena. He was an All-Star in 1971-72. He was waived on December 1, 1975.

BENJAMIN, BENOIT

Benoit Benjamin was a 7-foot, 250-pound center for the Cavaliers in 1999-2000. He was signed as a free agent on November 1, 1999. He played three games with Cleveland. He was waived on November 18, 1999.

BENNETT, ANTHONY

Anthony Bennett was a 6-foot-8, 245-pound power forward for the Cavaliers in 2013-14. He was a first-round draft choice—the number one overall pick—in 2013 out of the University of Nevada, Las Vegas. In his one season with the Cavs, he averaged 4.2 points, three rebounds, .3 assists, .4 steals, and .2 blocked shots per game. He scored 19 points in a 109–99 triumph over Sacramento on February 11 at Quicken Loans Arena. He was traded to Minnesota on August 23, 2014.

BENNETT, ELMER

Elmer Bennett was a 6-foot, 170-pound point guard for the Cavaliers in 1994-95. He signed the first of two 10-day contracts on January 26, 1995. He played four games with the Cavs. He became a free agent again on February 23, 1995, and was not re-signed.

BENNETT, MELVIN

Melvin Bennett was a 6-foot-7, 200-pound power forward for Cleveland in 1981-82. Signed as a free agent on December 12, 1981, he played three games with the Cavs. He was waived on December 22, 1981.

BENNETT, WINSTON

Winston Bennett was a 6-foot-7, 210-pound small forward for the Cavaliers from 1989-90 to 1991-92. He was a third-round draft choice in 1988 out of the University of Kentucky. In his three seasons with the Cavs he averaged 4.8 points, 3.1 rebounds, .9 assists, .4 steals, and .2 blocked shots per game. His best season as a Cavalier was 1989-90 when he averaged 6.1 points, 3.4 rebounds, one assist, .4 steals, and .2 blocked shots per contest.

Bennett scored 23 points in a 108–82 victory over the Nets on March 23, 1991, at The Coliseum, and 22 points in a 107–101 playoff loss to the 76ers on April 29, 1990, in Philadelphia. He was waived on March 27, 1992.

BENSON, KENT

Kent Benson was a 6-foot-10, 235-pound center for the Cavaliers in 1987-88. Traded from Utah on October 8, 1987, he played two games with the Cavs. He was waived on July 22, 1988.

BENTON, MAX

Max Benton was Cleveland's head trainer or trainer from 2001-02 to 2012-13.

BEST/HIGHEST SEASON PERFORMANCES

Please see Individual Statistics on page 185.

BEST/HIGHEST SEASON PERFORMANCES

Please see Team Statistics on page 215.

BICKERSTAFF, BERNIE

Bernie Bickerstaff was a Cavaliers assistant coach in 2013-14.

BLAIR, BILL

Bill Blair was a Cavaliers assistant coach in 1999-2000.

BLATT, DAVID

David Blatt was the Cavaliers' head coach in 2014-15 and for part of the 2015-16 season. In 2014-15, he led Cleveland to a 53-29 record and an appearance in the Finals after a 19-20 start. In 2015-16, the Cavs were 30-11 when he—incredibly—was fired. His overall record as Cavaliers head coach was 83-40. His postseason mark was 14-6.

BLOUNT, CORIE

Corie Blount was a 6-foot-9, 240-pound power forward for the Cavaliers in 1998-99. Signed as a free agent on March 13, 1999, he averaged 3.4 points, 5.3 rebounds, .5 assists, .9 steals, and .6 blocked shots per game in his one season with the Cavs. He scored 11 points in a 113–86 victory over Boston on March 23 at Gund Arena. He became a free agent again on July 1, 1999, and was not re-signed.

BOHANNON, ETDRICK

Etdrick Bohannon was a 6-foot-9, 220-pound power forward for Cleveland in 2000-01. He signed the first of two 10-day contracts on January 7, 2001. In six games with the Cavs he averaged 1.3 points, 1.2 rebounds, and .3 blocked shots per contest. He scored four points in a 119–107 defeat to the Grizzlies in Vancouver on January 13. He became a free agent again on January 28, 2001, and was not re-signed.

BOLAND, JIM

Jim Boland was Cleveland's president from 1997-98 to 2001-02.

BOOZER, CARLOS

Carlos Boozer was a 6-foot-9, 258-pound power forward for Cleveland from 2002-03 to 2003-04. He was a second-round draft pick in 2002 from Duke University. In his two seasons with the Cavs he averaged 12.6 points, 9.4 rebounds, 1.6 assists, .9 steals, and .7 blocked shots per game. His best season as a Cavalier was 2003-04 when he averaged 15.5 points, 11.4 rebounds, two assists, one steal, and .7 blocked shots per contest.

Boozer scored 32 points twice—in a 102–96 overtime victory against the Jazz at Utah on January 17, 2004, and in a 99–94 triumph over Seattle on January 20, 2004, at Gund Arena. He became a free agent on July 1, 2004, and was not re-signed.

BOYKINS, EARL

Earl Boykins was a 5-foot-5, 135-pound point guard for Cleveland from 1998-99 to 1999-2000. He signed the first of two 10-day contracts on March 10, 1999, and on April 2, 1999, signed a contract for the rest of the 1998-99 season. He was waived on October 28, 1999. On February 8, 2000, he signed the first of two more 10-day contracts and on February 28, 2000, signed a contract for the rest of the 1999-2000 season.

In his two seasons with the Cavs Boykins averaged 4.2 points, 1.7 assists, .9 rebounds, and .4 steals per game. His best season as a Cavalier was 1999-2000 when he averaged 5.3 points, 1.8 assists, one rebound, and .5 steals per contest. He scored 22 points in a 119–101 victory over the Nuggets on February 17, 2000, at Gund Arena. He became a free agent again on July 1, 2000, and was not re-signed.

BOYLAN, JIM

Jim Boylan was a Cavaliers assistant coach from 1993-94 to 1996-97 and has been since 2013-14.

BRAMLETT, A. J.

A. J. Bramlett was a 6-foot-10, 227-pound center for the Cavaliers in 1999-2000. He was a second-round draft pick in 1999 from the University of Arizona. In eight games with the Cavs he averaged one point, 2.8 rebounds, and .1 steals per contest. He scored two points on four occasions. He was waived on January 5, 2000.

BRANDON, TERRELL

Terrell Brandon was a 5-foot-11, 180-pound point guard for the Cavaliers from 1991-92 to 1996-97. A first-round draft pick in 1991 out of the University of Oregon, he averaged 12.7 points, 4.9 assists, 2.7 rebounds, 1.4 steals, and .3 blocked shots per game in his six seasons with Cleveland. His best season as a Cavalier was 1996-97 when he averaged 19.5 points, 6.3 assists, 3.9 rebounds, 1.8 steals, and .4 blocked shots per contest.

Brandon scored 33 points in a 100–94 victory over Utah on December 22, 1996, at Gund Arena. He scored 32 points twice—in a 100–95 win over Minnesota on December 19, 1995, also at Gund Arena, and in a 99–91 triumph over Indiana on January 4, 1997, yet again at Gund Arena. He had 21 points in an 84–80 playoff loss to the Knicks on April 27, 1996, likewise at Gund Arena. He was an All-Star from 1995-96 to 1996-97. He was traded to Milwaukee on September 25, 1997.

BRANSON, BRAD

Brad Branson was a 6-foot-10, 220-pound power forward for the Cavaliers in 1981-82. Signed as a free agent on March 30, 1982, he averaged 5.3 points, 3.3 rebounds, .6 assists, .5 steals, and .4 blocked shots per contest in 10 games with Cleveland. He scored 13 points in a 117–114 defeat to New York on April 10 at The Coliseum. He was traded to Indiana on October 25, 1982.

BRATZ, MIKE

Mike Bratz was a 6-foot-2, 185-pound point guard for the Cavaliers in 1980-81. Traded from Dallas on September 16, 1980, he averaged 10 points, 5.7 assists, 2.5 rebounds, 1.7 steals, and .2 blocked shots per game in his one season with the Cavs. He scored 23 points in a 130–122 triumph over Denver on December 18 at The Coliseum. He was traded to San Antonio on October 28, 1981. He was a Cavaliers assistant coach in 2002-03 and 2004-05.

BREMER, J. R.

J. R. Bremer was a 6-foot-2, 185-pound point guard for Cleveland in 2003-04. Traded from Boston on July 29, 2003, in his one season with the Cavs he averaged 3.5 points, 1.3 assists, 1.1 rebounds, .6 steals, and .1 blocked shots

Terrell Brandon drives to the bucket against the Knicks, 1995-96. (AndersonsClevelandDesign.com)

per game. He scored 20 points in a 106–92 defeat to the Kings in Sacramento on October 29. He was released on March 3, 2004.

BREWER, JIM

Jim Brewer was a 6-foot-9, 210-pound power forward for the Cavaliers from 1973-74 to 1978-79. The uncle of Los Angeles Clippers head coach and president of basketball operations Doc Rivers, he was a first-round draft choice in 1973 from the University of Minnesota. He averaged 7.5 points, 7.7 rebounds, 1.8 assists, .9 steals, and .8 blocked shots per game in his six seasons with Cleveland. His best season as a Cavalier was 1975-76 when he averaged 11.5 points, 10.9 rebounds, 2.5 assists, 1.1 steals, and 1.1 blocked shots per contest. The previous season Brewer averaged 8.4 points, 6.2 rebounds, 1.6 assists, .9 steals, and .5 blocked shots per game. In 1976-77, he averaged 8.5 points, 9.4 rebounds, 2.4 assists, 1.2 steals, and one blocked shot per contest.

Brewer scored 25 points in a 106–104 win over Washington on January 11, 1976, at The Coliseum and 24 points in a 113–111 victory over the Jazz on March 16, 1975, in New Orleans. He had 15 points in a 102–98 overtime playoff defeat to the Bullets at Washington on April 26, 1976. He was traded to the Pistons on February 15, 1979.

BREWER, RON

Ron Brewer was a 6-foot-4, 180-pound shooting guard for the Cavaliers from 1981-82 to 1982-83 and in 1985-86. He was traded from San Antonio on December 23, 1981, was traded to Golden State on December 15, 1982, and was re-signed as a free agent on January 11, 1986.

In his three seasons with the Cavs Brewer averaged 12.6 points, 1.7 assists, 1.9 rebounds, .9 steals, and .3 blocked shots per game. His best season as a Cavalier was 1981-82 when he averaged 19.4 points, 2.6 assists, 2.4 rebounds, 1.3 steals, and .5 blocked shots per contest. He scored 33 points in a 132–120 overtime victory against the Warriors on November 10, 1982, at Golden State. He became a free agent again on July 1, 1986, and was not re-signed.

BRIELMAIER, BRET

Bret Brielmaier has been a Cavaliers assistant coach since 2013-14.

BRIGGS, GARY

Gary Briggs was the Cavaliers' head trainer or trainer from 1981-82 to 1999-2000.

BRINSON, JIM

Jim Brinson was a Cavaliers local television broadcaster from 1985-86 to 1986-87.

Jim Brewer against the Warriors with Austin Carr below, 1976. (AndersonsClevelandDesign.com)

BROKAW, GARY

Gary Brokaw was a 6-foot-4, 178-pound shooting guard for Cleveland in 1976-77. Traded from Milwaukee on January 13, 1977, he averaged 7.2 points, three assists, 1.5 rebounds, .4 steals, and .3 blocked shots per game in his one season with the Cavs. He scored 21 points in a 113–107 victory over Kansas City on April 3 at The Coliseum. He scored 14 points in a 109–100 playoff loss to the Bullets on April 13 at Washington. He was traded to Buffalo on October 17, 1977.

BROOKS, SCOTT

Scott Brooks was a 5-foot-11, 165-pound point guard for the Cavaliers in 1997-98. He was signed as a free agent on December 12, 1997. In his one season with Cleveland he averaged 1.8 points, 1.1 assists, .7 rebounds, .4 steals, and .1 blocked shots per game. He scored 10 points in a 108–94 defeat to Atlanta on February 5 at Gund Arena. He scored two points in a 106–77 playoff loss to the Pacers on April 23 at Indiana. He became a free agent again on July 1, 1998, and was not re-signed.

BROWN, BOB

Bob Brown was a Cavaliers local radio and television broadcaster in 1970-71.

BROWN, CHUCKY

Chucky Brown was a 6-foot-7, 214-pound small forward for the Cavaliers from 1989-90 to 1991-92 and in 2000-01. He was a second-round draft pick in 1989 out of North Carolina State University. He was waived on December 2, 1991. On January 29, 2001, he signed the first of two 10-day contracts and on February 22, 2001, signed a contract for the rest of the 2000-01 season.

In his four seasons with the Cavs Brown averaged 7.2 points, 2.8 rebounds, .8 assists, .4 steals, and .3 blocked shots per game. His best season as a Cavalier was 1990-91 when he averaged 8.5 points, 2.9 rebounds, 1.1 assists, .4 steals, and .3 blocked shots per contest. He scored 30 points in a 123–112 triumph over the Magic on January 6, 1990, at Orlando. He became a free agent again on July 1, 2001, and was not re-signed.

BROWN, DEVIN

Devin Brown was a 6-foot-5, 220-pound shooting guard for Cleveland in 2007-08. Signed as a free agent on September 27, 2007, he averaged 7.5 points, 2.2 assists, 3.4 rebounds, .7 steals, and .1 blocked shots per game in his one season with the Cavs. He scored 20 points twice—in a 93–91 win over the Kings on November 9 at Sacramento and in a 118–114 victory over the Bobcats on April 2 in Charlotte. He scored 10 points in a 108–72 playoff loss to the Wizards at Washington on April 24. He became a free agent again on July 1, 2008, and was not re-signed.

BROWN, KEDRICK

Kedrick Brown was a 6-foot-7, 222-pound small forward for the Cavaliers in 2003-04. Traded from the Celtics on December 15, 2003, he averaged 5.3 points, 2.3 rebounds, 1.1 assists, .4 steals, and .1 blocked shots per game in his one season with Cleveland. He scored 13 points twice—in a 99–94 victory over Seattle on January 20 at Gund Arena and in a 107–89 loss to the Bucks on April 2 at Milwaukee. He was traded to Philadelphia on July 20, 2004.

BROWN, MIKE

Mike Brown was Cleveland's head coach from 2005-06 to 2009-10 and in 2013-14. He led the Cavs to playoff berths in each of his first five seasons, including a Finals appearance in 2006-07. He led Cleveland to a franchise-best 66-16 record in 2008-09, but the Cavs fell to Orlando in the Eastern Conference Finals. He was Coach of the Year that season. Also that year, he was the Eastern Conference head coach in the All-Star Game.

The next season Brown led the Cavaliers to a 61-21 record, but they lost to Boston in the conference semifinals. He was fired after the season. In his second stint as Cleveland's head coach, the Cavs finished 33-49 in 2013-14. Again, he was fired after the season. His overall record as Cavaliers head coach was 305-187. His postseason mark was 42-29.

BROWN, SHANNON

Shannon Brown was a 6-foot-4, 205-pound shooting guard for Cleveland from 2006-07 to 2007-08. A first-round draft choice in 2006 from Michigan State University, in his two seasons with the Cavs he averaged 4.7 points, .7 assists, one rebound, .4 steals, and .1 blocked shots per game. His best season as a Cavalier was 2007-08 when he averaged seven points, 1.1 assists, 1.2 rebounds, .7 steals, and .1 blocked shots per contest. He scored 20 points in a 100–79 loss to the Nets at Quicken Loans Arena on December 4, 2007. He was traded to Chicago on February 21, 2008.

BROWN, TIERRE

Tierre Brown was a 6-foot-2, 189-pound point guard for the Cavaliers in 2002-03. He signed a 10-day contract on March 3, 2003, and on March 24, 2003, signed a contract for the rest of the 2002-03 season. In 15 games with Cleveland, he averaged 4.3 points, 2.6 assists, two rebounds, and .9 steals per contest. He scored 16 points in a 96–86 victory over Toronto on April 16 at Gund Arena. He became a free agent again on July 1, 2003, and was not re-signed.

BRYANT, MARK

Mark Bryant was a 6-foot-9, 245-pound power forward for the Cavaliers in 1999-2000. Signed as a free agent on August 12, 1999, in his one season with Cleveland he averaged 5.7 points, 4.7 rebounds, .8 assists, .4 steals, and .4 blocked shots per game. He scored 18 points in a 113–102 defeat to the Kings in Sacramento on January 16. He was waived on November 15, 2000.

BUCKNER, QUINN

Quinn Buckner was a Cavaliers local television broadcaster from 1994-95 to 1996-97.

BUTLER, MITCHELL

Mitchell Butler was a 6-foot-5, 210-pound shooting guard for the Cavaliers from 1997-98 to 1998-99. He was signed as a free agent on October 2, 1997. In his two seasons with Cleveland, he averaged 4.2 points, .8 assists, 1.3 rebounds, .5 steals, and .1 blocked shots per game. His best season as a Cavalier was 1998-99 when he averaged 5.4 points, .7 assists, 1.4 rebounds, .5 steals, and .1 blocked shots per contest. He scored 21 points in a 96–87 loss to the Raptors on May 5, 1999, at Toronto. He became a free agent again on July 1, 1999, and was not re-signed.

BYNUM, ANDREW

Andrew Bynum was a 7-foot, 285-pound center for Cleveland in 2013-14. Signed as a free agent on July 19, 2013, he averaged 8.4 points, 5.3 rebounds, 1.1 assists, .3 steals, and 1.2 blocked shots per game in his one season with the Cavs. He scored 20 points twice—in a 97–93 victory over the Bulls on November 30 at Quicken Loans Arena and in a 108–89 loss to the Hawks in Atlanta on December 6. He was traded to Chicago on January 6, 2014.

C

CAGE, MICHAEL

Michael Cage was a 6-foot-9, 224-pound center for the Cavaliers from 1994-95 to 1995-96. Signed as a free agent on August 2, 1994, he averaged 5.5 points, 7.9 rebounds, .7 assists, .9 steals, and .9 blocked shots per game in his two seasons with Cleveland. His best season as a Cavalier was 1995-96 when he averaged six points, 8.9 rebounds, .6 assists, 1.1 steals, and one blocked shot per contest.

Cage scored 20 points in a 92–86 defeat to the Spurs in San Antonio on January 10, 1996. He scored 10 points in an 84–80 playoff loss to New York on April 27, 1996, at Gund Arena. He became a free agent again on July 1, 1996, and was not re-signed.

CALVIN, MACK

Mack Calvin was a 6-foot, 165-pound point guard for the Cavaliers in 1980-81. Signed as a free agent on December 19, 1980, he averaged 2.5 points, 1.3 assists, .6 rebounds, and .2 steals per game in his one season with Cleveland. He scored six points on three occasions. He became a free agent again on July 1, 1981, and was not re-signed.

CAMPBELL, TONY

Tony Campbell was a 6-foot-7, 215-pound small forward for the Cavaliers in 1994-95. He was signed as a free agent on October 31, 1994. In his one season with Cleveland he averaged six points, two rebounds, .9 assists, .4 steals, and .1 blocked shots per game. He scored 23 points in a 105–102 victory over New Jersey on February 25 at Gund Arena. He scored 13 points in a 103–79 playoff loss to the Knicks on April 27 at New York. He became a free agent again on July 1, 1995, and was not re-signed.

CARR, AUSTIN

Austin Carr was a 6-foot-4, 200-pound shooting guard for the Cavaliers from 1971-72 to 1979-80. He was a first-round draft pick—the number one overall selection—in 1971 out of the University of Notre Dame, where he was a scoring machine and tallied 61 points—still an NCAA Tournament record—against Ohio University in 1970. Knee problems, especially from an injury in 1974-75, kept him from attaining true greatness in the NBA, but he still managed to put up impressive numbers.

In his nine seasons with Cleveland Carr averaged 16.2 points, 2.9 assists, three rebounds, .8 steals, and .1 blocked shots per game. His best season as a Cavalier was 1973-74 when he averaged 21.9 points, 3.8 assists, 3.6 rebounds, 1.1 steals, and .2 blocked shots per contest. In his rookie season, he averaged 21.2 points, 3.4 assists, and 3.5 rebounds per game. The next season, he averaged 20.5 points, 3.4 assists, and 4.5 rebounds per contest.

Carr scored 42 points in a 115–105 loss to the Celtics on April 10, 1977, in Boston and 40 points in a 109–108 defeat to Houston on October 13, 1972, at the Cleveland Arena. He had 27 points in a 102–98 overtime playoff loss to the Bullets in Washington on April 26, 1976. He was an All-Star in 1973-74. In 1979-80, he won the J. Walter Kennedy Citizenship Award. He was selected by Dallas in the 1980 Expansion Draft. His jersey number 34 was retired by the Cavaliers on January 3, 1981.

Carr was a Cavaliers local television broadcaster from 1981-82 to 1983-84 and has been since 1998-99. Known as "Mr. Cavalier" to viewers, he is loved by fans perhaps even on the same level as longtime Cavs local radio and television broadcaster Joe Tait was.

CARR, KENNY

Kenny Carr was a 6-foot-7, 220-pound power forward for Cleveland from 1979-80 to 1981-82. He was traded from Los Angeles on October 24, 1979. In his three seasons with the Cavs he averaged 14.1 points, nine rebounds, 1.6 assists, one steal, and .5 blocked shots per game. His best season as a Cavalier was 1980-81 when he averaged 15.2 points, 10.3 rebounds, 2.4 assists, .9 steals, and .5 blocked shots per contest. He scored 32 points on three occasions. He was traded to the Pistons on February 16, 1982.

CASSPI, OMRI

Omri Casspi was a 6-foot-9, 225-pound small forward for Cleveland from 2011-12 to 2012-13. He was traded from the Kings on June 30, 2011. In his two seasons with the Cavs he averaged 5.9 points, 3.2 rebounds, .9 assists, .6 steals, and .3 blocked shots per game. His best season as a Cavalier was 2011-12 when he averaged 7.1 points, 3.5 rebounds, one assist, .6 steals, and .3 blocked shots per contest. Casspi scored 15 points in a 110–108 defeat to the Heat on November 24, 2012, in Miami. He became a free agent on July 1, 2013, and was not re-signed.

CAVALETTES

The Cavalettes were the Cavaliers' dance team in the late 1970s.

CAVALIER GIRLS

The Cavalier Girls are the Cavs' dance team.

"CAVS BASKETBALL—TONIGHT'S THE NIGHT"

"Cavs Basketball—Tonight's the Night" was the Cavaliers' fight song in the late-1980s. The catchy, upbeat tune was written and performed by Cleveland music legend Michael Stanley.

CHANDLER, NEV

Nev Chandler was a Cavaliers local television broadcaster from 1982-83 to 1984-85.

CHAPPELL, LEN

Len Chappell was a 6-foot-8, 240-pound power forward for the Cavaliers in 1970-71. Selected from Milwaukee in the 1970 Expansion Draft, he averaged 6.8 points, three rebounds, and .2 assists per contest in six games with Cleveland. He scored 19 points in a 115–112 loss to the Trail Blazers in Portland on October 16. He was waived on October 27, 1970.

CHERRY, WILL

Will Cherry was a 6-foot, 185-pound point guard for the Cavaliers in 2014-15. Signed as a free agent on November 2, 2014, in eight games with Cleveland he averaged 1.9 points, one assist, .6 rebounds, .8 steals, and .1 blocked shots per contest. He scored five points in a 106–74 victory over

Orlando on November 24 at Quicken Loans Arena. He was waived on November 30, 2014.

CHESTNUT, TOM

Tom Chestnut was the Cavaliers' president from 1990-91 to 1994-95.

CHIEVOUS, DERRICK

Derrick Chievous was a 6-foot-7, 195-pound small forward for the Cavaliers from 1989-90 to 1990-91. Traded from Houston on February 21, 1990, in his two seasons with the Cavs he averaged 2.9 points, one rebound, .2 assists, .2 steals, and .1 blocked shots per game. His best season as a Cavalier was 1989-90 when he averaged 3.5 points, 1.1 rebounds, .3 assists, .2 steals, and .1 blocked shots per contest.

Chievous scored 12 points in a 145–105 defeat to the Warriors on March 8, 1990, at Golden State. He scored 13 points in a 122–95 playoff victory over Philadelphia on May 1, 1990, at The Coliseum. He became a free agent on July 1, 1991, and was not re-signed.

CHILCUTT, PETE

Pete Chilcutt was a 6-foot-10, 230-pound power forward for the Cavaliers in 1999-2000. He signed the first of two 10-day contracts on January 31, 2000. In six games with Cleveland he averaged 1.5 rebounds and .2 assists per contest. His second 10-day contract was terminated on February 22, 2000.

CHONES, JIM

Jim Chones was a 6-foot-11, 220-pound center for the Cavaliers from 1974-75 to 1978-79. Traded from Los Angeles on May 17, 1974, in his five seasons with Cleveland he averaged 14.3 points, 9.5 rebounds, 1.8 assists, .6 steals, and 1.1 blocked shots per game. His best season as a Cavalier was 1977-78 when he averaged 15 points, 10.3 rebounds, 1.6 assists, .6 steals, and .7 blocked shots per contest.

In 1975-76, Chones averaged 15.8 points, nine rebounds, two assists, .5 steals, and 1.1 blocked shots per game. That same season his broken right ankle two days before the start of the Eastern Conference Finals against the Celtics is what many Cavs fans say cost the team the NBA Championship. In his last season with Cleveland he averaged 13.4 points, 10.3 rebounds, 2.2 assists, .6 steals, and 1.2 blocked shots per contest.

Chones scored 31 points in a 101–95 victory over Golden State on December 18, 1977, at The Coliseum. He scored 29 points three times. He had 23 points in a 100–95 playoff loss to Washington on April 13, 1976, at The Coliseum. He was traded back to the Lakers on October 5, 1979.

Chones was a Cavaliers local television broadcaster from 1987-88 to 1996-97. He has been a Cavs local radio broadcaster since 2010-11.

CLARK, EARL

Earl Clark was a 6-foot-10, 225-pound power forward for the Cavaliers in 2013-14. Signed as a free agent on July 12, 2013, he averaged 5.2 points, 2.8 rebounds, .4 assists, .4 steals, and .4 blocked shots per game in his one season with Cleveland. He scored 15 points in an 86–80 loss to Charlotte on November 15 at Quicken Loans Arena. He was traded to Philadelphia on February 20, 2014.

CLEAMONS, JIM

Jim Cleamons was a 6-foot-3, 185-pound point guard for the Cavaliers from 1972-73 to 1976-77. Traded from Los Angeles on August 31, 1972, in his five seasons with Cleveland he averaged 9.4 points, 4.1 assists, 3.6 rebounds, 1.1 steals, and .3 blocked shots per game. His best season as a Cavalier was 1975-76 when he averaged 12.2 points, 5.2 assists, 4.3 rebounds, 1.5 steals, and .2 blocked shots per contest. The season before, Cleamons averaged 11.9 points, 5.1 assists, 4.4 rebounds, 1.1 steals, and .3 blocked shots per game. In his last season with Cleveland he averaged 10.4 points, 5.1 assists, 4.6 rebounds, 1.1 steals, and .4 blocked shots per contest.

Cleamons scored 29 points twice—in a 119–106 triumph over the Lakers on December 17, 1974, at Los Angeles and in a 105–85 victory over Phoenix on January 17, 1976, at The Coliseum. He scored 18 points three times in the playoffs. He became a free agent on July 1, 1977, and was not re-signed.

CLEAVES, MATEEN

Mateen Cleaves was a 6-foot-2, 205-pound point guard for Cleveland in 2003-04. He signed a 10-day contract on March 29, 2004, and played four games with the Cavs. He was waived on April 6, 2004.

CLEMENS, BARRY

Barry Clemens was a 6-foot-6, 210-pound small forward for the Cavaliers from 1972-73 to 1973-74. Traded from Seattle on August 23, 1972, in his two seasons with Cleveland he averaged six points, 2.6 rebounds, 1.4 assists, and .5 steals per game. His best season as a Cavalier was 1972-73 when he averaged 6.5 points, 2.9 rebounds, and 1.6 assists per contest. Clemens scored 24 points in a 103–100 loss to the Warriors on December 10, 1972, at the Cleveland Arena. He was chosen by New Orleans in the 1974 Expansion Draft.

CLEVELAND ARENA

The Cleveland Arena was the Cavaliers' home from 1970-71 to 1973-74. The building was a showpiece when it opened in 1937, but by the time the Cavs moved in, it had become decrepit. It was also in a bad area of town. Its seating capacity was 11,000.

A choked-up Bill Fitch (left) and Nick Mileti prior to Fitch's Coach of the Year trophy presentation before Game 6 of the Eastern Conference Finals, May 18, 1976. (The Cleveland Press Collection, Michael Schwartz Library, Cleveland State University)

CLEVELAND CLINIC COURTS

Cleveland Clinic Courts in Independence has been the Cavaliers' practice facility and team headquarters since 2007-08. It replaced the former single-court center the team used within Quicken Loans Arena.

CLIFTON, ALLIE

Allie Clifton has been the Cavaliers' local television sideline reporter since 2012-13.

COACH OF THE YEAR

Bill Fitch (1975-76)

Mike Brown (2008-09)

COLES, BIMBO

Vernell "Bimbo" Coles was a 6-foot-1, 180-pound point guard for Cleveland from 2000-01 to 2002-03. He was signed as a free agent on August 12, 2000. In his three seasons with the Cavs he averaged 4.2 points, 2.6 assists, 1.3 rebounds, .4 steals, and .1 blocked shots per game. His best season as a Cavalier was 2002-03 when he averaged 4.9 points, 2.7 assists, 2.3 rebounds, .5 steals, and .2 blocked shots per contest. Coles scored 17 points in a 99–97 victory over the Knicks on November 8, 2000, at New York. He was waived on February 28, 2003.

COLISEUM, THE

The Coliseum in Richfield was the Cavaliers' home from 1974-75 to 1993-94. Its seating capacity was 20,900 from 1974-75 to 1987-88 and 20,273 from 1988-89 to 1993-94. The Coliseum was ahead of its time. Besides the main

The Coliseum, spring 1975. (AndersonsClevelandDesign.com)

arena, it had two full-sized practice courts, a weight room, loges, suites, office space, and more.

COLTER, STEVE

Steve Colter was a 6-foot-3, 165-pound point guard for the Cavaliers in 1994-95. Signed as a free agent on October 5, 1994, in his one season with the Cavs he averaged 3.4 points, 1.8 assists, one rebound, .5 steals, and .1 blocked shots per game. He scored 16 points in a 101–100 double-overtime victory against the Nuggets on January 21 at Denver. He scored five points in a 93–80 playoff defeat to New York at Gund Arena on May 4. He became a free agent again on July 1, 1995, and was not re-signed.

"COME ON CAVS – GOT TO MAKE IT HAPPEN"

"Come On Cavs—Got to Make It Happen" was the Cavaliers' fight song from 1974-75 to 1979-80. The groovy anthem, written by Cleveland radio legend Larry Morrow and performed by some of the finest musicians in New York City, was a smash hit. Some 10,000 copies of the record album were sold.

COMPOSITE WIN-LOSS RECORDS VS. OTHER TEAMS, BEST TO WORST (POSTSEASON)

Please see Team Statistics on page 215.

COMPOSITE WIN-LOSS RECORDS VS. OTHER TEAMS, BEST TO WORST (REGULAR SEASON)

Please see Team Statistics on page 215.

COOK, JEFF

Jeff Cook was a 6-foot-10, 215-pound power forward and center for the Cavaliers from 1982-83 to 1984-85. Traded from Phoenix on February 7, 1983, he averaged 6.1 points, 6.2 rebounds, 1.5 assists, .8 steals, and .6 blocked shots per game in his three seasons with Cleveland. His best season as a Cavalier was 1982-83 when he averaged 7.1 points, 6.9 rebounds, 1.5 assists, .9 steals, and .6 blocked shots per contest. Cook scored 18 points in a 104–92 defeat to the Bucks on January 3, 1984, at Milwaukee. He was traded to San Antonio on December 14, 1984.

COOKE, JOE

Joe Cooke was a 6-foot-3, 175-pound shooting guard for the Cavaliers in 1970-71. A sixth-round draft pick in 1970 out of Indiana University, he averaged 4.3 points, 1.3 assists, and 1.6 rebounds per game in his one season with the Cavs. He scored 23 points in a 123–105 loss to the Trail Blazers in Portland on February 21. He became a free agent on July 1, 1971, and was not re-signed.

CORBIN, TYRONE

Tyrone Corbin was a 6-foot-6, 210-pound small forward for the Cavaliers from 1986-87 to 1987-88. Signed as a free agent on January 24, 1987, he averaged 6.1 points, 3.7 rebounds, .8 assists, .7 steals, and .2 blocked shots per game in his two seasons with Cleveland. His best season as a Cavalier was 1987-88 when he averaged 7.3 points, 4.1 rebounds, one assist, .8 steals, and .3 blocked shots per contest. Corbin scored 23 points in a 101–88 victory over Philadelphia on November 21, 1987, at The Coliseum. He was traded to Phoenix on February 25, 1988.

CORRIGAN, JACK

Jack Corrigan was a Cavaliers local television broadcaster from 1984-85 to 1987-88.

COURTNEY, JOE

Joe Courtney was a 6-foot-8, 235-pound power forward for the Cavaliers in 1995-96. Signed as a free agent on October 5, 1995, in his one season with Cleveland he averaged 1.7 points, 2.1 rebounds, .4 assists, .2 steals, and .3 blocked shots per game. He scored five points in a 108–100 win over the Bullets on January 2 at Washington. He was waived on March 5, 1996.

CREGER, LARRY

Larry Creger was a Cavaliers assistant coach in 1980-81.

CROMPTON, GEOFF

Geoff Crompton was a 6-foot-11, 280-pound center for Cleveland in 1983-84. He was signed as a free agent on March 10, 1984. In seven games with the Cavaliers he averaged .7 points, 1.3 rebounds, .1 assists, .1 steals, and

.1 blocked shots per contest. He scored two points twice—in a 108–97 loss to Kansas City on March 18 at The Coliseum and in a 124–97 defeat to the Nets on April 8 at New Jersey. He was waived on October 23, 1984.

CROTTY, JOHN

John Crotty was a 6-foot-1, 185-pound point guard for the Cavaliers in 1995-96. Signed as a free agent on October 23, 1995, in his one season with the Cavs he averaged three points, 1.8 assists, .9 rebounds, .4 steals, and .1 blocked shots per game. Crotty scored 19 points in a 95–86 win over the Bucks on February 29 at Milwaukee. He scored two points in a 106–83 playoff loss to New York on April 25 at Gund Arena. He was released on August 13, 1996.

CROWDS, LARGEST TO SMALLEST (POSTSEASON)

Please see Attendance Statistics on page 272.

C-TOWN THROWDOWNS

C-Town Throwdowns has been the Cavaliers' high-flying slam dunk team since 2010-11. The team members unite at center court in a huddle to prepare for gravity-defying performances during timeouts, launching themselves acrobatically off of trampolines high into the air and then dunking basketballs.

CULP, RON

Ron Culp was the Cavaliers' trainer from 1970-71 to 1973-74.

CUNNINGHAM, JARED

Jared Cunningham was a 6-foot-4, 195-pound shooting guard for the Cavaliers in 2015-16. He was selected in the first round of the 2012 draft out of Oregon State University and was traded to Dallas on June 29, 2012. He was re-signed as a free agent on September 28, 2015. In his one season with Cleveland, Cunningham averaged 2.6 points, .5 assists, .7 rebounds, .3 steals, and .1 blocked shots per game. He scored 12 points in a 106–76 win over the Grizzlies on October 28 at Memphis. He was traded again to Orlando on February 18, 2016.

CURRY, DELL

Dell Curry was a 6-foot-4, 190-pound shooting guard for Cleveland in 1987-88. The father of Golden State superstar Stephen Curry and Dallas's—and ex-Cavalier—Seth Curry, he was traded from the Jazz on October 8, 1987. In his one season with the Cavs he averaged 10 points, 1.9 assists, 2.1 rebounds, 1.2 steals, and .3 blocked shots per game. He scored 27 points in a 113–112 defeat to the Warriors on December 9 at Golden State. He scored two points in a 104–93 playoff loss to the Bulls in Chicago on April 28. He was chosen by Charlotte in the 1988 Expansion Draft.

CURRY, SETH

Seth Curry was a 6-foot-2, 185-pound point guard for the Cavaliers in 2013-14. The son of ex-Cavalier Dell Curry and the younger brother of Warrior superstar Stephen Curry, he signed a 10-day contract on March 21, 2014. He played one game with Cleveland. He became a free agent again on March 31, 2014, and was not re-signed.

D

DALY, CHUCK

Chuck Daly was a Cavaliers head coach in 1981-82. He led the Cavs to a 9-32 record after replacing Bob Kloppenburg, who had lost his only game after taking over for Don Delaney, who had started the season 4-13. Daly was fired. He was inducted into the Naismith Memorial Basketball Hall of Fame in 1994.

DAUGHERTY, BRAD

Brad Daugherty was a 7-foot, 245-pound center for the Cavaliers from 1986-87 to 1993-94. He was a first-round draft pick—the number one overall selection—in 1986 out of the University of North Carolina. In his eight seasons with Cleveland he averaged 19 points, 9.5 rebounds, 3.7 assists, .8 steals, and .7 blocked shots per game. His best season as a Cavalier was 1990-91 when he averaged 21.6 points, 10.9 rebounds, 3.3 assists, one steal, and .6 blocked shots per contest. The next season, he averaged 21.5 points, 10.4 rebounds, 3.6 assists, .9 steals, and 1.1 blocked shots per game. The season after that, he averaged 20.2 points, 10.2 rebounds, 4.4 assists, .7 steals, and .8 blocked shots per contest.

On April 15, 1988, Daugherty scored 44 points in a 120–109 victory over Boston at The Coliseum. He scored 38 points in a 128–120 loss to the Nuggets on January 12, 1991, at Denver. He had 40 points in a 120–113 playoff win over New Jersey on April 23, 1992, at The Coliseum. He was an All-Star from 1987-88 to 1988-89 and 1990-91 to 1992-93. He retired on July 22, 1996. His jersey number 43 was retired by the Cavaliers on March 1, 1997.

Daugherty was a Cavaliers local television broadcaster in 1997-98.

DAVID, KORNEL

Kornel David was a 6-foot-9, 235-pound small forward for the Cavaliers in 1999-2000. He signed the first of two 10-day contracts on January 6, 2000.

Brad Daugherty in action with Kareem Abdul-Jabbar defending, January 13, 1989. (AndersonsClevelandDesign.com)

In six games with Cleveland he averaged 1.8 points, 1.3 rebounds, .2 assists, .7 steals, and .2 blocked shots per contest. He scored five points in a 95–86 defeat to the Lakers on January 19 at Los Angeles. He became a free agent again on January 26, 2000, and was not re-signed.

DAVIS, BARON

Baron Davis was a 6-foot-3, 209-pound point guard for Cleveland in 2010-11. Traded from the Clippers on February 24, 2011, in 15 games with the Cavaliers he averaged 13.9 points, 6.1 assists, 2.4 rebounds, 1.1 steals, and .4 blocked shots per contest. He scored 22 points in a 123–107 loss to the Knicks in New York on April 3. He was waived on December 14, 2011.

DAVIS, CHARLIE

Charlie Davis was a 6-foot-2, 160-pound shooting guard for the Cavaliers from 1971-72 to 1972-73. An eighth-round draft choice in 1971 out of Wake Forest University, he averaged 9.6 points, two assists, and 1.4 rebounds per game in his two seasons with the Cavs. His best season as a Cavalier was 1971-72 when he averaged 9.8 points, two assists, and 1.5 rebounds per contest. He scored 30 points in a 120–106 loss to the 76ers on October 27, 1971, at Philadelphia. He was traded to Portland on October 24, 1972.

DAVIS, DWIGHT

Dwight Davis was a 6-foot-8, 220-pound power forward for the Cavaliers from 1972-73 to 1974-75. A first-round draft pick in 1972 out of the University of Houston, he averaged 10.5 points, 7.1 rebounds, 1.9 assists, .7 steals, and .7 blocked shots per game in his three seasons with Cleveland. His best season as a Cavalier was 1973-74 when he averaged 12.5 points, 8.5 rebounds, 2.4 assists, .8 steals, and one blocked shot per contest.

Davis scored 25 points twice—in a 109–98 victory over Atlanta on November 19, 1972, at the Cleveland Arena and in an 89–75 triumph over the 76ers on December 5, 1973, in Philadelphia. He was traded to the Warriors on May 29, 1975.

DAVIS, HARRY

Harry Davis was a 6-foot-7, 220-pound small forward for Cleveland in 1978-79. He was a second-round draft choice in 1978 out of Florida State University. In his one season with the Cavaliers he averaged 4.1 points, 1.7 rebounds, .4 assists, .3 steals, and .2 blocked shots per game. He scored 12 points twice—in a 111–109 victory over Boston on March 27 at The Coliseum and in a 102–95 defeat to the Pacers on April 4 at Indiana. He was waived on October 10, 1979.

DAVIS, JOHNNY

Johnny Davis was a 6-foot-2, 170-pound point guard and shooting guard for the Cavaliers from 1984-85 to 1985-86. He was traded from Atlanta on August 8, 1984, and averaged 10.6 points, 4.6 assists, 1.3 rebounds, .6 steals, and .1 blocked shots per game in his two seasons with Cleveland. His best season as a Cavalier was 1984-85 when he averaged 12.4 points, 5.6 assists, 1.6 rebounds, .6 steals, and .1 blocked shots per contest.

Davis scored 33 points in a 124–107 loss to the Pistons on October 30, 1984, at Detroit. He scored 15 points in a 108–106 playoff defeat to the Celtics in Boston on April 20, 1985. He was traded back to the Hawks on February 10, 1986.

DAVIS, RICKY

Ricky Davis was a 6-foot-6, 195-pound shooting guard and small forward for the Cavaliers from 2001-02 to 2003-04. Traded from Miami on October 26, 2001, in his three seasons with Cleveland he averaged 16 points, four assists, 4.1 rebounds, 1.2 steals, and .4 blocked shots per game. His best season as a Cavalier was 2002-03 when he averaged 20.6 points, 5.5 assists, 4.9 rebounds, 1.6 steals, and .5 blocked shots per contest. He scored 45 points in a 140–133 double-overtime loss to the Bucks on December 9, 2002, at Gund Arena. He was traded to Boston on December 15, 2003.

DECEMBER

The following are five memorable Cavaliers games that were played in the month of December:

DECEMBER 19, 1975

Cleveland won a thriller over the Phoenix Suns 128–124 in double overtime before 6,809 fans at the Arizona Veterans Memorial Coliseum. The Cavaliers recovered from a 10-point halftime deficit to tie the score at 82 entering the fourth quarter. It was 105–105 after regulation and 116–116 after the first overtime. Campy Russell led the Cavs with 27 points. Bingo Smith scored 22. Dick Van Arsdale and Keith Erickson each led the Suns with 26 points.

DECEMBER 17, 1991

In their most lopsided victory ever, the Cavaliers routed the Miami Heat 148–80 in front of 10,487 fans at The Coliseum. The Cavs led 34–24 after one quarter, 73–53 at halftime, and 106–67 after three quarters. Remarkably, not one Cavalier scored 20 points. Mark Price and John Battle each led Cleveland with 18 points, while Brad Daugherty and Henry James both had 17. Steve Smith led Miami with 15 points.

DECEMBER 19, 2003

Behind a team-leading 36 points from LeBron James, Cleveland earned its first road win in almost a year by beating the Philadelphia 76ers 88–81 before 20,761 fans at the Wachovia Center. The Cavs trailed 29–20 after one quarter but chipped away at the deficit and were even with Philly at 62 heading into the fourth quarter. Glenn Robinson led the Sixers with 18 points.

DECEMBER 25, 2003

In one of the most anticipated matchups in recent memory, the Cavaliers, led by heralded rookie LeBron James, were beaten 113–101 in overtime by the Orlando Magic, who were led by three-time All-Star Tracy McGrady, in front of 17,283 fans at the TD Waterhouse Center. It was a close game until the extra session, when the Magic outscored the Cavs 16–4. James led Cleveland with 34 points. McGrady led Orlando with 41 points.

DECEMBER 2, 2010

In LeBron James's return to Cleveland some five months after "The Decision," which landed him in South Florida, the Cavaliers were crushed by the Miami Heat 118–90 before 20,562 unmerciful booing fans inside Quicken Loans Arena. The Cavs trailed 31–23 after the first quarter, 59–40 at halftime, and 95–65 after the third quarter. Daniel Gibson was tops on Cleveland with 21 points. James led Miami with 38 points.

"DECISION, THE"

"The Decision" occurred on the evening of July 8, 2010, when LeBron James told Jim Gray on ESPN that, after seven seasons with the team, he was leaving the Cavaliers to join forces with Dwyane Wade and Chris Bosh in Miami with the Heat.

"DECISION II, THE"

"The Decision II" occurred on July 11, 2014, when LeBron James announced by way of a letter on SI.com that he would return to the Cavaliers, his original team, after four seasons with the Miami Heat.

DECLERCQ, ANDREW

Andrew DeClercq was a 6-foot-10, 230-pound center for the Cavaliers from 1998-99 to 1999-2000. Traded from Boston on March 11, 1999, in his two seasons with Cleveland he averaged 7.3 points, 5.5 rebounds, .7 assists, .9 steals, and .7 blocked shots per game. His best season as a Cavalier was 1998-99 when he averaged nine points, 5.8 rebounds, .6 assists, 1.1 steals, and .6 blocked shots per contest. He scored 19 points in a 109–103 loss to Seattle on November 11, 1999, at Gund Arena. He was traded to Orlando on August 3, 2000.

DELANEY, DON

Don Delaney was a Cavaliers head coach from 1980-81 to 1981-82. He had a 3-8 record in 1980-81 after replacing the fired Bill Musselman with the team's record at 25-46, for a final mark of 28-54. The Cavaliers began the next season 4-13 under Delaney, when he was fired. His overall record as Cavs head coach was 7-21. He was a Cavs assistant coach in 1982-83. He was the team's general manager from 1980-81 to 1982-83.

DELLAVEDOVA, MATTHEW

Matthew Dellavedova was a 6-foot-4, 198-pound shooting guard and point guard for the Cavaliers from 2013-14 to 2015-16. He was signed as a free agent on August 5, 2013. In his three seasons with Cleveland he averaged 5.7 points, 3.4 assists, 1.9 rebounds, .5 steals, and .1 blocked shots per game. His best season as a Cavalier was 2015-16 when he averaged 7.5 points, 4.4 assists, 2.1 rebounds, .6 steals, and .1 blocked shots per contest. The season before, he averaged 4.8 points, three assists, 1.9 rebounds, and .4 steals per game. In his first season with the Cavs he averaged 4.7 points, 2.6 assists, 1.7 rebounds, .5 steals, and .1 blocked shots per contest.

Dellavedova scored 21 points in a 97–96 win over the Pistons on March 26, 2014, at Detroit. He scored 20 points in a 96–91 Finals victory over Golden State on June 9, 2015, at Quicken Loans Arena. He was traded to Milwaukee on July 7, 2016.

DENG, LUOL

Luol Deng was a 6-foot-9, 220-pound small forward for Cleveland in 2013-14. Traded from the Bulls on January 6, 2014, he averaged 14.3 points, 5.1 rebounds, 2.5 assists, one steal, and .1 blocked shots per game in his one season with the Cavs. He scored 27 points in a 120–118 victory over the Lakers in Los Angeles on January 14. He won the 2013-14 J. Walter Kennedy Citizenship Award. He became a free agent on July 1, 2014, and was not re-signed.

DICKENS, KANIEL

Kaniel Dickens was a 6-foot-8, 215-pound power forward for Cleveland in 2007-08. He signed the first of two 10-day contracts on February 22, 2008. In five games with the Cavs he averaged .4 points, .2 rebounds, .2 assists, and .2 blocked shots per contest. He scored two points in a 107–96 loss to the Bulls in Chicago on March 6. He became a free agent again on March 13, 2008, and was not re-signed.

DILLARD, MICKEY

Mickey Dillard was a 6-foot-3, 170-pound point guard for the Cavaliers in 1981-82. He was a third-round draft pick in 1981 from Florida State University. In his one season with Cleveland he averaged 2.2 points, one assist, .5 rebounds, .2 steals, and .1 blocked shots per game. He scored eight points in a 98–89 loss to the Bulls at Chicago on December 15. He was waived on January 18, 1982.

DIOP, DESAGANA

DeSagana Diop was a 7-foot, 300-pound center and power forward for the Cavaliers from 2001-02 to 2004-05. A first-round draft pick in 2001 out of Oak Hill Academy, he averaged 1.6 points, 2.6 rebounds, .5 assists, .4 steals, and .9 blocked shots per game in his four seasons with Cleveland. His best season as a Cavalier was 2003-04 when he averaged 2.3 points, 3.6 rebounds, .6 assists, .5 steals, and .9 blocked shots per contest. He scored 10 points in a 97–84 loss to New Orleans on November 23, 2002, at Gund Arena. He became a free agent on July 1, 2005, and was not re-signed.

DOLEAC, MICHAEL

Michael Doleac was a 6-foot-11, 262-pound center for the Cavaliers in 2001-02. Traded from Orlando on June 27, 2001, he averaged 4.6 points, four rebounds, .6 assists, .4 steals, and .3 blocked shots per game in his one season with Cleveland. He scored 17 points in a 107–94 loss to the Mavericks on November 14 at Gund Arena. He became a free agent on July 1, 2002, and was not re-signed.

DONEWALD, BOB

Bob Donewald was a Cavaliers assistant coach in 2003-04.

DRAFT CHOICES BY SCHOOL (TOP TEN)

1.	North Carolina	6
2.	Florida State	5
	Kentucky	5
	Notre Dame	5
5.	California	4
	Duke	4
	Michigan	4
	Ohio State	4
	UCLA	4
10.	Arizona	3
	Indiana	3
	Kansas	3
	Kansas State	3
	LSU	3
	Nevada–Las Vegas	3
	Richmond	3
	Villanova	3
	Western Kentucky	3

DREILING, GREG

Greg Dreiling was a 7-foot-1, 250-pound center for the Cavaliers in 1994-95. Signed as a free agent on October 5, 1994, in his one season with Cleveland he averaged 1.9 points, two rebounds, .4 assists, .1 steals, and .4

blocked shots per game. He scored 11 points in a 96–90 loss to the Bullets in Washington on March 19. He became a free agent again on July 1, 1995, and was not re-signed.

DRENNAN, BRUCE

Bruce Drennan was a Cavaliers local television broadcaster from 1980-81 to 1981-82.

DREW, LARRY

Larry Drew has been a Cavaliers assistant coach since 2014-15.

DUDLEY, CHRIS

Chris Dudley was a 6-foot-11, 235-pound center and power forward for the Cavaliers from 1987-88 to 1989-90. A fourth-round draft pick in 1987 from Yale University, he averaged 3.5 points, 3.3 rebounds, .4 assists, .3 steals, and .5 blocked shots per game in his three seasons with Cleveland. His best season as a Cavalier was 1989-90 when he averaged five points, 5.5 rebounds, .5 assists, .5 steals, and 1.1 blocked shots per contest.

Dudley, who was known for his extremely poor free throw shooting, scored 15 points twice—in a 113–110 overtime victory against the Jazz on December 11, 1989, at Utah and in a 120–101 triumph over the SuperSonics on December 15, 1989, at The Coliseum. He scored two points in the playoffs twice—in a 106–101 loss to the Bulls on May 1, 1988, at Chicago and in a 110–102 win over the Bulls on May 3, 1988, at The Coliseum. He was traded to New Jersey on February 21, 1990.

DUMAS, TONY

Tony Dumas was a 6-foot-6, 190-pound shooting guard for Cleveland in 1997-98. Traded from the Suns on October 1, 1997, in seven games with the Cavs he averaged two points, .7 assists, and .7 rebounds per contest. He scored five points in a 100–70 victory over Houston on January 6 at Gund Arena. He was waived on January 29, 1998.

E

EAVES, JERRY

Jerry Eaves was a Cavaliers assistant coach from 2001-02 to 2002-03.

EDWARDS, JAMES

James Edwards was a 7-foot, 225-pound center for the Cavaliers from 1981-82 to 1982-83. He was signed as a free agent on May 25, 1981. In his two seasons with Cleveland he averaged 16 points, 7.4 rebounds, 1.5 assists, .3 steals, and 1.4 blocked shots per game. His best season as a Cavalier was 1981-82 when he averaged 16.7 points, 7.5 rebounds, 1.6 assists, .3 steals, and 1.5 blocked shots per contest. He scored 31 points in a 123–113 defeat to the Pistons in Detroit on February 11, 1982. He was traded to the Suns on February 7, 1983.

EDWARDS, SHANE

Shane Edwards was a 6-foot-7, 220-pound small forward for Cleveland in 2013-14. Signed to a 10-day contract on March 12, 2014, he played two games with the Cavs. He was waived on March 21, 2014.

EGAN, HANK

Hank Egan was a Cavaliers assistant coach from 2005-06 to 2009-10.

EGAN, JOHNNY

Johnny Egan was a 5-foot-11, 180-pound point guard for the Cavaliers in 1970-71. He was chosen in the 1970 Expansion Draft from the Lakers. In his one season with Cleveland he averaged four points, 2.2 assists, and 1.2 rebounds per game. He scored 16 points in a 115–112 loss to the Trail Blazers on October 16 in Portland. He was traded to San Diego on December 9, 1970.

EHLO, CRAIG

Craig Ehlo was a 6-foot-6, 180-pound shooting guard for the Cavaliers from 1986-87 to 1992-93. Signed as a free agent on January 13, 1987, he averaged 9.9 points, 3.5 assists, 4.4 rebounds, 1.3 steals, and .4 blocked shots per game in his seven seasons with Cleveland. His best season as a Cavalier was 1989-90 when he averaged 13.6 points, 4.6 assists, 5.4 rebounds, 1.6 steals, and .3 blocked shots per contest.

Ehlo scored 31 points in a 131–125 overtime victory against Atlanta on November 17, 1989, at The Coliseum. He scored 27 points in a 123–114 defeat to the Celtics in Boston on March 21, 1990. He had 25 points in a 122–95 playoff win over Philadelphia on May 1, 1990, at The Coliseum. He became a free agent again on July 1, 1993, and was not re-signed.

EKKER, RON

Ron Ekker was a Cavaliers assistant coach from 2001-02 to 2002-03.

ELLINGTON, WAYNE

Wayne Ellington was a 6-foot-4, 200-pound shooting guard for the Cavaliers in 2012-13. Traded from the Grizzlies on January 22, 2013, in his one season with Cleveland he averaged 10.4 points, 1.6 assists, three rebounds, .8 steals, and .1 blocked shots per game. He scored 21 points in a 119–113 loss to the Spurs at San Antonio on March 16. He became a free agent on July 1, 2013, and was not re-signed.

EMBRY, WAYNE

Wayne Embry was the Cavaliers' general manager from 1986-87 to 1998-99. Although he will always be remembered for his moves on draft day in 1986 that brought to town Brad Daugherty, Ron Harper, and Mark Price, he pocketed Executive of the Year awards in 1991-92 and 1997-98. He was inducted into the Naismith Memorial Basketball Hall of Fame in 1999.

ERDEN, SEMIH

Semih Erden was a 7-foot, 240-pound center for Cleveland from 2010-11 to 2011-12. Traded from Boston on February 24, 2011, in his two seasons with the Cavs he averaged 3.5 points, 2.6 rebounds, .3 assists, .4 steals, and .3 blocked shots per game. His best season as a Cavalier was 2010-11 when he averaged 3.3 points, 2.8 rebounds, .3 assists, .5 steals, and .8 blocked shots per contest. He scored 18 points in a 98–87 victory over the Pacers on February 15, 2012, at Quicken Loans Arena. He became a free agent on July 1, 2012, and was not re-signed.

EVANS, MIKE

Mike Evans was a 6-foot-1, 170-pound point guard for the Cavaliers in 1981-82. He was signed as a free agent on February 20, 1982. In eight games with Cleveland he averaged 3.4 points, 2.5 assists, 1.3 rebounds, and .5 steals per contest. He scored 12 points in a 147–127 defeat to the Nuggets on March 7 at Denver. He was waived on October 11, 1982.

EXECUTIVE OF THE YEAR

- Wayne Embry (1991-92)
- Wayne Embry (1997-98)
- Danny Ferry (2008-09)

EYENGA, CHRISTIAN

Christian Eyenga was a 6-foot-5, 210-pound small forward for the Cavaliers from 2010-11 to 2011-12. A first-round draft pick in 2009 from the Democratic Republic of the Congo, he averaged 6.2 points, 2.7 rebounds, .8 assists, .7 steals, and .6 blocked shots per game in his two seasons with the Cavs. His best season as a Cavalier was 2010-11 when he averaged 6.9 points, 2.8 rebounds, .8 assists, .8 steals, and .6 blocked shots per contest. He scored 16 points in a 120–105 loss to the Raptors on January 5, 2011, at Quicken Loans Arena. He was traded to the Lakers on March 15, 2012.

F

FAN CLUBS

WINE & GOLD NATION

Wine & Gold Nation is the official fan club of the Cavaliers. The club is for passionate Cavs fans who are 18 years of age and older and want to show off their pride and connect with Cavs fans across the nation.

CAVALRY

Cavalry is the official fan club of the Cavaliers for Cavs fans who are 13–17 years old.

KIDS CLUB

Kids Club is the official fan club of the Cavaliers for Cavs fans who are 6–12 years old.

CAVALITTLES

Cavalittles is the official fan club of the Cavaliers for Cavs fans who are 5 years old and younger.

FEBRUARY

The following are five memorable Cavaliers games that were played in the month of February:

FEBRUARY 20, 1972

In perhaps the greatest victory of the franchise's brief history up to that point, the Cavaliers shocked the New York Knicks 111–109 before 8,877 fans at the Cleveland Arena. The victory was even more remarkable because the Cavs trailed 32–13 after one quarter. Austin Carr led Cleveland with 25 points and Butch Beard had 21. Leading the Knicks with 28 points was Dave DeBusschere.

FEBRUARY 20, 1977

The Cavaliers blew an 89–67 lead after three quarters and fell 112–111 to the Philadelphia 76ers before 15,875 fans at The Spectrum. Leading the way for the Cavs were Austin Carr with 26 points, Bingo Smith with 22, and Jim Chones with 20. Julius Erving led the Sixers with 34 points.

FEBRUARY 23, 1984

In what very well may have been their most impressive performance during the brief Gunds' ownership of the franchise, the Cavaliers defeated the Philadelphia 76ers 116–109 in overtime before 14,517 fans at The Coliseum. The Cavs were led by World B. Free's 35 points. Moses Malone was tops on the Sixers with 29 points.

FEBRUARY 27, 1997

Despite scoring only 11 points in the fourth quarter, the Cavaliers beat the 49-6 Chicago Bulls 73–70 in front of a crowd of 20,562 at Gund Arena. Terrell Brandon led the Cavs with 23 points. Also scoring 23 points, tops on the Bulls, was Michael Jordan.

FEBRUARY 25, 2010

The Cavaliers broke open a close game by outscoring the Boston Celtics 35–14 in the fourth quarter en route to a 108–88 triumph in front of 18,624 fans at TD Garden. LeBron James led the Cavs with 36 points. Ray Allen led the Celtics with 21 points.

FELIX, CARRICK

Carrick Felix was a 6-foot-6, 201-pound shooting guard for the Cavaliers in 2013-14. A second-round draft pick in 2013 out of Arizona State University, he averaged 2.7 points, .6 assists, and .9 rebounds per contest in seven games with Cleveland. He scored 10 points in a 114–85 victory over Brooklyn on April 16 at Quicken Loans Arena. He was traded to Utah on July 22, 2014.

FERNSTEN, ERIC

Eric Fernsten was a 6-foot-10, 205-pound center for the Cavaliers in 1975-76. A fourth-round draft choice in 1975 out of the University of San Francisco, he played four games with the Cavs. He was traded to Chicago on November 27, 1975.

FERRY, DANNY

Danny Ferry was a 6-foot-10, 230-pound power forward for Cleveland from 1990-91 to 1999-2000. Traded on November 16, 1989, from the Clippers, he averaged 7.8 points, three rebounds, 1.4 assists, .5 steals, and .3 blocked shots per game in his 10 seasons with the Cavs. His best season as a Cavalier was 1995-96, when he averaged 13.3 points, 3.8 rebounds, 2.3 assists, .7 steals, and .5 blocked shots per contest.

Ferry scored 32 points in a 101–97 triumph over the Knicks in New York on April 11, 1996. He scored 20 points in a 103–79 playoff loss to the Knicks on April 27, 1995, also at New York. He became a free agent on July 1, 2000, and was not re-signed.

Ferry was the Cavaliers' general manager from 2005-06 to 2009-10. He was Executive of the Year in 2008-09.

FINALS MVP

LeBron James (2015-16)

FIRST-ROUND DRAFT CHOICES

1970	John Johnson (Iowa)
1971	Austin Carr (Notre Dame)
1972	Dwight Davis (Houston)
1973	Jim Brewer (Minnesota)
1974	Campy Russell (Michigan)
1975	John Lambert (Southern California)
1976	Chuckie Williams (Kansas State)
1978	Mike Mitchell (Auburn)
1980	Chad Kinch (North Carolina–Charlotte)
1982	John Bagley (Boston College)
1983	Roy Hinson (Rutgers), Stewart Granger (Villanova)
1984	Tim McCormick (Michigan)

1985	Charles Oakley (Virginia Union)
1986	Brad Daugherty (North Carolina), Ron Harper (Miami [Ohio])
1987	Kevin Johnson (California)
1988	Randolph Keys (Southern Mississippi)
1989	John Morton (Seton Hall)
1991	Terrell Brandon (Oregon)
1993	Chris Mills (Arizona)
1995	Bob Sura (Florida State)
1996	Vitaly Potapenko (Wright State), Zydrunas Ilgauskas (Lithuania)
1997	Derek Anderson (Kentucky), Brevin Knight (Stanford)
1999	Andre Miller (Utah), Trajan Langdon (Duke)
2000	Jamal Crawford (Michigan)
2001	DeSagana Diop (Oak Hill Academy), Brendan Haywood (North Carolina)
2002	Dajuan Wagner (Memphis)
2003	LeBron James (St. Vincent-St. Mary)
2004	Luke Jackson (Oregon)
2006	Shannon Brown (Michigan State)
2008	J. J. Hickson (North Carolina State)
2009	Christian Eyenga (Democratic Republic of the Congo)
2011	Kyrie Irving (Duke), Tristan Thompson (Texas)
2012	Dion Waiters (Syracuse), Jared Cunningham (Oregon State)
2013	Anthony Bennett (Nevada–Las Vegas), Sergey Karasav (Russia)
2014	Andrew Wiggins (Kansas)
2015	Tyus Jones (Duke)

FITCH, BILL

Bill Fitch was the Cavaliers' head coach from 1970-71 to 1978-79. His first four seasons were tough to stomach—15-67, 23-59, 32-50, and 29-53, respectively. He did his best to deflect all of the attention on his team's lousy play by entertaining the press with his witty sense of humor, including jokes and one-liners.

By 1974-75, the Cavaliers had a decent team and finished 40-42, missing the postseason on the final day of the season. The next season, the team finished 49-33 and shocked the Washington Bullets in a memorable seven-game playoff series that spawned the Miracle of Richfield moniker and advanced them to the Eastern Conference Finals. That season Fitch was named Coach of the Year. The next two seasons brought playoff berths but first-round failure each time. Fitch resigned after the 1978-79 season in which the Cavaliers finished just 30-52. His overall record as Cleveland's head coach was 304-434. His postseason mark was 7-11. He was also the team's general manager from 1973-74 to 1978-79.

FIVE HIGHEST/LOWEST-SCORING GAMES (POSTSEASON)

Please see Team Statistics on page 215.

FIVE LARGEST HOME CROWDS

Please see Attendance Statistics on page 272.

FIVE MOST ONE-SIDED GAMES (POSTSEASON)

Please see Team Statistics on page 215.

FLOWERS, BRUCE

Bruce Flowers was a 6-foot-8, 225-pound power forward for the Cavaliers in 1982-83. He was a second-round draft pick in 1979 from the University of Notre Dame. In his one season with Cleveland he averaged 4.9 points, 3.4 rebounds, .9 assists, .4 steals, and .2 blocked shots per game. He scored 14 points twice—in a 132–121 defeat to the Nuggets on March 1 at Denver and in a 124–102 loss to the Celtics on March 25 in Boston. He became a free agent on July 1, 1983, and was not re-signed.

FORD, DON

Don Ford was a 6-foot-9, 215-pound small forward for Cleveland from 1979-80 to 1981-82. Traded from Los Angeles on February 15, 1980, in his three seasons with the Cavs he averaged 3.8 points, 2.7 rebounds, 1.2 assists, .3 steals, and .2 blocked shots per game. His best season as a Cavalier was 1979-80 when he averaged 7.3 points, 4.1 rebounds, 1.4 assists, .5 steals, and .3 blocked shots per contest. He scored 17 points in a 111–104 victory over the Kings in Kansas City on March 7, 1980. He was waived on January 19, 1982.

FOSTER, FRED

Fred Foster was a 6-foot-5, 210-pound small forward for the Cavaliers from 1973-74 to 1974-75. Signed as a free agent on October 29, 1973, in his two seasons with Cleveland he averaged six points, 1.7 rebounds, 1.3 assists, .3 steals, and .1 blocked shots per game. His best season as a Cavalier was 1974-75 when he averaged 6.9 points, 1.5 rebounds, 1.4 assists, and .3 steals per contest. He scored 23 points in a 110–103 victory over Philadelphia on November 28, 1974, at The Coliseum. He was traded to Chicago on September 5, 1975.

FOX SPORTS NET OHIO

Fox Sports Net Ohio was a Cavaliers local television station from 2000-01 to 2003-04.

FOX SPORTS OHIO

Fox Sports Ohio was a Cavaliers local television station from 1998-99 to 1999-2000 and has been since 2008-09.

FRATELLO, MIKE

Mike Fratello was the Cavaliers' head coach from 1993-94 to 1998-99. Under him, the Cavs had winning records in five of six seasons, including three 47-win campaigns and four playoff berths. Unfortunately, Cleveland lost in the first round each time. He was fired after the 1998-99 season. His overall record as Cavs head coach was 248-212. His postseason mark was 2-12.

FRAZIER, WALT

Walt Frazier was a 6-foot-4, 200-pound point guard for the Cavaliers from 1977-78 to 1979-80. Signed on October 10, 1977, as compensation for Jim Cleamons signing with New York as a free agent, in his three seasons with Cleveland he averaged 14.6 points, 3.8 assists, 3.5 rebounds, 1.4 steals, and .2 blocked shots per game. His best season as a Cavalier was 1977-78 when he averaged 16.2 points, 4.1 assists, 4.1 rebounds, 1.5 steals, and .3 blocked shots per contest.

Frazier scored 29 points in a 113–102 loss to New Orleans on December 27, 1977, at The Coliseum. He was waived on October 19, 1979. He was inducted into the Naismith Memorial Basketball Hall of Fame in 1987.

FREE, WORLD B.

World B. Free was a 6-foot-2, 185-pound shooting guard for Cleveland from 1982-83 to 1985-86. Traded from Golden State on December 15, 1982, in his four seasons with the Cavs he averaged 23 points, 3.9 assists, 2.9 rebounds, 1.2 steals, and .2 blocked shots per game. His best season as a Cavalier was 1982-83 when he averaged 24.2 points, 3.7 assists, 2.9 rebounds, 1.5 steals, and .2 blocked shots per contest.

Free scored 45 points in a 122–115 defeat to the Rockets on February 16, 1985, at The Coliseum and 43 points in a 123–105 victory over the Hawks on March 29, 1986, at Atlanta. He had 32 points in a 105–98 playoff win over Boston on April 23, 1985, at The Coliseum. He became a free agent on July 1, 1986, and was not re-signed.

FREEMAN, GARY

Gary Freeman was a 6-foot-9, 210-pound small forward for the Cavaliers in 1970-71. Traded from the Bucks on February 1, 1971, in 11 games with Cleveland he averaged 1.4 points, .7 rebounds, and .4 assists per contest. He scored four points twice—in a 107–90 loss to the Lakers on February 28 at Los Angeles and in a 120–109 defeat to the Braves on March 6 in Buffalo. He became a free agent on July 1, 1971, and was not re-signed.

FRYE, CHANNING

Channing Frye has been a 6-foot-11, 255-pound center for the Cavaliers since 2015-16. Traded from the Magic on February 18, 2016, in his one season

World B. Free in action against the Sixers. (AndersonsClevelandDesign.com)

with the Cavs he has averaged 7.5 points, 3.6 rebounds, one assist, .3 steals, and .3 blocked shots per game. He scored 21 points in a 120–108 triumph over the Lakers on March 10 at Los Angeles. He scored 27 points in a 121–108 playoff victory over the Hawks on May 6 at Atlanta.

FSN OHIO

FSN Ohio was a Cavaliers local television station from 2004-05 to 2007-08.

FURLOW, TERRY

Terry Furlow was a 6-foot-4, 190-pound shooting guard for the Cavaliers from 1977-78 to 1978-79. Traded from Philadelphia on October 3, 1977, in his two seasons with Cleveland he averaged 11 points, 1.7 assists, two rebounds, .6 steals, and .3 blocked shots per game. His best season as a Cavalier was 1978-79 when he averaged 13.3 points, 2.1 assists, two rebounds, .8 steals, and .3 blocked shots per contest.

Furlow scored 25 points on three occasions. He scored 20 points in a 132–114 playoff defeat to New York on April 12, 1978, at The Coliseum. He was traded to Atlanta on January 31, 1979.

G

GARRETT, ROWLAND

Rowland Garrett was a 6-foot-6, 210-pound small forward for the Cavaliers from 1975-76 to 1976-77. Traded from the Bulls on November 27, 1975, he averaged 3.1 points, 1.2 rebounds, .2 assists, .3 steals, and .1 blocked shots per game in his two seasons with Cleveland. His best season as a Cavalier was 1976-77 when he averaged 3.4 points, 1.4 rebounds, .2 assists, .2 steals, and .1 blocked shots per contest.

Garrett scored 15 points in a 132–89 victory over Milwaukee on January 24, 1976, at The Coliseum. He scored two points in a 111–99 playoff loss to the Celtics on May 6, 1976, in Boston. He was traded to the Bucks on January 13, 1977.

GARRIS, JOHN

John Garris was a 6-foot-8, 205-pound power forward for the Cavaliers in 1983-84. A second-round draft pick in 1984 out of Boston College, he averaged four points, 2.3 rebounds, .3 assists, .2 steals, and .2 blocked shots per game in his one season with Cleveland. He scored 20 points in a 130–98 loss to the Bucks in Milwaukee on March 28. He was traded to Atlanta on August 8, 1984.

GATLING, CHRIS

Chris Gatling was a 6-foot-10, 220-pound power forward for Cleveland in 2000-01. Traded from Miami on August 30, 2000, in his one season with the Cavs he averaged 11.4 points, 5.3 rebounds, .8 assists, .7 steals, and .4 blocked shots per game. He scored 38 points in a 108–103 loss to the Kings in Sacramento on January 10. He was traded back to the Heat on October 26, 2001.

GEARY, REGGIE

Reggie Geary was a 6-foot-2, 187-pound point guard for the Cavaliers in 1996-97. A second-round draft choice in 1996 from the University of Arizona, he averaged 1.5 points, .9 assists, .4 rebounds, .3 steals, and .1 blocked shots per game in his one season with the Cavs. He scored 11 points in a 94–74 loss to the Jazz in Utah on January 20. He became a free agent on July 1, 1997, and was not re-signed.

GEE, ALONZO

Alonzo Gee was a 6-foot-6, 225-pound small forward and shooting guard for the Cavaliers from 2010-11 to 2013-14. He was signed as a free agent on December 28, 2010. In his four seasons with Cleveland he averaged 8.2 points, 3.8 rebounds, 1.3 assists, one steal, and .3 blocked shots per game. His best season as a Cavalier was 2011-12 when he averaged 10.6 points, 5.1 rebounds, 1.8 assists, 1.3 steals, and .3 blocked shots per contest.

Gee scored 22 points on two occasions—in a 122–117 overtime defeat to the Nets in New Jersey on April 8, 2012, and in a 118–117 double-overtime loss to Portland on December 1, 2012, at Quicken Loans Arena. He was traded to Charlotte on June 27, 2014.

GENERAL MANAGERS

Nick Mileti (1970-71 to 1972-73)
Bill Fitch (1973-74 to 1978-79)
Ron Hrovat (1979-80)
Don Delaney (1980-81 to 1982-83)
Harry Weltman (1983-84 to 1985-86)
Wayne Embry (1986-87 to 1998-99)
Jim Paxson (1999-2000 to 2004-05)
Danny Ferry (2005-06 to 2009-10)
Chris Grant (2010-11 to 2013-14)
David Griffin (2014-15 to present)

GIBSON, DANIEL

Daniel Gibson was a 6-foot-2, 190-pound point guard and shooting guard for the Cavaliers from 2006-07 to 2012-13. A second-round draft choice in 2006 out of the University of Texas, in his seven seasons with Cleveland he averaged 7.8 points, two assists, two rebounds, .6 steals, and .2 blocked shots per game. His best season as a Cavalier was 2010-11 when he averaged 11.6 points, three assists, 2.6 rebounds, .7 steals, and .3 blocked shots per contest.

Gibson scored 29 points in a 101–90 loss to Utah on December 20, 2010, at Quicken Loans Arena. He scored 31 points in a 98–82 playoff victory over the Pistons on June 2, 2007, also at Quicken Loans Arena. He became a free agent on July 1, 2013, and was not re-signed.

GILBERT, DAN

Dan Gilbert has been the Cavaliers' majority owner since 2004-05. With LeBron James leading the way, his first Cavs team finished 42-40, barely missing the postseason. What followed were five straight playoff seasons, including two seasons of 66 and 61 wins, respectively, and an appearance in the Finals in 2007. After James left as a free agent for Miami, the Cavs won just 19, 21, 24, and 33 games, respectively, from 2010-11 to 2013-14. After James returned to the Cavaliers in 2014, the team has played in two straight Finals—losing to Golden State in six games in 2014-15 and then beating the Warriors in seven games in 2015-16.

GOODEN, DREW

Drew Gooden was a 6-foot-10, 250-pound power forward for the Cavaliers from 2004-05 to 2007-08. Traded from Orlando on July 23, 2004, in his four seasons with Cleveland he averaged 11.9 points, 8.6 rebounds, 1.1 assists, .8 steals, and .6 blocked shots per game. His best season as a Cavalier was 2004-05 when he averaged 14.4 points, 9.2 rebounds, 1.6 assists, .9 steals, and .9 blocked shots per contest.

Gooden scored 33 points in a 104–87 triumph over Milwaukee on January 30, 2005, at Gund Arena and 31 points in a 95–86 victory over the Bucks again on January 5, 2007, in Milwaukee. He scored 24 points in the playoffs twice—in an 89–84 loss to Washington on April 25, 2006, at Quicken Loans Arena and in a 109–102 win over the Wizards on April 25, 2007, again at Quicken Loans Arena. He was traded to Chicago on February 21, 2008.

GRAHAM, GREG

Greg Graham was a 6-foot-4, 174-pound shooting guard for the Cavaliers in 1997-98. Traded from the Nuggets on October 20, 1997, in six games with Cleveland he averaged 2.7 points, one assist, .2 rebounds, and .2 steals per contest. He scored 10 points in a 96–93 overtime defeat to the Magic on November 19 at Gund Arena. He was waived on December 2, 1997.

GRAHAM, JOEY

Joey Graham was a 6-foot-7, 225-pound small forward for Cleveland in 2010-11. Signed as a free agent on July 30, 2010, he averaged 5.2 points, 2.2 rebounds, .5 assists, .2 steals, and .2 blocked shots per game in his one season with Cleveland. He scored 14 points on two occasions—in a 103–101 defeat to the Nets in New Jersey on January 24 and in a 117–103 loss to Denver at Quicken Loans Arena on January 28. He was waived on December 9, 2011.

GRAHAM, STEPHEN

Stephen Graham was a 6-foot-6, 215-pound shooting guard for the Cavaliers in 2005-06. He signed the first of two 10-day contracts on February 6, 2006, and on February 24, 2006, signed a contract for the rest of the 2005-06 season. In 13 games with Cleveland he averaged 2.8 points, .2 assists, 1.3 rebounds, .2 steals, and .2 blocked shots per contest. He scored eight points twice—in a 101–87 victory over the Spurs on February 13 at Quicken Loans Arena and in a 100–99 win over Atlanta on April 19 again at Quicken Loans Arena. He was waived on October 24, 2006.

GRANGER, STEWART

Stewart Granger was a 6-foot-3, 190-pound point guard for the Cavaliers in 1983-84. A first-round draft pick in 1983 from Villanova University, he averaged 4.5 points, 2.4 assists, one rebound, and .4 steals per game in his one season with the Cavs. He scored 16 points in a 115–103 loss to the Mavericks in Dallas on March 7. He was traded to Atlanta on August 8, 1984.

GRANT, CHRIS

Chris Grant was the Cavaliers' general manager from 2010-11 to 2013-14.

GRAVES, BUTCH

Earl "Butch" Graves was a 6-foot-3, 200-pound shooting guard for the Cavaliers in 1984-85. Signed to the first of two 10-day contracts on January

10, 1985, he played four games with Cleveland. He became a free agent again on January 30, 1985, and was not re-signed.

GREEN, DANNY

Danny Green was a 6-foot-6, 215-pound shooting guard for the Cavaliers in 2009-10. A 2009 second-round draft pick out of the University of North Carolina, he averaged two points, .3 assists, .9 rebounds, .3 steals, and .2 blocked shots per game in his one season with Cleveland. He scored six points in a 109–95 victory over Minnesota on January 27 at Quicken Loans Arena. He was waived on October 19, 2010.

GREEN, LITTERIAL

Litterial Green was a 6-foot-1, 185-pound point guard for Cleveland in 1998-99. Signed as a free agent on January 21, 1999, he played one game with the Cavs. He was waived on February 17, 1999.

GRIFFIN, DAVID

David Griffin has been the Cavaliers' general manager since 2014-15.

GUIDINGER, JAY

Jay Guidinger was a 6-foot-10, 255-pound center for the Cavaliers from 1992-93 to 1993-94. He was signed as a free agent on October 8, 1992. He was waived on December 23, 1993, re-signed to the first of two 10-day contracts on January 19, 1994, and on February 8, 1994, signed a contract for the rest of the 1993-94 season.

In his two seasons with Cleveland Guidinger averaged 1.5 points, 1.5 rebounds, .3 assists, .2 steals, and .2 blocked shots per game. His best season as a Cavalier was 1992-93 when he averaged 1.6 points, two rebounds, .5 assists, .3 steals, and .3 blocked shots per contest. He scored seven points in a 115–102 loss to the SuperSonics on November 11, 1993, at Seattle. He scored two points in a 114–98 playoff win over New Jersey on April 29, 1993, at The Coliseum. He became a free agent again on July 1, 1994, and was not re-signed.

GUMBEL, GREG

Greg Gumbel was a Cavaliers local television broadcaster in 1992-93.

GUND, GEORGE AND GORDON

Brothers Gordon and George Gund were the Cavaliers' majority owners from 1983-84 to 2004-05. They purchased the Cavs from Ted Stepien, who in three years had turned the franchise into a disaster. It took some time, but the Gunds brought better times to the team, starting with an improvement from 23 wins in Stepien's last season of 1982-83 to 28 wins in their first season as owners, a year in which Gordon Gund doubled as team president. After a 2-19 start, the 1984-85 Cavaliers finished 36-46 and gave the heavily-favored Boston Celtics a huge scare before they died in the first round of the playoffs.

The Mark Price-Brad Daugherty-John Williams era brought even more excitement, including a berth in the 1992 Eastern Conference Finals. The rest of the 1990s brought several playoff appearances but very little advancement. The Cavaliers eventually dropped to just 17 wins in 2002-03. That dreadful season, however, resulted in the team winning that spring's NBA Draft Lottery, which brought LeBron James to town. In James's first season, the Cavaliers more than doubled their win total from the year before. In the Gunds' final season as owners, the Cavs improved to 42-40, barely missing the playoffs.

GUND ARENA

Gund Arena, or "The Gund" as it was also known, has been the Cavaliers' home since 1994-95. It became known as Quicken Loans Arena in 2005-06. Its seating capacity was 20,562.

GUOKAS, MATT

Matt Guokas was a Cavaliers local television broadcaster from 1997-98 to 2003-04.

H

HALL OF FAMERS

The following individuals from Cavaliers history are members of the Naismith Memorial Basketball Hall of Fame (includes the years they were inducted and the roles they played with the Cavs):

Nate Thurmond (1985, player)
Walt Frazier (1987, player)
Lenny Wilkens (1989, player; 1998, coach)
Chuck Daly (1994, coach)
Wayne Embry (1999, contributor)
Shaquille O'Neal (2016, player)

HAMILTON, ZENDON

Zendon Hamilton was a 6-foot-11, 250-pound center for Cleveland in 2005-06. Signed as a free agent on September 27, 2005, in 11 games with the Cavs he averaged 2.3 points, one rebound, and .3 steals per contest. He scored six points in a 102–76 defeat to the Spurs in San Antonio on November 4. He became a free agent again on January 30, 2006, and was not re-signed.

HANDY, PHIL

Phil Handy has been a Cavaliers assistant coach since 2015-16.

HARANGODY, LUKE

Luke Harangody was a 6-foot-8, 246-pound power forward for the Cavaliers from 2010-11 to 2011-12. Traded on February 24, 2011, from the Celtics, in his two seasons with the Cavs he averaged 4.5 points, 3.4 rebounds, .6 assists, .4 steals, and .3 blocked shots per game. His best season as a Cavalier was 2010-11 when he averaged 6.2 points, 4.2 rebounds, one assist, .5 steals, and .5 blocked shots per contest. He scored 18 points in a 119–115 victory over the Knicks on March 4, 2011, at New York. He was waived on November 29, 2012.

HARPER, RON

Ron Harper was a 6-foot-6, 185-pound shooting guard for the Cavaliers from 1986-87 to 1989-90. A first-round draft choice in 1986 out of Miami University, in his four seasons with Cleveland he averaged 19.4 points, 5.1 assists, 4.7 rebounds, 2.3 steals, and one blocked shot per game. His best season as a Cavalier was 1989-90 when he averaged 22 points, seven assists, 6.9 rebounds, two steals, and 1.3 blocked shots per contest.

Harper scored 40 points in a 104–102 loss to the Celtics in Boston on February 4, 1987. He scored 37 points in a 103–101 defeat to the Pistons on January 13, 1987, at The Coliseum. He had 31 points in a 96–88 playoff win over the Bulls on April 30, 1989, again at The Coliseum. He was traded to the Clippers on November 16, 1989.

Ron Harper goes for two, 1988-89. (AndersonsClevelandDesign.com)

HARPRING, MATT

Matt Harpring was a 6-foot-7, 231-pound shooting guard for the Cavaliers in 2000-01. Traded from the Magic on August 3, 2000, in his one season with Cleveland he averaged 11.1 points, 1.8 assists, 4.3 rebounds, .8 steals, and .3 blocked shots per game. He scored 28 points in a 114–109 triumph over the Hornets on March 16 at Gund Arena. He was traded to Philadelphia on August 3, 2001.

HARRIS, JOE

Joe Harris was a 6-foot-6, 219-pound shooting guard for the Cavaliers from 2014-15 to 2015-16. A second-round draft pick in 2014 from the University of Virginia, he averaged 2.5 points, .5 assists, .8 rebounds, and .1 steals per game in his two seasons in Cleveland. His best season as a Cavalier was 2014-15 when he averaged 2.7 points, .5 assists, .8 rebounds, and .1 steals per contest.

Harris scored 16 points in a 95–92 defeat to the 76ers on January 5, 2015, at Philadelphia. He scored seven points in a 118–88 playoff victory over Atlanta on May 26, 2015, at Quicken Loans Arena. He was traded to Orlando on January 12, 2016.

HARRIS, LUCIOUS

Lucious Harris was a 6-foot-5, 190-pound shooting guard for the Cavaliers in 2004-05. Signed as a free agent on October 1, 2004, in his one season with the Cavs he averaged 4.3 points, .7 assists, 1.7 rebounds, .4 steals, and .1 blocked shots per game. He scored 16 points in a 104–79 victory over New York on January 8 at Gund Arena. He became a free agent again on June 23, 2005, and was not re-signed.

HARRIS, MANNY

Manny Harris was a 6-foot-5, 185-pound shooting guard for the Cavaliers from 2010-11 to 2011-12. He was signed as a free agent on September 25, 2010. He was waived on December 22, 2011, signed the first of two 10-day contracts on February 21, 2012, and on March 17, 2012, signed a contract for the rest of the 2011-12 season.

In his two seasons with Cleveland Harris averaged 6.2 points, 1.5 assists, 2.6 rebounds, .6 steals, and .2 blocked shots per game. His best season as a Cavalier was 2011-12 when he averaged 6.7 points, 1.2 assists, 2.7 rebounds, .5 steals, and .2 blocked shots per contest. He scored 27 points in a 108–100 loss to the Suns on January 9, 2011, at Phoenix. He was waived again on July 1, 2012.

HAWES, SPENCER

Spencer Hawes was a 7-foot-1, 245-pound center for the Cavaliers in 2013-14. Traded on February 20, 2014, from Philadelphia, in his one season with Cleveland he averaged 13.5 points, 7.7 rebounds, 2.4 assists, .5 steals, and one blocked shot per game. He scored 22 points in a 103–94 win over the Warriors on March 14 at Golden State. He became a free agent on July 1, 2014, and was not re-signed.

HAWKINS, MICHAEL

Michael Hawkins was a 6-foot, 178-pound point guard for Cleveland in 2000-01. He was signed as a free agent on October 16, 2000, was waived on October 26, 2000, and was re-signed as a free agent again on November 22, 2000. In 10 games with the Cavs he averaged .8 points, 1.3 assists, .5 rebounds, and .2 steals per contest. He scored three points twice—in an 86–67 victory over the Heat on November 22 at Miami and in a 99–92 triumph over Utah on December 16 at Gund Arena. He was waived again on January 2, 2001.

HAYES, STEVE

Steve Hayes was a 7-foot, 205-pound center for the Cavaliers in 1982-83. He was traded from Detroit on October 7, 1982. In his one season with Cleveland he averaged 3.6 points, 3.6 rebounds, .6 assists, .3 steals, and .6 blocked shots per game. He scored 15 points in a 101–94 loss to the SuperSonics in Seattle on November 19. He was waived on October 19, 1983.

HAYWOOD, BRENDAN

Brendan Haywood was a 7-foot, 268-pound center for Cleveland in 2014-15. He was a first-round draft pick in 2001 out of the University of North Carolina. That same day, he was traded to Orlando. He was re-signed on June 27, 2014, in a trade with Charlotte. In his one season with the Cavs, he averaged 1.6 points, 1.3 rebounds, .1 assists, .1 steals, and .5 blocked shots per game. He scored seven points in a 103–80 loss to the Pistons on December 28 at Quicken Loans Arena. He was traded to Portland on July 27, 2015.

HEAD COACHES' WIN-LOSS RECORDS, BEST TO WORST (POSTSEASON)

Please see Individual Statistics on page 185.

HEAD COACHES' WIN-LOSS RECORDS, BEST TO WORST (REGULAR SEASON)

Please see Individual Statistics on page 185.

HELM, DICK

Dick Helm was a Cavaliers assistant coach from 1986-87 to 1992-93.

HENDERSON, ALAN

Alan Henderson was a 6-foot-9, 235-pound center for the Cavaliers in 2005-06. Signed as a free agent on September 17, 2005, he averaged 2.5 points, 2.7 rebounds, .2 assists, .2 steals, and .2 blocked shots per game in his one season with Cleveland. He scored 16 points in a 90–89 defeat to the Nuggets on January 18 at Denver. He became a free agent again on July 1, 2006, and was not re-signed.

HENDERSON, CEDRIC

Cedric Henderson was a 6-foot-7, 215-pound small forward for Cleveland from 1997-98 to 2000-01. A second-round draft pick in 1997 from the University of Memphis, he averaged 7.5 points, three rebounds, 1.7 assists, .9 steals, and .4 blocked shots per game in his four seasons with the Cavs. His best season as a Cavalier was 1997-98 when he averaged 10.1 points, four rebounds, two assists, 1.2 steals, and .5 blocked shots per contest.

Henderson scored 30 points in a 106–101 victory over Vancouver on February 25, 1998, at Gund Arena. He scored nine points in an 86–77 playoff win over Indiana on April 27, 1998, again at Gund Arena. He was traded to Philadelphia on August 3, 2001.

HENDERSON, KEVIN

Kevin Henderson was a 6-foot-4, 195-pound shooting guard for the Cavaliers in 1987-88. He was a third-round draft pick in 1986 out of California State University, Fullerton. He was waived on October 28, 1986. He was re-signed as a free agent on March 29, 1988. In five games with the Cavs he averaged 1.8 points, .4 assists, and .8 rebounds per contest. He scored seven points in a 116–103 victory over Atlanta on April 12 at The Coliseum. He became a free agent again on July 1, 1988, and was not re-signed.

HENDRICKSON, MARK

Mark Hendrickson was a 6-foot-9, 220-pound power forward for the Cavaliers in 1999-2000. He was signed as a free agent on December 27, 1999, waived on January 5, 2000, and signed the first of two 10-day contracts on January 8, 2000. In 10 games with Cleveland he averaged 1.2 points, 1.1 rebounds, .3 assists, .2 steals, and .1 blocked shots per contest. He scored four points twice—in a 91–90 defeat to the Bucks in Milwaukee on December 30 and in a 111–107 loss to Sacramento on January 4 at Gund Arena. He became a free agent again on January 28, 2000, and was not re-signed.

HERNANDEZ BRITO, RAFAEL

Rafael Hernandez Brito has been a Cavaliers local radio broadcaster since 2014-15.

HERRON, KEITH

Keith Herron was a 6-foot-6, 195-pound shooting guard for the Cavaliers in 1981-82. Signed as a free agent on December 30, 1981, in his one season with Cleveland he averaged 2.8 points, .8 assists, .7 rebounds, .3 steals, and .1 blocked shots per game. He scored 12 points in a 108–104 win over the Pacers on February 3 at The Coliseum. He was waived on October 8, 1982.

HICKSON, J. J.

J. J. Hickson was a 6-foot-9, 242-pound center and power forward for the Cavaliers from 2008-09 to 2010-11. A first-round draft pick in 2008 out of North Carolina State University, he averaged 9.1 points, 5.7 rebounds, .6 assists, .4 steals, and .6 blocked shots per game in his three seasons with the Cavs. His best season as a Cavalier was 2010-11 when he averaged 13.8 points, 8.7 rebounds, 1.1 assists, .6 steals, and .7 blocked shots per contest.

Hickson scored 31 points on two occasions—in a 100–88 defeat to Atlanta on November 2, 2010, at Quicken Loans Arena and in a 112–105 loss to the Grizzlies on February 4, 2011, at Memphis. He scored 13 points in a 104–86 playoff defeat to Boston on May 3, 2010, at Quicken Loans Arena. He was traded to the Kings on June 30, 2011.

HIGGINS, ROD

Rod Higgins was a 6-foot-7, 200-pound small forward for the Cavaliers in 1993-94. Signed as a free agent on December 23, 1993, in his one season with Cleveland he averaged 5.4 points, 2.3 rebounds, one assist, .7 steals, and .4 blocked shots per game. He scored 20 points in a 105–99 triumph over Charlotte on April 5 at The Coliseum. He scored five points in a 105–96 playoff loss to the Bulls in Chicago on May 1. He became a free agent again on July 1, 1994, and was not re-signed.

HIGGS, KENNY

Kenny Higgs was a 6-foot, 180-pound point guard for Cleveland in 1978-79. A third-round draft choice in 1978 from LSU, he averaged five points, 2.1 assists, 1.5 rebounds, one steal, and .2 blocked shots per game in his one season with the Cavs. He scored 21 points in a 111–107 win over Kansas City on February 22 at The Coliseum. He was waived on October 8, 1979.

HILL, TYRONE

Tyrone Hill was a 6-foot-9, 240-pound power forward and center for the Cavaliers from 1993-94 to 1996-97 and 2001-02 to 2002-03. He was traded from Golden State on July 15, 1993. He was traded to Milwaukee on September 25, 1997. He was re-signed on August 3, 2001, in a trade with Philadelphia.

In his six seasons with Cleveland Hill averaged 10.8 points, 9.2 rebounds, .9 assists, .8 steals, and .5 blocked shots per game. His best season as a Cavalier was 1994-95 when he averaged 13.8 points, 10.9 rebounds, .8 assists, .8 steals, and .6 blocked shots per contest. He scored 29 points in a 102–100 double-overtime defeat to Dallas on March 20, 1995, at Gund Arena. He scored 16 points in a 104–96 playoff loss to the Bulls in Chicago on April 29, 1994. He was an All-Star in 1994-95. He was waived on February 27, 2003.

HINSON, ROY

Roy Hinson was a 6-foot-9, 210-pound small forward and power forward for Cleveland from 1983-84 to 1985-86. A first-round draft choice in 1983 out of Rutgers University, he averaged 13.6 points, 7.3 rebounds, one assist, .6 steals, and 1.8 blocked shots per game in his three seasons with the Cavs. His best season as a Cavalier was 1985-86 when he averaged 19.6 points, 7.8 rebounds, 1.2 assists, .8 steals, and 1.4 blocked shots per contest.

Hinson scored 39 points in a 116–109 loss to the Rockets on January 28, 1986, at Houston. He scored 24 points in a 126–123 playoff defeat to the Celtics in Boston on April 18, 1985. He was traded to the 76ers on June 16, 1986.

HOLLINS, RYAN

Ryan Hollins was a 7-foot, 240-pound center for the Cavaliers from 2010-11 to 2011-12. Traded from the Timberwolves on July 26, 2010, in his two seasons with Cleveland he averaged 4.9 points, 2.6 rebounds, .3 assists, .3 steals, and .6 blocked shots per game. His best season as a Cavalier was 2010-11 when he averaged 5.3 points, 2.7 rebounds, .4 assists, .3 steals, and .6 blocked shots per contest. He scored 16 points in a 99–89 victory over Charlotte on April 5, 2011, at Quicken Loans Arena. He was waived on March 20, 2012.

HOPSON, SCOTTY

Scotty Hopson was a 6-foot-7, 204-pound shooting guard for the Cavaliers in 2013-14. Signed as a free agent on March 31, 2014, he played two games with Cleveland. He was traded to the Hornets on July 12, 2014.

HOWARD, GREG

Greg Howard was a 6-foot-9, 215-pound power forward for the Cavaliers in 1971-72. Traded on August 13, 1971, from Phoenix, in his one season with the Cavs he averaged 2.9 points, 2.3 rebounds, and .6 assists per game. He scored 12 points three times. He was waived on July 28, 1972.

HOWARD, MO

Mo Howard was a 6-foot-2, 170-pound shooting guard for Cleveland in 1976-77. A second-round draft pick in 1976 out of the University of Maryland, he averaged 2.3 points, .6 assists, .6 rebounds, .1 steals, and .2 blocked shots per contest in nine games with the Cavs. He scored eight points in a 123–112 loss to the Pistons in Detroit on November 10. He was waived on December 10, 1976.

HROVAT, RON

Ron Hrovat was the Cavaliers' general manager in 1979-80.

HUBBARD, PHIL

Phil Hubbard was a 6-foot-8, 215-pound small forward for the Cavaliers from 1981-82 to 1988-89. Traded from Detroit on February 16, 1982, in his eight seasons with Cleveland he averaged 10.6 points, five rebounds, 1.2 assists, .9 steals, and .1 blocked shots per game. His best season as a Cavalier was 1984-85 when he averaged 15.8 points, 6.3 rebounds, 1.5 assists, 1.1 steals, and .1 blocked shots per contest.

Hubbard scored 37 points in a 116–112 loss to the Lakers on December 4, 1984, at The Coliseum and 31 points in a 109–107 defeat to Philadelphia on January 18, 1984, also at The Coliseum. He had 23 points in a 117–115 playoff loss to Boston on April 25, 1985, again at The Coliseum. He became a free agent on July 1, 1989, and was not re-signed.

HUDSON, LESTER

Lester Hudson was a 6-foot-3, 190-pound point guard for the Cavaliers in 2011-12. He signed the first of two 10-day contracts on March 30, 2012. In 13 games with Cleveland he averaged 12.7 points, 2.7 assists, 3.5 rebounds, 1.1 steals, and .2 blocked shots per contest. He scored 26 points in a 122–117 overtime loss to the Nets in New Jersey on April 8. He became a free agent again on April 19, 2012, and was not re-signed.

HUGHES, KIM

Kim Hughes was a 6-foot-11, 220-pound center for the Cavaliers in 1980-81. Traded from Denver on October 31, 1980, he averaged .7 points, 1.7 rebounds, .5 assists, .4 steals, and .5 blocked shots per game in his one season with Cleveland. He scored six points in a 118–109 loss to the Rockets on December 3 in Houston. He became a free agent on July 1, 1981, and was not re-signed.

HUGHES, LARRY

Larry Hughes was a 6-foot-5, 184-pound shooting guard and point guard for Cleveland from 2005-06 to 2007-08. Signed as a free agent on August 2, 2005, he averaged 14.3 points, 3.3 assists, 3.9 rebounds, 1.4 steals, and .4 blocked shots per game in his three seasons with the Cavs. His best season as a Cavalier was 2005-06 when he averaged 15.5 points, 3.6 assists, 4.5 rebounds, 1.5 steals, and .6 blocked shots per contest.

Hughes scored 40 points in a 118–111 victory over the Magic on February 11, 2008, at Orlando. He scored 27 points in a 97–82 playoff win over the Wizards on April 22, 2007, at Quicken Loans Arena. He was traded to Chicago on February 21, 2008.

HUNT, MELVIN

Melvin Hunt was a Cavaliers assistant coach from 2005-06 to 2009-10.

HUSTON, GEOFF

Geoff Huston was a 6-foot-2, 175-pound point guard for the Cavaliers from 1980-81 to 1984-85. He was traded from the Mavericks on February 7, 1981. In his five seasons with Cleveland he averaged 10.4 points, 6.1 assists, 1.7 rebounds, .7 steals, and .1 blocked shots per game. His best season as a Cavalier was 1982-83 when he averaged 12.2 points, 6.1 assists, two rebounds, .9 steals, and .1 blocked shots per contest. He scored 31 points in a 124–119 loss to the Bulls on January 26, 1983, at The Coliseum. He was waived on December 7, 1984.

I

IAVARONI, MARC

Marc Iavaroni was a Cavaliers assistant coach from 1997-98 to 1998-99.

ILGAUSKAS, ZYDRUNAS

Zydrunas Ilgauskas was a 7-foot-3, 238-pound center for the Cavaliers from 1997-98 to 1998-99 and 2000-01 to 2009-10. He was a first-round draft pick from Lithuania in 1996. In his 12 seasons with Cleveland he averaged 13.8 points, 7.7 rebounds, 1.2 assists, .5 steals, and 1.6 blocked shots per game. His best season as a Cavalier was 2004-05 when he averaged 16.9 points, 8.6 rebounds, 1.3 assists, .7 steals, and 2.1 blocked shots per contest. In 2002-03, Ilgauskas averaged 17.2 points, 7.5 rebounds, 1.6 assists, .7 steals, and 1.9 blocked shots per game. In 2007-08, he averaged 14.1 points, 9.3 rebounds, 1.4 assists, .5 steals, and 1.6 blocked shots per contest.

Zydrunas Ilgauskas battles Tim Duncan underneath, 2006-07. (AndersonsClevelandDesign.com)

Ilgauskas, who suffered a myriad of foot and ankle injuries during the early part of his career, scored 35 points twice—in a 103–94 loss to Orlando on January 21, 2003, at Gund Arena and in a 109–104 double-overtime defeat to Indiana on November 3, 2004, again at Gund Arena. He scored 25 points in a 92–86 playoff loss to the Pacers on April 25, 1998, at Indiana. He was an All-Star in 2002-03 and 2004-05. He was traded to Washington on February 17, 2010. His jersey number 11 was retired by the Cavaliers on March 8, 2014.

IRVING, KYRIE

Kyrie Irving has been a 6-foot-3, 193-pound point guard for the Cavaliers since 2011-12. He was a first-round draft pick—the number one overall selection—in 2011 from Duke University. In his five seasons with Cleveland he has averaged 20.8 points, 5.5 assists, 3.4 rebounds, 1.4 steals, and .3 blocked shots per game. His best season as a Cavalier has been 2012-13 when he averaged 22.5 points, 5.9 assists, 3.7 rebounds, 1.5 steals, and .4 blocked shots per contest. The next season, he averaged 20.8 points, 6.1 assists, 3.6 rebounds, 1.5 steals, and .3 blocked shots per game. The season after that, he averaged 21.7 points, 5.2 assists, 3.2 rebounds, 1.5 steals, and .3 blocked shots per contest.

Kyrie Irving goes for a layup against the Sixers, 2015-16. (AndersonsClevelandDesign.com)

Irving scored a team-record 57 points in a 128–125 overtime victory against the Spurs on March 12, 2015, at San Antonio and 55 points in a 99–94 triumph over the Trail Blazers on January 28, 2015, at Quicken Loans Arena. He had 41 points in a 112–97 Finals win over the Warriors on June 13, 2016, at Golden State. Irving was the Rookie of the Year in 2011-12. He was an All-Star from 2012-13 to 2014-15 and the All-Star Game MVP in 2013-14.

J

J. WALTER KENNEDY CITIZENSHIP AWARD

Austin Carr (1979-80)
Eric Snow (2004-05)
Luol Deng (2013-14)

JACK, JARRETT

Jarrett Jack was a 6-foot-3, 200-pound point guard for the Cavaliers in 2013-14. Signed as a free agent on July 12, 2013, in his one season with Cleveland he averaged 9.5 points, 4.1 assists, 2.8 rebounds, .7 steals, and .3 blocked shots per game. He scored 31 points in a 106–100 win over the Knicks at New York on March 23. He was traded to the Nets on July 10, 2014.

JACKSON, CEDRIC

Cedric Jackson was a 6-foot-3, 191-pound point guard for the Cavaliers in 2009-10. Signed to the first of two 10-day contracts on January 23, 2010, in five games with the Cavs he averaged .2 points, .4 assists, and .2 rebounds per contest. He scored one point in a 94–73 victory over the Pacers on January 29 in Indiana. He became a free agent again on February 12, 2010, and was not re-signed.

JACKSON, DARNELL

Darnell Jackson was a 6-foot-9, 253-pound power forward for the Cavaliers from 2008-09 to 2009-10. Traded from Miami on June 26, 2008, he averaged 1.5 points, 1.4 rebounds, .2 assists, .2 steals, and .1 blocked shots per game in his two seasons with Cleveland. His best season as a Cavalier was 2008-09 when he averaged 1.9 points, 1.7 rebounds, .2 assists, .2 steals, and .1 blocked shots per contest.

Jackson scored 15 points in a 111–110 overtime loss to Philadelphia on April 15, 2009, at Quicken Loans Arena. He scored two points in a 105–85 playoff win over Atlanta on May 7, 2009, again at Quicken Loans Arena. He was waived on March 23, 2010.

JACKSON, JIM

Jim Jackson was a 6-foot-6, 220-pound small forward for the Cavaliers in 2000-01. Traded from the Hawks on January 2, 2001, he averaged 10.3 points, 3.7 rebounds, 2.9 assists, .9 steals, and .2 blocked shots per game in his one season with Cleveland. He scored 23 points in a 92–90 defeat to the Pacers on February 23 at Gund Arena. He became a free agent on July 1, 2001, and was not re-signed.

JACKSON, LUKE

Luke Jackson was a 6-foot-7, 215-pound small forward for the Cavaliers from 2004-05 to 2005-06. A first-round draft choice in 2004 out of the University of Oregon, he averaged 2.7 points, one rebound, .6 assists, and .2 steals per game in his two seasons with Cleveland. His best season as a Cavalier was 2005-06 when he averaged 2.7 points, 1.1 rebounds, .7 assists, .3 steals, and .1 blocked shots per contest. He scored 14 points in a 110–85 triumph over Utah on December 20, 2005, at Quicken Loans Arena. He was traded to Boston on October 13, 2006.

JAMES, HENRY

Henry James was a 6-foot-8, 220-pound power forward and small forward for the Cavaliers from 1990-91 to 1991-92 and in 1997-98. He signed the first of two 10-day contracts on December 31, 1990, and on January 21, 1991, signed a contract for the rest of the 1990-91 season. He became a free agent again on July 1, 1992. The Cavs re-signed him as a free agent again on September 22, 1997.

In his three seasons with Cleveland James averaged 6.1 points, 1.6 rebounds, .5 assists, .2 steals, and .1 blocked shots per game. His best season as a Cavalier was 1990-91 when he averaged 8.1 points, 2.1 rebounds, .9 assists, .4 steals, and .1 blocked shots per contest. He scored 25 points in a 108–92 loss to the Bulls on January 5, 1991, in Chicago and four points in a 107–81 playoff win over the Bulls on May 21, 1992, again at Chicago. He became a free agent again on July 1, 1998, and was not re-signed.

JAMES, LEBRON

LeBron James was a 6-foot-8, 250-pound small forward and shooting guard for the Cavaliers from 2003-04 to 2009-10 and has been since 2014-15. He was a first-round draft pick—the number one overall selection—in 2003 out of St. Vincent-St. Mary High School. On July 10, 2010, two days after "The Decision" in which he announced to Jim Gray on ESPN that he would be leaving for Miami, he completed a sign-and-trade deal with the Heat. On July 12, 2014, a day after "The Decision II," in which he announced by way of a letter on SI.com that he would be returning to Cleveland, he was re-signed as a free agent.

In his nine seasons with Cleveland James has averaged 27.3 points, seven rebounds, seven assists, 1.7 steals, and .8 blocked shots per game. His best season as a Cavalier has been 2009-10 when he averaged 29.7 points, 7.3 rebounds, 8.6 assists, 1.6 steals, and one blocked shot per contest. In 2005-06, he averaged 31.4 points, seven rebounds, 6.6 assists, 1.6 steals, and .8 blocked shots per game. In 2007-08 he averaged 30 points, 7.9 rebounds, 7.2 assists, 1.8 steals, and 1.1 blocked shots per contest.

James scored 56 points in a 105–98 loss to the Raptors on March 20, 2005, at Toronto. He scored 55 points in a 111–103 victory over the Bucks on February 20, 2009, at Milwaukee. He had 49 points, a team postseason record, in a 107–106 playoff defeat to the Magic on May 20, 2009, at Quicken Loans Arena.

James was the Rookie of the Year in 2003-04. He was an All-Star from 2004-05 to 2009-10 and has been since 2014-15. He was the NBA MVP from 2008-09 to 2009-10. He was the Finals MVP in 2015-16 and the All-Star Game MVP in 2005-06 and 2007-08.

JAMISON, ANTAWN

Antawn Jamison was a 6-foot-8, 223-pound power forward for the Cavaliers from 2009-10 to 2011-12. Traded from the Wizards on February 17, 2010, in his three seasons with Cleveland he averaged 17.3 points, 6.7 rebounds, 1.8 assists, .9 steals, and .6 blocked shots per game. His best season as a Cavalier was 2010-11 when he averaged 18 points, 6.7 rebounds, 1.7 assists, .9 steals, and .5 blocked shots per contest.

Jamison scored 35 points twice—in a 104–95 defeat to Dallas on January 2, 2011, at Quicken Loans Arena and in a 126–119 overtime victory against the Clippers on February 11, 2011, again at Quicken Loans Arena. He scored 25 points in a 96–94 playoff win over Chicago on April 27, 2010, also at Quicken Loans Arena. He became a free agent on July 1, 2012, and was not re-signed.

JANUARY

The following are five memorable Cavaliers games that were played in the month of January:

JANUARY 22, 1974

The Cavaliers recovered from a seven-point deficit after three quarters to beat the Los Angeles Lakers 111–110 in overtime before 13,856 fans at The Forum. Lenny Wilkens led the Cavs with 24 points. Austin Carr and Luke Witte each added 17. Jim Price led the Lakers with 24 points.

JANUARY 19, 1978

Despite a team-leading 43 points from Julius Erving—"Dr. J."—the Cavaliers defeated the Philadelphia 76ers 117–109 before 14,170 fans at The Coliseum. Elmore Smith led the Cavs with 27 points. Jim Chones had 21 and Walt Frazier had 18.

JANUARY 29, 1980

The Cavaliers defeated the Los Angeles Lakers 154–153 in four overtimes before 13,820 fans at The Coliseum. The Cavs were led by Mike Mitchell's 34 points, Dave Robisch's 32, and Randy Smith's 31, the only time in team history that three players scored 30 points or more in a game. Kareem Abdul-Jabbar led the Lakers with 42 points and Magic Johnson had 30.

JANUARY 11, 2011

The Cavaliers were routed 112–57 by the Los Angeles Lakers in front of 18,997 fans at the Staples Center. The Cavs were down 27–12 after one quarter, 57–25 at halftime, and 92–41 after three quarters. Alonzo Gee (12 points) and Ramon Sessions (10 points) were the only Cavs to score in double figures. Andrew Bynum and Metta World Peace led the Lakers with 15 points apiece.

JANUARY 18, 2016

The Cavaliers were routed by the Golden State Warriors 132–98 in front of 20,562 fans at Quicken Loans Arena. The Cavs were outscored 70–44 in the first half. LeBron James led Cleveland with 16 points. Stephen Curry was tops on the Warriors with 35 points.

JEFFERSON, RICHARD

Richard Jefferson has been a 6-foot-7, 233-pound small forward for the Cavaliers since 2015-16. Signed as a free agent on August 5, 2015, in his one season with Cleveland he has averaged 5.5 points, 1.7 rebounds, .8 assists, .4 steals, and .2 blocked shots per game. He scored 20 points in a 122–101 loss to the Heat in Miami on March 19. He scored 12 points in a 110–77 Finals defeat to the Warriors on June 5 at Golden State.

JENT, CHRIS

Chris Jent was a Cavaliers assistant coach from 2006-07 to 2010-11.

JERSEY NUMBERS

0

Lari Ketner
Kevin Love
Jeff McInnis
C. J. Miles

00

Milos Babic
Benoit Benjamin
Darnell Jackson

1

Carlos Boozer
Terrell Brandon
Daniel Gibson
Stephen Graham
Kenny Higgs
Jarrett Jack
James Jones
Wesley Person
Darnell Valentine

2

Scott Brooks
Mark Bryant
Reggie Geary
Mo Howard
Kyrie Irving
Jim Jackson
Flip Murray
Dajuan Wagner
Mike Woodson
Mo Williams
Reggie Williams

3

J. R. Bremer
Tierre Brown
Craig Ehlo
Eddie Johnson
Sasha Pavlovic
Kendrick Perkins
Ramon Sessions
Elmore Smith
Bob Sura
Sebastian Telfair
Jeff Trepagnier
Dion Waiters
Ennis Whatley

4

Tony Battie
Ron Harper
Antawn Jamison
Shawn Kemp
Steve Kerr
Chris Mihm
Harold Miner
Campy Russell
Iman Shumpert
Sedric Toney
Ben Wallace
Luke Walton
David Wesley

5

John Bagley
Earl Boykins
Kedrick Brown
Will Cherry
Jim Cleamons
Steve Colter
Mike Evans
Ryan Hollins
Kevin Jones
Coby Karl
Steve Kerr
Bobby Lewis
J. R. Smith

6

Shannon Brown
Mitchell Butler
Earl Clark
Manny Harris
Jerome Moiso
Larry Nance
Ben Uzoh

7

Bingo Smith

8

Mateen Cleaves
Matthew Dellavedova
Christian Eyenga
Tim Kempton
Tarence Kinsey
Jeremy Pargo
Lonnie Shelton
Brian Skinner
Scott Wedman

9

Tony Campbell
Jared Cunningham
Matthew Dellavedova
Luol Deng
Mickey Dillard
Semih Erden
Channing Frye
Litterial Green
Cedric Jackson
Larry Kenon
Dan Majerle
Randy Smith

10

John Battle
Ron Brewer
Joe Cooke
Walt Frazier
Stewart Granger
Butch Graves
Anthony Johnson
Sergey Karasev
Milt Palacio
Robert Smith

Dick Snyder
Ryan Stack
Wally Szczerbiak

11

Terrell Brandon
John Crotty
Walt Frazier
Zydrunas Ilgauskas
Kevin Johnson
Cliff Robinson
Mike Sanders
Willie Smith
John Warren

12

Elmer Bennett
Bimbo Coles
Joey Graham
Joe Harris
Lucious Harris
Kevin Henderson
D. J. Kennedy
Brevin Knight
Gerald Madkins
Jordan McRae
Kevin Ollie
Billy Thomas
Kevin Williams

13

John Amaechi
Donny Marshall
James Silas
Michael Stewart
Tristan Thompson
Delonte West

14

Danny Green
Mark Hendrickson
Lester Hudson
Sasha Kaun
Shaun Livingston
Dirk Minniefield
Lowes Moore
Ira Newble
Bobby Phills
Henry Sims
Foots Walker

15

Anthony Bennett
Matt Harpring
Keith Herron
Butch Lee
Jamario Moon
Roger Phegley
Cedric Simmons
Donald Sloan
Dave Sorenson
Marreese Speights
Cornell Warner
Chuckie Williams

16

Gary Alexander
Johnny Davis

17

Michael Hawkins
Smush Parker
Anderson Varejao
Bobby Washington

18

Kornel David
Charlie Davis
McCoy McLemore
Mike Miller
Anthony Parker
John Williams

19

Damon Jones
Lenny Wilkens

20

Winston Bennett
Greg Graham
Geoff Huston
Chad Kinch
Scooter McCray
Timofey Mozgov
Johnny Newman
Chris Quinn
Larry Robinson
Campy Russell
Eric Snow
Bryant Stith

21

Butch Beard
Andrew Bynum
Mack Calvin
Johnny Egan
World B. Free
Daniel Gibson
J. J. Hickson
Antonio Lang
Trajan Langdon
Darius Miles
Roger Phegley
A. J. Price
Campy Russell
Mychel Thompson
Gerald Wilkins

22

Cliff Anderson
Austin Carr
Jim Chones
Chris Dudley
Larry Nance
Johnny Newman
Carl Nicks
Mike Wilson

23

Derek Anderson
Mike Bratz
Tyrone Corbin
Bruce Flowers
Gary Freeman
Rowland Garrett
Rod Higgins
LeBron James
John Morton
Carl Thomas

24

Chris Dudley
Shane Edwards
Fred Foster
Scotty Hopson
Richard Jefferson
Trey Johnson
Jason Kapono
John Lambert
Keith Lee
Donyell Marshall

Andre Miller
Chris Mills
Jimmy Oliver
Gerald Paddio
Kevin Restani
Samardo Samuels

25

Ron Anderson
Gary Brokaw
Terry Furlow
Ben McDonald
Mark Price
Dave Robisch
Darren Tillis

27

Tony Dumas
Dwayne Jones

29

Mike Wilks

30

Dell Curry
Greg Dreiling
Carrick Felix
Darryl Johnson
Dahntay Jones
Eddie Jordan
Jerome Lane
Jon Leuer
David Magley
Larry Mikan
Mike Mitchell
Lamond Murray
Jackie Ridgle
Tree Rollins
Carl Thomas

31

Seth Curry
Ricky Davis
Zendon Hamilton
Randolph Keys
Shawn Marion
Scot Pollard
J. R. Reid
Fred Roberts
Richard Washington
Jawad Williams

32

Kenny Carr
Pete Chilcutt
Chris Gatling
Spencer Hawes
Tyrone Hill
Roy Hinson
Larry Hughes
Henry James
John Johnson
Jelani McCoy
Johnny Rogers
Joe Smith
Robert Traylor
Luke Walton
John Warren

33

Devin Brown
Derrick Chievous
Alonzo Gee
Brendan Haywood
Luke Jackson
Kannard Johnson
Jumaine Jones
Donny Marshall

Shaquille O'Neal
Mike Sanders
Bobby Wilkerson
Bill Willoughby
Paul Thompson

34

Austin Carr

35

Jim Cleamons
Danny Ferry
Don Ford
Phil Hubbard
Demetris Nichols
Rick Roberson
Clarence Weatherspoon

36

Omri Casspi
Paul Thompson

40

Barry Clemens
Joe Courtney
Harry Davis
James Edwards
Greg Howard
Walter Jordan
Gary Suiter
Tyler Zeller

41

Lance Allred
Etdrick Bohannon
Geoff Crompton
Eric Fernsten
Steve Hayes
Bill Laimbeer
Bruno Sundov
Mark West

42

Dwight Davis
Nate Thurmond

43

Brad Daugherty
Earl Tatum

44

Corie Blount
Michael Cage
Luke Harangody
Alan Henderson
Kim Hughes
Reggie Johnson
Edgar Jones
Paul Mokeski
Leon Powe
Shawnelle Scott
Jiri Welsch
Walt Wesley
Luke Witte

45

Jeff Cook
Kaniel Dickens
Cedric Henderson
Luther Rackley
Bob Rule

47

A. J. Bramlett
Scott Williams

50

Len Chappell
Bimbo Coles
Arinze Onuaku
Steve Patterson
Ben Poquette
Bill Robinzine

51

Michael Doleac

52

Melvin Bennett
Brad Branson
Jim Brewer
Chucky Brown
DeSagana Diop
Sam Lacey
Bill Laimbeer
Vitaly Potapenko
Jerome Whitehead
Mo Williams

53

Alex Kirk

54

Kent Benson
Jay Guidinger
Lee Nailon
Robert Traylor
Melvin Turpin
Gary Voce

55

Andrew DeClercq
John Garris
Eric Williams
Lorenzen Wright

85

Baron Davis

89

Lou Amundson

90

Drew Gooden

JOHNSON, ANTHONY

Anthony Johnson was a 6-foot-3, 190-pound point guard for the Cavaliers in 2000-01. Traded from Atlanta on January 2, 2001, in his one season with Cleveland he averaged 2.4 points, 1.6 assists, .8 rebounds, and .2 steals per game. He scored 16 points in a 107–101 victory over the Warriors on January 15 at Golden State. He became a free agent on July 1, 2001, and was not re-signed.

JOHNSON, DARRYL

Darryl Johnson was a 6-foot-1, 170-pound point guard for the Cavaliers in 1995-96. He signed the first of two 10-day contracts on March 5, 1996. In

11 games with Cleveland he averaged 1.1 points, .1 assists, and .2 rebounds per contest. He scored two points on six occasions. He was released on August 22, 1996.

JOHNSON, EDDIE

Eddie Johnson was a 6-foot-2, 180-pound shooting guard for the Cavaliers in 1985-86. Traded from the Hawks on February 10, 1986, in his one season with Cleveland he averaged 9.8 points, 3.6 assists, 1.4 rebounds, and .3 steals per game. He scored 25 points in a 128–114 loss to the Bullets on March 12 at The Coliseum. He became a free agent on July 1, 1986, and was not re-signed.

JOHNSON, GUS

Gus Johnson was a Cavaliers assistant coach in 1981-82.

JOHNSON, JIM

Jim Johnson was a Cavaliers local radio broadcaster from 1989-90 to 1991-92.

JOHNSON, JOHN

John Johnson was a 6-foot-7, 200-pound small forward for the Cavaliers from 1970-71 to 1972-73. He was a first-round draft choice—the franchise's first-ever draft pick—in 1970 out of the University of Iowa. In his three seasons with Cleveland, he averaged 15.9 points, 7.1 rebounds, and 4.5 assists per game. His best season as a Cavalier was 1971-72 when he averaged 17 points, 7.7 rebounds, and 5.1 assists per contest.

Johnson scored 40 points in a 108–102 victory over Baltimore on December 26, 1971, at the Cleveland Arena. He was an All-Star in 1970-71 and 1971-72. He was traded to Portland on April 24, 1973.

JOHNSON, KANNARD

Kannard Johnson was a 6-foot-9, 220-pound small forward for the Cavaliers in 1987-88. A second-round draft pick in 1987 out of Western Kentucky University, he played four games with Cleveland. He was waived on December 29, 1987.

JOHNSON, KEVIN

Kevin Johnson was a 6-foot-1, 180-pound point guard for the Cavaliers in 1987-88. A first-round draft pick in 1987 out of the University of California, in his one season with Cleveland he averaged 7.3 points, 3.7 assists, 1.4 rebounds, 1.2 steals, and .3 blocked shots per game. He scored 15 points in a 106–102 win over the Bullets on December 22 at Washington. He was traded to the Suns on February 25, 1988.

JOHNSON, REGGIE

Reggie Johnson was a 6-foot-9, 205-pound power forward for the Cavaliers in 1981-82. Traded from San Antonio on December 23, 1981, in his one season with Cleveland he averaged 9.7 points, 5.4 rebounds, one assist, .3 steals, and .7 blocked shots per game. He scored 19 points twice—in a 109–100 defeat to Washington on January 7 at The Coliseum and in a 100–99 victory over the Bullets on February 2 at Washington. He was traded to the Kings on February 16, 1982.

JOHNSON, TREY

Trey Johnson was a 6-foot-5, 218-pound shooting guard for the Cavaliers in 2008-09. He signed the first of two 10-day contracts on February 3, 2009, and played four games with Cleveland. He became a free agent again on March 2, 2009, and was not re-signed.

JONES, DAHNTAY

Dahntay Jones was a 6-foot-6, 225-pound small forward for the Cavaliers in 2015-16. Signed on April 13, 2016, as a free agent, he played one game with Cleveland. He was waived on July 30, 2016.

JONES, DAMON

Damon Jones was a 6-foot-3, 185-pound point guard and shooting guard for the Cavaliers from 2005-06 to 2007-08. He was signed as a free agent on September 8, 2005. In his three seasons with Cleveland he averaged 6.6 points, 1.9 assists, 1.3 rebounds, and .3 steals per game. His best season as a Cavalier was 2005-06 when he averaged 6.7 points, 2.1 assists, 1.6 rebounds, and .5 steals per contest.

Jones scored 29 points in a 102–96 victory over the Knicks on November 13, 2006, at New York. He scored nine points in an 83–82 Finals loss to the Spurs on June 14, 2007, at Quicken Loans Arena. He was traded to Milwaukee on August 13, 2008.

JONES, DWAYNE

Dwayne Jones was a 6-foot-11, 250-pound power forward for the Cavaliers from 2006-07 to 2007-08. Traded from Boston on October 13, 2006, in his two seasons with Cleveland he averaged 1.4 points, 2.4 rebounds, .2 assists, .2 steals, and .4 blocked shots per game. His best season as a Cavalier was 2007-08 when he averaged 1.4 points, 2.5 rebounds, .2 assists, .2 steals, and .4 blocked shots per contest.

Jones scored nine points in a 100–79 loss to New Jersey on December 4, 2007, at Quicken Loans Arena. He scored two points in a 116–86 playoff win over Washington on April 21, 2008, again at Quicken Loans Arena. He became a free agent on July 1, 2008, and was not re-signed.

JONES, EDGAR

Edgar Jones was a 6-foot-10, 225-pound power forward for the Cavaliers from 1984-85 to 1985-86. Traded from the Spurs on December 14, 1984, in his two seasons with the Cavs he averaged 9.2 points, four rebounds, .7 assists, .5 steals, and .6 blocked shots per game. His best season as a Cavalier was 1985-86 when he averaged 9.7 points, 3.9 rebounds, .8 assists, .6 steals, and .7 blocked shots per contest.

Jones scored 24 points in a 129–111 victory over the Lakers in Los Angeles on November 5, 1985. He scored 14 points in a 117–115 playoff defeat to Boston on April 25, 1985, at The Coliseum. He was waived on October 8, 1986.

JONES, HARRY

Harry Jones was a Cavaliers local television broadcaster from 1976-77 to 1978-79.

JONES, JAMES

James Jones has been a 6-foot-8, 218-pound small forward for Cleveland since 2014-15. Signed as a free agent on August 5, 2014, in his two seasons with the Cavs he has averaged 4.1 points, 1.1 rebounds, .4 assists, .2 steals, and .2 blocked shots per game. His best season as a Cavalier has been 2014-15, when he averaged 4.4 points, 1.1 rebounds, .4 assists, .2 steals, and .1 blocked shots per contest. Jones scored 15 points in a 111–76 victory over the Magic on December 11, 2015, at Orlando. He scored 17 points in a 106–91 playoff win over Chicago on May 6, 2015, at Quicken Loans Arena.

JONES, JUMAINE

Jumaine Jones was a 6-foot-8, 218-pound power forward and small forward for the Cavaliers from 2001-02 to 2002-03. Traded from Philadelphia on August 3, 2001, he averaged nine points, 5.6 rebounds, 1.4 assists, .9 steals, and .4 blocked shots per game in his two seasons with Cleveland. His best season as a Cavalier was 2002-03 when he averaged 9.8 points, 5.1 rebounds, 1.4 assists, .8 steals, and .3 blocked shots per contest. Jones scored 28 points in a 98–88 victory over New York on December 28, 2001, at Gund Arena. He was traded to the Celtics on July 29, 2003.

JONES, KEVIN

Kevin Jones was a 6-foot-8, 251-pound power forward for the Cavaliers in 2012-13. Signed as a free agent on November 29, 2012, in his one season with Cleveland he averaged three points, 2.4 rebounds, .3 assists, .3 steals, and .2 blocked shots per game. He scored 11 points in a 91–77 loss to the 76ers in Philadelphia on April 14. He was waived on July 19, 2013.

JORDAN, EDDIE

Eddie Jordan was a 6-foot-1, 170-pound point guard for the Cavaliers in 1977-78. A second-round draft pick in 1977 out of Rutgers University, in his one season with the Cavs he averaged 2.3 points, 1.5 assists, .5 rebounds, and .5 steals per game. He scored 11 points in a 91–88 loss to the Bulls on October 18, 1977, at The Coliseum. He was waived on December 10, 1977.

JORDAN, WALTER

Walter Jordan was a 6-foot-7, 198-pound small forward for the Cavaliers in 1980-81. Signed as a free agent on August 13, 1980, he averaged 2.3 points, 1.4 rebounds, .4 assists, .4 steals, and .2 blocked shots per game in his one season with Cleveland. He scored eight points in a 137–119 defeat to the 76ers on January 16 at Philadelphia. He became a free agent again on July 1, 1981, and was not re-signed.

JUNE

The following are five memorable Cavaliers games that were played in the month of June:

JUNE 2, 2007

The Cavaliers were crowned Eastern Conference champions for the first time by beating the Detroit Pistons 98–82 in Game 6 of the conference finals in front of 20,562 crazed fans at Quicken Loans Arena. The Cavs turned a tight game into a rout by outscoring Detroit 31–16 in the fourth quarter. Daniel Gibson led the Cavs with 31 points. LeBron James scored 20. Richard Hamilton led the Pistons with 29 points.

JUNE 7, 2007

In its first-ever NBA Finals game, Cleveland lost to the San Antonio Spurs 85–76 in front of 18,797 fans at the AT&T Center. The Cavaliers trailed by five points at halftime and by 15 after three quarters. Daniel Gibson led the Cavs with 16 points. Tony Parker was tops on the Spurs with 27 points.

JUNE 7, 2015

The Cavaliers defeated the Golden State Warriors 95–93 in overtime before 19,596 fans at Oracle Arena to tie the NBA Finals at a game apiece. It was the Cavs' first-ever victory in the championship round. Two free throws by Matthew Dellavedova, and one by LeBron James, helped Cleveland down the stretch. James led the Cavaliers with 39 points. Klay Thompson led Golden State with 34 points.

JUNE 13, 2016

Trailing three games to one in the NBA Finals, the Cavaliers staved off elimination by beating the Golden State Warriors 112–97 before 19,596 fans at Oracle Arena. LeBron James and Kyrie Irving each led the Cavs with 41 points, becoming the first teammates to ever score 40 or more points in a Finals game. Stephen Curry led Golden State with 25 points.

JUNE 19, 2016

In front of 19,596 screaming fans at Oracle Arena, the Cavaliers did what was thought to be the impossible by winning their third straight game against the Golden State Warriors 93–89 to win the NBA Finals four games to three. It was the first time ever a team came back from a 3–1 series deficit to win the Finals. It was also the city of Cleveland's first major pro sports championship in 52 years. In the last minute, Kyrie Irving hit a key three-pointer and LeBron James a free throw that was the dagger. James led the Cavs with 27 points, while Irving had 26. Draymond Green led the Warriors with 32 points.

K

KAPONO, JASON

Jason Kapono was a 6-foot-8, 213-pound small forward for the Cavaliers in 2003-04. A second-round draft pick in 2003 from UCLA, in his one season with Cleveland he averaged 3.5 points, 1.3 rebounds, .3 assists, and .3 steals per game. He scored 19 points in a 104–100 victory over New Orleans on February 23 at Gund Arena. He was selected by the Bobcats in the 2004 Expansion Draft.

KARASEV, SERGEY

Sergey Karasev was a 6-foot-7, 208-pound small forward for Cleveland in 2013-14. A first-round draft choice in 2013 from Russia, he averaged 1.7 points, .7 rebounds, .3 assists, and .1 steals per game in his one season with the Cavs. He scored eight points in a 126–96 loss to the Spurs on November 23 at San Antonio. He was traded to Brooklyn on July 10, 2014.

KARL, COBY

Coby Karl was a 6-foot-5, 215-pound shooting guard for the Cavaliers in 2009-10. Signed as a free agent on October 1, 2009, he played three games with Cleveland. He was waived on January 6, 2010. He is the son of ex-Cavs head coach George Karl

KARL, GEORGE

George Karl was the Cavaliers' head coach in 1984-85 and a Cavs head coach in 1985-86. His 1984-85 squad got off to a 2-19 start but recovered and qualified for the playoffs with a 36-46 record. They put up a valiant fight against a heavily favored Boston team the opening round before succumbing. The 1985-86 Cavs were 25–42 when he was fired. Karl's overall record as Cleveland's head coach was 61-88. His postseason mark was 1-3. He is the father of ex-Cavalier Coby Karl.

KAUN, SASHA

Sasha Kaun was a 6-foot-11, 260-pound center for the Cavaliers in 2015-16. Signed as a free agent on September 8, 2015, in his one season with Cleveland, he averaged .9 points, one rebound, .1 assists, .2 steals, and .2 blocked shots per game. He scored four points on three occasions. He was traded to Philadelphia on July 15, 2016.

KELLEMAN, HOWARD

Howard Kelleman was a Cavaliers local radio broadcaster in 1988-89.

KEMP, SHAWN

Shawn Kemp was a 6-foot-10, 230-pound power forward and center for the Cavaliers from 1997-98 to 1999-2000. He was traded from Seattle on September 25, 1997. In his three seasons with Cleveland he averaged 18.5 points, 9.1 rebounds, 2.1 assists, 1.3 steals, and 1.1 blocked shots per game. His best season as a Cavalier was 1998-99 when he averaged 20.5 points, 9.2 rebounds, 2.4 assists, 1.1 steals, and 1.1 blocked shots per contest.

Kemp scored 36 points in a 111–101 loss to the Nets on December 15, 1999, in New Jersey and 35 points in a 96–94 win over the Bullets on December 29, 1999, at Gund Arena. He had 31 points in an 86–77 playoff victory over the Pacers on April 27, 1998, again at Gund Arena. He was an All-Star in 1997-98. He was traded to the Trail Blazers on August 30, 2000.

KEMPTON, TIM

Tim Kempton was a 6-foot-10, 245-pound power forward for the Cavaliers in 1993-94. Signed as a free agent on April 15, 1994, he played four games with Cleveland. He became a free agent again on July 1, 1994, and was not re-signed.

KENNEDY, D. J.

D. J. Kennedy was a 6-foot-6, 215-pound small forward for the Cavaliers in 2011-12. Signed as a free agent on April 21, 2012, he played two games with the Cavs. He was traded to Memphis on July 25, 2012.

KENON, LARRY

Larry Kenon was a 6-foot-9, 205-pound power forward for Cleveland in 1982-83. Traded from the Warriors on January 10, 1983, he averaged 7.3

points, 3.7 rebounds, 1.1 assists, .7 steals, and .3 blocked shots per game in his one season with the Cavs. He scored 22 points in a 110–107 victory over San Diego on February 6 at The Coliseum. He was waived on March 21, 1983.

KERR, STEVE

Steve Kerr was a 6-foot-3, 175-pound point guard for the Cavaliers from 1989-90 to 1992-93. Traded from Phoenix on September 5, 1989, in his four seasons with Cleveland he averaged six points, 2.7 assists, 1.2 rebounds, .5 steals, and .1 blocked shots per game. His best season as a Cavalier was 1989-90 when he averaged 6.7 points, 3.2 assists, 1.3 rebounds, .6 steals, and .1 blocked shots per contest.

Kerr scored 24 points in a 107–102 victory over the Pacers on April 17, 1992, at Indiana. He scored nine points in a 109–104 playoff loss to the Nets on April 28, 1992, at New Jersey. He was traded to Orlando on December 2, 1992.

KETNER, LARI

Lari Ketner was a 6-foot-9, 277-pound power forward for the Cavaliers in 1999-2000. He signed the first of two 10-day contracts on February 22, 2000, and on March 13, 2000, signed a contract for the rest of the 1999-2000 season. In 16 games with Cleveland he averaged 1.5 points, 1.7 rebounds, .2 steals, and .1 blocked shots per contest. He scored four points three times. He was waived on September 28, 2000.

KEYS, RANDOLPH

Randolph Keys was a 6-foot-7, 195-pound small forward for the Cavaliers from 1988-89 to 1989-90. A first-round draft pick in 1988 out of the University of Southern Mississippi, he averaged 5.9 points, 2.1 rebounds, .6 assists, .6 steals, and .1 blocked shots per game in his two seasons with Cleveland. His best season as a Cavalier was 1989-90 when he averaged 7.6 points, 2.9 rebounds, .8 assists, and .8 steals per contest. He scored 22 points twice—in a 102-89 defeat to the Celtics on December 1, 1989, at Boston and in a 104–101 loss to the Spurs on January 19, 1990, in San Antonio. He was traded to Charlotte on February 22, 1990.

KINCH, CHAD

Chad Kinch was a 6-foot-4, 190-pound shooting guard for the Cavaliers in 1980-81. A first-round draft pick in 1980 from the University of North

Carolina Charlotte, in his one season with Cleveland he averaged 2.8 points, 1.2 assists, .8 rebounds, .3 steals, and .2 blocked shots per game. He scored 10 points on three occasions. He was traded to Dallas on February 7, 1981.

KINSEY, TARENCE

Tarence Kinsey was a 6-foot-6, 185-pound shooting guard for the Cavaliers in 2008-09. Signed as a free agent on August 4, 2008, in his one season with Cleveland he averaged two points, .2 assists, .8 rebounds, and .2 steals per game. He scored 11 points on three occasions. He scored two points in the playoffs twice—in a 102–84 victory over Detroit on April 18 at Quicken Loans Arena and in a 99–72 triumph over Atlanta on May 5, again at Quicken Loans Arena. He was waived on July 29, 2009.

KIRK, ALEX

Alex Kirk was a 7-foot, 245-pound center for the Cavaliers in 2014-15. Signed as a free agent on August 11, 2014, in five games with Cleveland he averaged .8 points, .2 rebounds, and .2 assists per contest. He scored two points twice—in a 101–82 loss to the Trail Blazers on November 4 in Portland and in a 109–97 win over Indiana on November 29 at Quicken Loans Arena. He was traded to the Knicks on January 5, 2015.

KLOPPENBURG, BOB

Bob Kloppenburg was a Cavaliers head coach in 1981-82. He had an 0-1 record after replacing the fired Don Delaney, who had started the season 4-13. He was relieved of his duties. He was also a Cavs assistant coach in 1981-82.

KNIGHT, BREVIN

Brevin Knight was a 5-foot-10, 173-pound point guard for the Cavaliers from 1997-98 to 2000-01. A first-round draft pick in 1997 out of Stanford University, in his four seasons with the Cavs he averaged nine points, 7.6 assists, 3.1 rebounds, two steals, and .2 blocked shots per game. His best season as a Cavalier was 1997-98 when he averaged nine points, 8.2 assists, 3.2 rebounds, 2.5 steals, and .2 blocked shots per contest.

Knight scored 22 points in a 91–85 victory over Chicago on April 9, 1998, at Gund Arena. He scored 11 points in an 86–77 playoff win over Indiana on April 27, 1998, again at Gund Arena. He was traded to Atlanta on January 2, 2001.

KOKOSKOV, IGOR

Igor Kokoskov was a Cavaliers assistant coach in 2013-14.

KOMOROSKI, LEN

Len Komoroski was the Cavaliers' president from 2002-03 to 2004-05 and 2009-10 to 2010-11.

KUESTER, JOHN

John Kuester was a Cavaliers assistant coach from 2007-08 to 2008-09.

KULL, HERMAN

Herman Kull was a Cavaliers assistant coach in 1985-86.

L

LACEY, SAM

Sam Lacey was a 6-foot-10, 235-pound center for the Cavaliers in 1982-83. Signed as a free agent on December 6, 1982, in his one season with Cleveland he averaged 4.2 points, 3.9 rebounds, two assists, .5 steals, and .4 blocked shots per game. He scored 16 points in a 107–106 victory over the Pistons on January 28 at Detroit. He was waived on May 18, 1983.

LAIMBEER, BILL

Bill Laimbeer was a 6-foot-11, 245-pound center for the Cavaliers from 1980-81 to 1981-82. A third-round draft choice in 1979 out of the University of Notre Dame, he averaged 8.6 points, 7.4 rebounds, two assists, .6 steals, and .8 blocked shots per game in his two seasons with Cleveland. His best season as a Cavalier was 1980-81 when he averaged 9.8 points, 8.6 rebounds, 2.7 assists, .7 steals, and one blocked shot per contest. He scored 30 points in a 114–95 win over Kansas City on December 23, 1981, at The Coliseum. He was traded to Detroit on February 16, 1982.

LAMBERT, JOHN

John Lambert was a 6-foot-10, 225-pound power forward for Cleveland from 1975-76 to 1980-81. A first-round draft pick in 1975 out of the University of Southern California, in his six seasons with the Cavs he averaged 3.9 points, 3.6 rebounds, .6 assists, .4 steals, and .4 blocked shots per game. His best season as a Cavalier was 1979-80 when he averaged 5.4 points, 4.8 rebounds, .8 assists, .6 steals, and .6 blocked shots per contest.

Lambert scored 18 points in a 114–91 triumph over the Bullets on January 22, 1980, at The Coliseum. He scored four points in a 99–94 playoff defeat to the Celtics on May 16, 1976, at Boston. He was waived on December 19, 1980.

LANE, JEROME

Jerome Lane was a 6-foot-6, 230-pound power forward for the Cavaliers in 1992-93. Signed as a free agent on August 31, 1992, in his one season with Cleveland he averaged 2.8 points, 2.5 rebounds, .8 assists, .6 steals, and .1 blocked shots per game. He scored eight points twice—in a 124–97 win over Houston on December 15 at The Coliseum and in a 122–107 victory over Denver on March 8, likewise at The Coliseum. He became a free agent again on July 1, 1993, and was not re-signed.

LANG, ANTONIO

Antonio Lang was a 6-foot-8, 205-pound power forward and small forward for the Cavaliers from 1995-96 to 1996-97 and in 1998-99. He was traded from Phoenix on October 7, 1995. He became a free agent on July 1, 1997. He was re-signed as a free agent on January 21, 1999.

In his three seasons with the Cavs Lang averaged 2.6 points, 1.7 rebounds, .4 assists, .4 steals, and .4 blocked shots per game. His best season as a Cavalier was 1996-97 when he averaged 2.7 points, two rebounds, .5 assists, .5 steals, and .5 blocked shots per contest. He scored 14 points twice—in an 88–86 loss to the Hornets at Charlotte on January 29, 1996, and in a 93–81 defeat to the Pistons in Detroit on December 6, 1996. He was waived on March 10, 1999.

LANGDON, TRAJAN

Trajan Langdon was a 6-foot-3, 197-pound shooting guard for the Cavaliers from 1999-2000 to 2001-02. A first-round draft choice in 1999 out of Duke University, he averaged 5.4 points, 1.3 assists, 1.3 rebounds, .5 steals, and .1 blocked shots per game in his three seasons with Cleveland. His best season as a Cavalier was 2000-01 when he averaged six points, 1.2 assists, 1.4 rebounds, .6 steals, and .1 blocked shots per contest. He scored 31 points in a 117–98 victory over Detroit at Gund Arena on November 21, 2000. He became a free agent on July 1, 2002, and was not re-signed.

LARGEST HOME CROWDS FOR EACH SEASON, HIGHEST TO LOWEST

Please see Attendance Statistics on page 272.

LEBOVITZ, HAL

Hal Lebovitz was a Cavaliers local television broadcaster from 1970-71 to 1974-75.

LEE, BUTCH

Alfred "Butch" Lee was a 6-foot, 185-pound point guard for the Cavaliers from 1978-79 to 1979-80. Traded from Atlanta on January 31, 1979, in his two seasons with Cleveland he averaged 10.6 points, 3.6 assists, 1.9 rebounds, and .8 steals per game. His best season as a Cavalier was 1978-79, when he averaged 11.5 points, 3.8 assists, two rebounds, and .9 steals per contest. He scored 22 points in a 106–103 loss to the Lakers on February 9, 1979, at Los Angeles. He was traded to the Lakers on February 15, 1980.

LEE, KEITH

Keith Lee was a 6-foot-10, 215-pound power forward for the Cavaliers from 1985-86 to 1986-87. He was traded from the Bulls on June 18, 1985. In his two seasons with Cleveland he averaged 6.7 points, 4.8 rebounds, 1.1 assists, .4 steals, and .6 blocked shots per game. His best season as a Cavalier was 1985-86 when he averaged 7.4 points, 6.1 rebounds, 1.2 assists, .5 steals, and .6 blocked shots per contest. He scored 25 points in a 121–114 loss to Philadelphia on January 24, 1986, at The Coliseum. He was traded to New Jersey on October 8, 1987.

LESSIG, JIM

Jim Lessig was the Cavaliers' assistant coach in 1970-71. He was a Cavs local television broadcaster in 1975-76.

LEUER, JON

Jon Leuer was a 6-foot-10, 228-pound center for the Cavaliers in 2012-13. Signed as a free agent on July 20, 2012, in nine games with Cleveland, he averaged 2.4 points, 1.4 rebounds, .6 assists, and .2 steals per contest. He scored seven points in a 106–96 defeat to the Warriors on November 7 at Golden State. He was traded to Memphis on January 22, 2013.

LEWIS, BOBBY

Bobby Lewis was a 6-foot-3, 175-pound shooting guard for the Cavaliers in 1970-71. He was chosen in the 1970 Expansion Draft from San Francisco. In his one season with Cleveland he averaged 5.9 points, 3.1 assists, and 2.6 rebounds per game. He scored 15 points in a 113–110 loss to Portland on March 21 at the Cleveland Arena. He became a free agent on July 1, 1971, and was not re-signed.

LITTLES, GENE

Gene Littles was a Cavaliers head coach in 1985-86. He had a 4-11 record after replacing the fired George Karl with the team's record at 25-42 for a final mark of 29-53. He was relieved of his duties after the season. He was a Cavs assistant coach from 1982-83 to 1985-86.

LIVINGSTON, SHAUN

Shaun Livingston was a 6-foot-7, 182-pound point guard for Cleveland in 2012-13. Signed as a free agent on December 25, 2012, in his one season with the Cavs he averaged 7.2 points, 3.6 assists, 2.5 rebounds, .8 steals, and .6 blocked shots per game. He scored 16 points in a 119–113 loss to the Spurs on March 16 in San Antonio. He became a free agent again on July 1, 2013, and was not re-signed.

Kevin Love against the Celtics in the 2015 playoffs. (AndersonsCleveland Design.com)

LONGABARDI, MIKE

Mike Longabardi has been a Cavaliers assistant coach since 2015-16.

LOVE, KEVIN

Kevin Love has been a 6-foot-10, 251-pound power forward for the Cavaliers since 2014-15. Traded from Minnesota on August 23, 2014, in his two seasons with Cleveland he has averaged 16.2 points, 9.8 rebounds, 2.3 assists, .7 steals, and .5 blocked shots per game. His best season as a Cavalier has been 2015-16 when he averaged 16 points, 9.9 rebounds, 2.4 assists, .8 steals, and .5 blocked shots per contest. In his first season with the Cavs he averaged 16.4 points, 9.7 rebounds, 2.2 assists, .7 steals, and .5 blocked shots per game.

Love scored 34 points in a 117–103 victory over Orlando on November 23, 2015, at Quicken Loans Arena. He scored 28 points in a 106–101 playoff win over Detroit on April 17, 2016, again at Quicken Loans Arena.

LOWE, SIDNEY

Sidney Lowe was a Cavaliers assistant coach from 1994-95 to 1998-99.

LUCAS, JOHN

John Lucas was the Cavaliers' head coach in 2001-02 and for the first half of the 2002-03 season. His first team went 29-53 and he was fired when the Cavs began the next season 8-34. His overall record as Cleveland's head coach was 37-87.

LUE, TYRONN

Tyronn Lue was a Cavaliers head coach in 2015-16 and has been their head coach since. He took over for David Blatt when the Cavs' record was 30-11. He led the team to a 27-14 record for a 57-25 overall record and the number one seed in the Eastern Conference playoffs. His Cavaliers wound up winning the NBA Finals, culminated by a record-setting comeback against Golden State in which the Cavs recovered from a 3–1 series deficit. His postseason record is 16-5. He was a Cavs assistant coach from 2014-15 to 2015-16. He was the Eastern Conference head coach in the All-Star Game.

M

MADKINS, GERALD

Gerald Madkins was a 6-foot-4, 200-pound shooting guard for the Cavaliers from 1993-94 to 1994-95. Signed as a free agent on June 15, 1993, in his two seasons with the Cavs he averaged 1.5 points, .7 assists, .4 rebounds, and .4 steals per game. His best season as a Cavalier was 1993-94 when he averaged 1.6 points, .9 assists, .5 rebounds, and .4 steals per contest. He scored 11 points in a 110–95 loss to the Hawks on April 13, 1994, at Atlanta. He was waived on December 6, 1994.

MAGLEY, DAVID

David Magley was a 6-foot-8, 202-pound small forward for the Cavaliers in 1982-83. A second-round draft choice in 1982 out of the University of Kansas, he averaged .9 points, .7 rebounds, .1 assists, and .1 steals per contest in 14 games with Cleveland. He scored four points in a 125–107 loss to the Lakers on January 6 at The Coliseum. He was waived on January 7, 1983.

MAJERLE, DAN

Dan Majerle was a 6-foot-6, 215-pound small forward for the Cavaliers in 1995-96. Traded on October 7, 1995, from the Suns, in his one season with the Cavs he averaged 10.6 points, 3.7 rebounds, 2.6 assists, one steal, and .4 blocked shots per game. He scored 25 points in a 116–104 defeat to the Magic on April 10 at Orlando. He scored 23 points in a 106–83 playoff loss to the Knicks on April 25 at Gund Arena. He was released on August 8, 1996.

MALONE, BRENDAN

Brendan Malone was a Cavaliers head coach in 2004-05. He took over a Cavs team that was 34-30 when Paul Silas was fired. He led the team to an 8-10 finish. Its 42-40 record left them just out of the postseason. He was also a Cavs assistant coach in 2004-05.

MALONE, MICHAEL

Michael Malone was a Cavaliers assistant coach from 2005-06 to 2009-10.

MARCH

The following are five memorable Cavaliers games that were played in the month of March:

MARCH 31, 1976

The Cavaliers clinched their first-ever playoff berth with a 110–101 victory over the New Orleans Jazz in front of a crowd of 8,734 at the Superdome. Jim Cleamons led Cleveland with 18 points, while Austin Carr and Jim Chones each had 17. Pete Maravich led the Jazz with 21 points.

MARCH 22, 1980

The Cavaliers continued their late-season push toward the playoffs with a 109–105 victory over the Boston Celtics—their eighth straight win—before a raucous crowd of 19,912 at The Coliseum. Randy Smith led the Cavs with 29 points. Mike Mitchell had 23. The Celtics were led by Larry Bird's 26 points.

MARCH 27, 1981

As longtime Cavaliers local radio broadcaster Joe Tait's war of words with team owner Ted Stepien, who was leading the team on a slow death march, came to a head and had Tait leaving town after the season, the Cavs honored their living legend with Joe Tait Night in their final home game of the season against the Philadelphia 76ers. The fact that 20,175 fans showed up at The Coliseum for a team that was 24 games below .500 was proof positive that Tait would be missed—big-time.

The angry crowd used the occasion to not only show support for its adored broadcaster, but also voice its discontent over the fact that Stepien was staying behind to run the team. It mattered little that the Cavs lost the game 138–117. Leading the way for Cleveland was Mike Mitchell with 30 points and Kenny Carr with 24. Also scoring 24 points, tops on the Sixers, was Andrew Toney.

MARCH 22, 1994

The Cavaliers defeated the Indiana Pacers 93–61 in front of 17,935 fans at The Coliseum. The Cavs held Indiana to just 29 points in the second half.

Cleveland was led by Terrell Brandon's 15 points. Rik Smits, the only Pacer to score in double figures, had 10 points.

MARCH 28, 2005

The Cavaliers made a remarkable recovery from a 15-point deficit after three quarters to defeat the New Orleans Hornets 109–108 in overtime before 16,118 fans at the New Orleans Arena. The Cavs, who outscored the Hornets 38–23 in the fourth quarter, were led by LeBron James's 44 points. The home team was led by J. R. Smith's 22 points.

MARION, SHAWN

Shawn Marion was a 6-foot-7, 220-pound small forward for the Cavaliers in 2014-15. Signed as a free agent on September 9, 2014, in his one season with Cleveland he averaged 4.8 points, 3.5 rebounds, .9 assists, .5 steals, and .5 blocked shots per game. He scored 13 points in a 109–90 loss to Dallas on January 4 at Quicken Loans Arena. He scored two points in a 94–82 playoff win over the Hawks on May 22 at Atlanta. He retired on June 18, 2015.

MARSHALL, DONNY

Donny Marshall was a 6-foot-7, 230-pound small forward for the Cavaliers from 1995-96 to 1996-97 and in 1999-2000. He was chosen in the second round of the 1995 draft from the University of Connecticut. He was waived on October 30, 1997. He was re-signed to the first of two 10-day contracts on February 25, 2000.

In his three seasons with Cleveland Marshall averaged 2.7 points, one rebound, .3 assists, .4 steals, and .1 blocked shots per game. His best season as a Cavalier was 1996-97 when he averaged 3.1 points, 1.3 rebounds, .4 assists, .4 steals, and .1 blocked shots per contest. He scored 17 points in a 106–73 victory over Charlotte on January 25, 1997, at Gund Arena. He was waived again on March 12, 2000.

MARSHALL, DONYELL

Donyell Marshall was a 6-foot-9, 218-pound power forward for the Cavaliers from 2005-06 to 2007-08. Signed as a free agent on August 2, 2005, in his three seasons with the Cavs he averaged 7.8 points, 4.9 rebounds, .6 assists, .6 steals, and .5 blocked shots per game. His best season as a Cavalier was 2005-06 when he averaged 9.3 points, 6.1 rebounds, .7 assists, .7 steals, and .5 blocked shots per contest.

Marshall scored 29 points in a 109–99 victory over the Bucks on December 29, 2006, at Quicken Loans Arena. He scored 28 points in a 114–113 overtime playoff win against the Wizards on May 5, 2006, at Washington. He was traded to Seattle on February 21, 2008.

MASCOTS

Whammer was the Cavaliers' first mascot. A polar bear who is said to have grown up in the tundra, Whammer debuted on November 9, 1995, during a game against the Chicago Bulls. At halftime, he used to dunk a basketball. He still makes occasional appearances at Cavs games.

Moondog has been the Cavaliers' mascot since November 5, 2003, when he debuted in a game against the Denver Nuggets. Moondog has a unique connection not only to the team, but to the city of Cleveland and its surrounding areas. Cleveland is known worldwide as the "Rock and Roll" city due to famed Cleveland radio disc jockey Alan Freed, who popularized the phrase "rock and roll," breaking new ground and sparking a music explosion. Freed called himself the "Moondog," and his listeners were "Moondoggers." When the Cavs looked to create a new mascot that would represent the city, Moondog was a natural selection. Like Freed, the mascot aims to be innovative, fun-loving, passionate, and controversial. Moondog is best known for his behind-the-back, halfcourt shot and fierce loyalty to the Cavaliers.

On November 27, 2010, during a game against the Memphis Grizzlies, a new mascot named Sir C.C., a swashbuckler character à la The Three Musketeers, debuted. He teams up with Moondog to provide gametime entertainment.

MAY

The following are five memorable Cavaliers games that were played in the month of May:

MAY 14, 1976

In perhaps their finest performance of their brief history, the Cavaliers defeated the Boston Celtics 106–87 in Game 4 of the Eastern Conference Finals in front of a Coliseum crowd of 21,564 to even the series at two wins apiece. The Cavs turned a 79–77 lead with eight minutes to go into a 97–83 advantage with 2:20 left. Bingo Smith led the Cavs with 27 points. Jo Jo White led Boston with 23 points.

MAY 7, 1989

The Cavaliers lost 101–100 to the Chicago Bulls in Game 5 of an Eastern Conference first-round playoff series before 20,273 fans at The Coliseum when Michael Jordan connected on what would soon become known simply as "The Shot"—an off-balance jumper from 15 feet away—at the buzzer. Moments earlier, Craig Ehlo had given the Cavs a 100–99 lead when he drove to the hoop for a layup. It was the second straight season in which the Cavs were ousted by the Bulls in Game 5 of the opening round of the playoffs. Leading the way for Cleveland were Ehlo with 24 points, Mark Price with 23, and Ron Harper with 22. Jordan led the Bulls with 44 points.

MAY 17, 1992

In Larry Bird's last game, the Cavaliers destroyed the Boston Celtics 122–104 in Game 7 of the Eastern Conference Semifinals before 20,273 fans at The Coliseum. The Cavs led by 14 points after the first quarter, by 18 at halftime, and by 24 after three quarters. Brad Daugherty led the Cavaliers with 28 points. John Williams scored 20. Reggie Lewis led Boston with 22 points.

MAY 5, 2006

Damon Jones nailed a 17-foot shot with 4.8 seconds to go in overtime that wound up giving the Cavaliers a series-clinching 114–113 win over the Washington Wizards before a crowd of 20,173 at the MCI Center in Game 6 of an Eastern Conference first-round playoff series. LeBron James led the Cavs with 32 points. Donyell Marshall scored 28. Gilbert Arenas led Washington with 36 points.

MAY 10, 2015

The Cavaliers recovered from a 68–61 deficit after three quarters to defeat the Chicago Bulls 86–84 in Game 4 of the Eastern Conference Semifinals before 22,256 fans at the United Center. LeBron James's 21-footer at the buzzer won the game and evened the series at two wins apiece. James led the Cavs with 25 points. Derrick Rose led the Bulls with 31 points.

MCCOY, JELANI

Jelani McCoy was a 6-foot-10, 245-pound center for the Cavaliers in 2003-04. Signed as a free agent on October 2, 2003, he played two games with Cleveland. He was waived on November 6, 2003.

MCCRAY, SCOOTER

Carlton "Scooter" McCray was a 6-foot-9, 215-pound power forward for the Cavaliers in 1986-87. Signed as a free agent on September 30, 1986, in his one season with Cleveland he averaged 3.3 points, 2.4 rebounds, one assist, .4 steals, and .2 blocked shots per game. He scored 11 points in a 111–99 loss to the Pacers on December 30 at Indiana. He was waived on February 10, 1987.

MCDONALD, BEN

Ben McDonald was a 6-foot-8, 210-pound small forward for the Cavaliers in 1985-86. He was a third-round draft pick in 1984 out of the University of California, Irvine. By then a free agent, on March 4, 1986, he signed the first of two 10-day contracts and on March 24, 1986, signed a contract for the rest of the 1985-86 season. In his one season with the Cavaliers he averaged 2.9 points, 1.8 rebounds, .4 assists, and .3 steals per game. He scored 10 points in a 114–93 loss to the Bucks in Milwaukee on April 3. He became a free agent again on July 1, 1986, and was not re-signed.

MCHONE, MORRIS

Morris McHone was the Cavaliers' assistant coach in 1979-80 and a Cavs assistant coach from 1984-85 to 1985-86.

MCINNIS, JEFF

Jeff McInnis was a 6-foot-4, 190-pound point guard for the Cavaliers from 2003-04 to 2004-05. Traded from Portland on January 21, 2004, in his two seasons with Cleveland he averaged 12.5 points, 5.8 assists, 2.2 rebounds, and .9 steals per game. His best season as a Cavalier was 2003-04 when he averaged 11.7 points, 7.5 assists, 2.6 rebounds, 1.2 steals, and .1 blocked shots per contest. He scored 26 points in a 120–101 loss to the Suns on December 1, 2004, in Phoenix. He became a free agent on July 1, 2005, and was not re-signed.

MCLEMORE, MCCOY

McCoy McLemore was a 6-foot-7, 230-pound small forward for the Cavaliers in 1970-71. Selected in the 1970 Expansion Draft from the Pistons, in his one season with Cleveland he averaged 11.7 points, eight rebounds, and three assists per game. He scored 25 points in a 116–112 defeat to the Celtics on November 20 in Boston. He was traded to Milwaukee on February 1, 1971.

MCLEOD, FRED

Fred McLeod was a Cavaliers local television broadcaster in 1979-80 and has been since 2006-07.

MCRAE, JORDAN

Jordan McRae has been a 6-foot-6, 185-pound point guard for the Cavaliers since 2015-16. He signed the first of two 10-day contracts on February 28, 2016. In 15 games with Cleveland he has averaged 4.1 points, one assist, .8 rebounds, and .1 blocked shots per contest. He scored 36 points in a 112–110 overtime defeat to Detroit on April 13 at Quicken Loans Arena. He scored five points in a 107–90 playoff win over the Pistons on April 20 again at Quicken Loans Arena.

MICHAEL, JOHN

John Michael has been a Cavaliers local radio broadcaster since 2011-12.

MIHM, CHRIS

Chris Mihm was a 7-foot, 265-pound center and power forward for the Cavaliers from 2000-01 to 2003-04. Traded from Chicago on June 28, 2000, in his four seasons with Cleveland he averaged 7.1 points, five rebounds, .4 assists, .3 steals, and one blocked shot per game. His best season as a Cavalier was 2003-04 when he averaged 6.9 points, 6.4 rebounds, .5 assists, .4 steals, and one blocked shot per contest. He scored 21 points in a 103–95 win over the Clippers on November 18, 2003, at Gund Arena. He was traded to Boston on December 15, 2003.

MIKAN, LARRY

Larry Mikan was a 6-foot-7, 210-pound small forward for the Cavaliers in 1970-71. The son of NBA Hall of Famer George Mikan and the nephew of ex-NBA player Ed Mikan, he was signed as a free agent on November 12, 1970. In his one season with Cleveland he averaged three points, 2.6 rebounds, and .8 assists per game. He scored 14 points in a 124–113 defeat to Philadelphia on March 9 at the Cleveland Arena. He became a free agent again on July 1, 1971, and was not re-signed.

MILES, C. J.

C. J. Miles was a 6-foot-6, 231-pound small forward and shooting guard for the Cavaliers from 2012-13 to 2013-14. He was signed as a free agent on August 8, 2012. In his two seasons with Cleveland he averaged 10.6 points, 2.4 rebounds, one assist, .8 steals, and .3 blocked shots per game. His best season as a Cavalier was 2012-13 when he averaged 11.2 points, 2.7 rebounds, one assist, .8 steals, and .3 blocked shots per contest. He scored 34 points in a 111–93 victory over Philadelphia on January 7, 2014, at Quicken Loans Arena. He became a free agent again on July 1, 2014, and was not re-signed.

MILES, DARIUS

Darius Miles was a 6-foot-9, 210-pound small forward for the Cavaliers from 2002-03 to 2003-04. Traded from the Clippers on July 30, 2002, in his two seasons with Cleveland he averaged 9.1 points, 5.1 rebounds, 2.5 assists, .9 steals, and .9 blocked shots per game. His best season as a Cavalier was 2002-03 when he averaged 9.2 points, 5.4 rebounds, 2.6 assists, one steal, and one blocked shot per contest. He scored 26 points in a 111–98 victory over Washington on November 8, 2003, at Gund Arena. He was traded to Portland on January 21, 2004.

MILETI, NICK

Nick Mileti founded the Cavaliers. His ownership group paid $3.7 million for the expansion team that began play in 1970-71. A name-the-team contest in the *Plain Dealer* that drew more than 14,000 entries was the driving force behind the name "Cavaliers." Mileti made the final call. The team colors of wine and gold emanated from the hues of his high school alma mater, John Adams.

Mileti was the Cavaliers' majority owner from 1970-71 to 1979-80. He was the one responsible for The Coliseum being built in time for the 1974-75 season. Under his ownership, the Cavs are best remembered for the 1975-76

Miracle of Richfield team that provided fans with a remarkable playoff run that nearly resulted in a Finals appearance.

At one time or another, Mileti also owned The Coliseum, the Cleveland Indians, the original Cleveland Barons, the Cleveland Crusaders, WKYC-FM 105.7, and WWWE-AM 1100, the latter of which became the home of the Cavaliers and Indians in 1973. He doubled as the Cavs' president for all 10 seasons he owned the team. He was also the club's general manager from 1970-71 to 1972-73. He sold the Cavaliers during the 1980 offseason. The sale eventually resulted in Ted Stepien becoming the majority owner.

MILLER, ANDRE

Andre Miller was a 6-foot-3, 200-pound point guard for the Cavaliers from 1999-2000 to 2001-02. A first-round draft pick in 1999 from the University of Utah, in his three seasons with the Cavs he averaged 14.5 points, 8.2 assists, 4.2 rebounds, 1.3 steals, and .3 blocked shots per game. His best season as a Cavalier was 2001-02 when he averaged 16.5 points, 10.9 assists, 4.7 rebounds, 1.6 steals, and .4 blocked shots per contest. He scored 37 points in a 114–107 overtime win against San Antonio on February 28, 2002, at Gund Arena. He was traded to the Clippers on July 30, 2002.

Andre Miller, 2000-01. (AndersonsClevelandDesign.com)

MILLER, MIKE

Mike Miller was a 6-foot-8, 218-pound small forward for Cleveland in 2014-15. Signed as a free agent on August 5, 2014, in his one season with Cleveland he averaged 2.1 points, 1.8 rebounds, .9 assists, .3 steals, and .1 blocked shots per game. He scored 21 points in a 95–91 win over Brooklyn on December 19 at Quicken Loans Arena. He scored three points in the playoffs on three occasions. He was traded to Portland on July 27, 2015.

MILLS, CHRIS

Chris Mills was a 6-foot-6, 215-pound small forward for the Cavaliers from 1993-94 to 1996-97. A first-round draft choice in 1993 out of the University of Arizona, he averaged 12.6 points, 5.4 rebounds, 2.1 assists, .9 steals, and .6 blocked shots per game in his four seasons with the Cavs. His best season as a Cavalier was 1995-96 when he averaged 15.1 points, 5.5 rebounds, 2.4 assists, .9 steals, and .7 blocked shots per contest.

Mills scored 30 points in a 98–73 triumph over Boston on March 14, 1996, at Gund Arena. He scored 25 points in a 95–92 overtime playoff defeat to the Bulls on May 3, 1994, at The Coliseum. He became a free agent on July 1, 1997, and was not re-signed.

MINER, HAROLD

Harold Miner was a 6-foot-5, 210-pound shooting guard for the Cavaliers in 1995-96. Traded from the Heat on June 14, 1995, in 19 games with the Cavs, he averaged 3.2 points, .4 assists, and .6 rebounds per contest. He scored 13 points in a 113–94 loss to the Bulls on November 15 in Chicago. He was released on August 8, 1996.

MINNIEFIELD, DIRK

Dirk Minniefield was a 6-foot-3, 180-pound point guard for the Cavaliers from 1985-86 to 1986-87. Signed as a free agent on September 11, 1985, he averaged 5.1 points, 3.2 assists, 1.6 rebounds, and .8 steals per game in his two seasons with Cleveland. His best season as a Cavalier was 1985-86 when he averaged 5.5 points, 3.5 assists, 1.7 rebounds, and .9 steals per contest. He scored 20 points in a 104–97 victory over Chicago on April 13, 1986, at The Coliseum. He was traded to Houston on December 9, 1986.

MIRACLE OF RICHFIELD

The Miracle of Richfield was a 35-day period during the spring of 1976 when the Cavaliers' first-ever appearance in the postseason resulted in a memorable seven-game series with the Washington Bullets in the Eastern Conference Semifinals—including three miraculous wins—and then a heartbreaking near-miss against the Boston Celtics in the Eastern Conference championship series.

The fans at The Coliseum, especially during the Washington series, were so loud, the building actually shook. Cavs head coach Bill Fitch several times had to hold team huddles closer to midfloor due to the noise. An hour before the games, the fans would yell over and over, "We want the Cavs! We want the Cavs!" It was incredible!

The Cavs lost Game 1 100–95 on April 13 at The Coliseum. The first miracle win occurred two nights later in Game 2 at Washington when Bingo Smith hit a 25-footer with two seconds to go to give the visitors an 80–79 lead and, after Elvin Hayes missed a last-second shot, their first-ever postseason win.

The Cavaliers won Game 3 at home 88–76 on April 16 but then fell 109–98 four nights later on the road. With the series tied 2–2, Game 5—and the second miracle win—was the next night, on April 22, at The Coliseum. With Washington leading 91–90 and just seven seconds left—and the three-point shot still four years away—Hayes was at the free throw line for two shots that, if made, likely would have put the dagger in the home team. Amid a thunderous din from the fans, the "Big E" missed both attempts. Two plays later, Smith threw up a running, off-balance air ball that fell right into the hands of Jim Cleamons, who was running to his left underneath the basket just to the right. Without even taking a step, Cleamons reached to the left and tried a reverse bank shot that sat on the rim—for minutes, it seemed—before falling through the net as the clock hit 0:00. The Cavs won 92–91 and the place went nuts.

Dick Snyder banks in the winning basket against the Bullets in Game 7 of the Eastern Conference Semifinals, April 29, 1976. (AndersonsClevelandDesign.com)

Four nights later in D.C., the Bullets won Game 6 102–98 in overtime to force a deciding Game 7 at The Coliseum on April 29. With the Cavaliers up 85–83 and 1:31 left, Hayes stood at the free throw line and, believe it or not, missed both attempts just like he did in the late stages of Game 5 seven nights earlier. Two exchange of possessions later, Phil Chenier hit a 15-footer from the wing to tie the game at 85 with 24 seconds remaining. A few moments after that, Dick Snyder banked in a running, one-handed shot from five feet out to give the Cavs an 87–85 lead with four seconds to go. Chenier missed a shot from the right corner and the buzzer sounded, and the Cavs won the game. Hundreds of fans rushed the court. The Cavs' basket stand was torn down. It was complete euphoria as 21,564 fans were delirious.

After the dust settled, it was time for the Cavs to think about their next opponent. Three days later, it was determined that their next foe would be the Boston Celtics. Unfortunately, Cavaliers starting center Jim Chones broke his right foot in a freak accident during a practice session two days before the start of the conference finals and was ruled out for the rest of the season. With Nate Thurmond, obtained in a trade early in the season, having to carry the load at center, it was just a little too much for the 34-year-old Akron native to handle. He did his best and almost led the Cavs to an upset of the Celtics.

Nate Thurmond attempts a hook shot over Dave Cowens as Jo Jo White watches during Game 4 of the Eastern Conference championship series, May 14, 1976. (The Cleveland Press Collection, Michael Schwartz Library, Cleveland State University)

Boston won Games 1 and 2 in the Boston Garden, 111–99 and 94–89, respectively. The Cavs won Game 3 at The Coliseum 83–78. With the help of a memorable six-minute-plus stretch in the fourth quarter, they won Game 4 going away 106–87 in what very well may have been the finest performance in their brief history to that point. The Celtics won Game 5 99–94 in Boston with the help of what many say was some shaky, to say the least, officiating. Game 6 at The Coliseum was a titanic battle that came down to the final few minutes. The Celtics wound up winning 94–87 and would go on to beat the

Phoenix Suns, a team that won only 42 games during the regular season, for the NBA championship.

It was a memorable ride for the Cavs and their fans that no one will ever forget.

MIRACLE IN RICHFIELD – THE CAVALIER HAPPENING

Miracle in Richfield—The Cavalier Happening is a record album released shortly after the 1975-76 season. Narrated by Joe Tait, it focuses on the Cavaliers' memorable playoff run that year.

MITCHELL, MIKE

Mike Mitchell was a 6-foot-7, 215-pound small forward for the Cavaliers from 1978-79 to 1981-82. A first-round draft choice in 1978 out of Auburn University, in his four seasons with the Cavs, he averaged 19.3 points, 5.8 rebounds, 1.2 assists, .8 steals, and .6 blocked shots per game. His best season as a Cavalier was 1980-81, when he averaged 24.5 points, 6.1 rebounds, 1.7 assists, .8 steals, and .6 blocked shots per contest.

Mitchell scored 46 points in a 105–104 loss to the Rockets on February 8, 1980, at Houston. He scored 42 points in a 110–108 defeat to the Nets on February 18, 1981, at New Jersey. He was an All-Star in 1980-81. He was traded to the Spurs on December 23, 1981.

Mike Mitchell, 1980. (AndersonsClevelandDesign.com)

MOISO, JEROME

Jerome Moiso was a 6-foot-10, 235-pound power forward for the Cavaliers in 2004-05. Signed to the first of two 10-day contracts on February 1, 2005, he played four games with Cleveland. He became a free agent again on February 21, 2005, and was not re-signed.

MOKESKI, PAUL

Paul Mokeski was a 7-foot, 250-pound center for the Cavaliers from 1981-82 to 1982-83 and in 1989-90. He was traded from Detroit on February 16, 1982. He was waived on December 20, 1982. He was re-signed as a free agent on September 26, 1989. In his three seasons with Cleveland he averaged 4.2 points, 3.6 rebounds, .6 assists, .4 steals, and .6 blocked shots per game. His best season as a Cavalier was 1982-83 when he averaged 5.5 points, six rebounds, 1.1 assists, .5 steals, and one blocked shot per contest.

Mokeski scored 14 points in a 131–125 overtime win against Atlanta on November 17, 1989, at The Coliseum. He scored two points in the playoffs on two occasions—in a 122–95 victory over Philadelphia on May 1, 1990, again at The Coliseum, and in a 113–97 defeat to the 76ers on May 5, 1990, at Philadelphia. He was released on July 1, 1990.

MOON, JAMARIO

Jamario Moon was a 6-foot-8, 205-pound small forward for the Cavaliers from 2009-10 to 2010-11. Signed as a free agent on July 24, 2009, in his two seasons with Cleveland he averaged 4.8 points, 3.1 rebounds, .9 assists, .6 steals, and .6 blocked shots per game. His best season as a Cavalier was 2010-11 when he averaged 4.7 points, three rebounds, 1.1 assists, .6 steals, and .7 blocked shots per contest.

Moon scored 15 points twice—in a 116–113 loss to Indiana on April 9, 2010, at Quicken Loans Arena and in a 99–83 defeat to the Hawks on April 14, 2010, in Atlanta. He scored 12 points in a 112–102 playoff win over Chicago on April 19, 2010, at Quicken Loans Arena. He was traded to the Clippers on February 24, 2011.

MOORE, LOWES

Lowes Moore was a 6-foot-1, 170-pound point guard for the Cavaliers in 1981-82. He was signed as a free agent on April 10, 1982, and played four games with Cleveland. He was waived on October 28, 1982.

MORTON, JOHN

John Morton was a 6-foot-3, 180-pound shooting guard and small forward for the Cavaliers from 1989-90 to 1991-92. A first-round draft choice in 1989 from Seton Hall University, he averaged 4.8 points, 2.9 assists, 1.3 rebounds, .7 steals, and .2 blocked shots per game in his three seasons with the Cavs. His best season as a Cavalier was 1990-91 when he averaged 5.4 points, 3.7 assists, 1.6 rebounds, .9 steals, and .3 blocked shots per contest.

Morton scored 21 points in a 113–111 overtime victory against the SuperSonics on March 5, 1991, at Seattle. He scored six points in a 122–95 playoff win over the 76ers on May 1, 1990, at The Coliseum. He was waived on November 14, 1991.

MOSLEY, JAMAHL

Jamahl Mosley was a Cavaliers assistant coach from 2010-11 to 2013-14.

MOST VALUABLE PLAYER

LeBron James (2008-09)
LeBron James (2009-10)

MOZGOV, TIMOFEY

Timofey Mozgov was a 7-foot-1, 275-pound center for the Cavaliers from 2014-15 to 2015-16. Traded from Denver on January 7, 2015, in his two seasons with the Cavs he averaged 7.9 points, 5.4 rebounds, .6 assists, .3 steals, and .9 blocked shots per game. His best season as a Cavalier was 2014-15 when he averaged 10.6 points, 6.9 rebounds, .8 assists, .4 steals, and 1.2 blocked shots per contest.

Mozgov scored 20 points in a 113–93 victory over Miami on February 11, 2015, at Quicken Loans Arena. He scored 28 points in a 103–82 Finals loss to the Warriors on June 11, 2015, again at Quicken Loans Arena. He became a free agent on July 1, 2016, and was not re-signed.

MUELLER, JIM

Jim Mueller was a Cavaliers local television broadcaster from 1976-77 to 1979-80.

MURRAY, FLIP

Ronald "Flip" Murray was a 6-foot-4, 190-pound shooting guard for Cleveland in 2005-06. Traded from Seattle on February 23, 2006, in his one season with the Cavs he averaged 13.5 points, 2.8 assists, 2.4 rebounds, 1.4 steals, and .3 blocked shots per game. He scored 25 points in a 103–101 victory over the Hornets on April 10 at Oklahoma City. He scored 21 points in a

114–113 overtime playoff win against the Wizards on May 5 at Washington. He became a free agent on July 1, 2006, and was not re-signed.

MURRAY, LAMOND

Lamond Murray was a 6-foot-7, 236-pound small forward for the Cavaliers from 1999-2000 to 2001-02. Traded from the Clippers on August 4, 1999, in his three seasons with Cleveland he averaged 15 points, 5.1 rebounds, 1.9 assists, 1.2 steals, and .5 blocked shots per game. His best season as a Cavalier was 2001-02 when he averaged 16.6 points, 5.2 rebounds, 2.2 assists, one steal, and .6 blocked shots per contest. He scored 40 points in a 113–98 victory over Golden State on January 2, 2002, at Gund Arena. He was traded to Toronto on September 25, 2002.

MUSSELMAN, BILL

Bill Musselman was a Cavaliers head coach from 1980-81 to 1981-82. The 1980-81 Cavaliers were 25-46 when he was relieved of his duties. He was rehired the next season with the team's record at 13-46, compiled by head coaches Don Delaney, Bob Kloppenburg, and Chuck Daly. With Musselman back at the helm, the Cavs lost 21 of their last 23 games to finish with a 15-67 record. He resigned eight days before the start of the following season. His overall record as Cleveland's head coach was 27-67.

N

NAILON, LEE

Lee Nailon was a 6-foot-9, 238-pound small forward for the Cavaliers in 2003-04. He signed the first of two 10-day contracts on March 3, 2004, and on March 23, 2004, signed a contract for the rest of the 2003-04 season. In his one season with Cleveland he averaged 7.7 points, three rebounds, .8 assists, and .2 steals per game. He scored 23 points in a 126–109 loss to the Mavericks in Dallas on March 30. He became a free agent again on July 1, 2004, and was not re-signed.

NANCE, LARRY

Larry Nance was a 6-foot-10, 205-pound power forward for the Cavaliers from 1987-88 to 1993-94. Traded from Phoenix on February 25, 1988, in his seven seasons with Cleveland he averaged 16.8 points, 8.2 rebounds, 2.6 assists, .8 steals, and 2.5 blocked shots per game. His best season as a Cavalier was 1990-91 when he averaged 19.2 points, 8.6 rebounds, three assists, .8 steals, and 2.5 blocked shots per contest. In 1988-89, Nance averaged 17.2 points, eight rebounds, 2.2 assists, .8 steals, and 2.8 blocked shots per game. In 1992-93, he averaged 16.5 points, 8.7 rebounds, 2.9 assists, .7 steals, and 2.6 blocked shots per contest.

Larry Nance, 1991-92.
(*AndersonsClevelandDesign.com*)

Nance scored 35 points in a 110–94 triumph over the Hawks on March 7,

1992, in Atlanta. He scored 34 points in a 128–120 defeat to the Nuggets on January 12, 1991, at Denver. He had 32 points in a 114–112 overtime playoff win against the Celtics on May 10, 1992, in Boston. He was an All-Star in 1988-89 and 1992-93. He became a free agent on July 1, 1994, and was not re-signed. His jersey number 22 was retired by the Cavaliers on January 30, 1995.

NATT, KENNY

Kenny Natt was a Cavaliers assistant coach from 2004-05 to 2006-07.

NBA CHAMPIONS

2015-16

NEUTRAL-SITE CROWDS, LARGEST TO SMALLEST

Please see Attendance Statistics on page 272.

NEUTRAL-SITE GAMES

Please see Team Statistics on page 215.

NEWBLE, IRA

Ira Newble was a 6-foot-7, 220-pound shooting guard and small forward for the Cavaliers from 2003-04 to 2007-08. Signed as a free agent on July 22, 2003, in his five seasons with Cleveland he averaged 4.2 points, .8 assists, 2.5 rebounds, .5 steals, and .2 blocked shots per game. His best season as a Cavalier was 2004-05 when he averaged 5.9 points, 1.2 assists, three rebounds, .7 steals, and .2 blocked shots per contest.

Newble scored 20 points in a 104–95 victory over the Raptors on April 20, 2005, at Toronto. He scored seven points in a 113–86 playoff loss to the Pistons on May 7, 2006, at Detroit. He was traded to Seattle on February 21, 2008.

NEWMAN, JOHNNY

Johnny Newman was a 6-foot-7, 190-pound small forward for Cleveland in 1986-87 and 1998-99. He was chosen in the second round of the 1986 draft from the University of Richmond. He was waived on November 5, 1987. He was re-signed as a free agent on January 24, 1999.

In his two seasons with the Cavs Newman averaged 5.5 points, 1.3 rebounds, .6 assists, .4 steals, and .2 blocked shots per game. His best season as a Cavalier was 1998-99 when he averaged 6.1 points, 1.5 rebounds, .8 assists, .6 steals, and .2 blocked shots per contest. He scored 22 points in a 109–107 loss to the 76ers on January 28, 1987, at Philadelphia. He was traded to the Clippers on August 4, 1999.

NICHOLS, DEMETRIS

Demetris Nichols was a 6-foot-8, 216-pound small forward for the Cavaliers in 2007-08. Signed as a free agent on October 29, 2007, he played three games with Cleveland. He was waived on December 5, 2007.

NICKNAMES

The following are 25 notable nicknames of Cavaliers players:

John Bagley	"Bags"
Jim Brewer	"Brew"
Austin Carr	"A.C."
Jim Cleamons	"Clem"
Brad Daugherty	"Hooch"
Dwight Davis	"Double D"
World B. Free	"Prince of Midair"
Alonzo Gee	"Zo"
Daniel Gibson	"Boobie"
Ron Harper	"Hollywood"
Zydrunas Ilgauskas	"Z"
Kyrie Irving	"Uncle Drew"
LeBron James	"King James"
John Johnson	"J. J."
Shawn Kemp	"Reign Man"
Trajan Langdon	"The Alaskan Assassin"
Dan Majerle	"Thunder Dan"
Andre Miller	"The Professor"
Ben Poquette	"Gentle Ben"
Vitaly Potapenko	"The Ukraine Train"
Dave Robisch	"Robo"
Dave Sorenson	"Sunshine"

Nate Thurmond	"Nate the Great"
Anderson Varejao	"Wild Thing"
John Williams	"Hot Rod"

NICKS, CARL

Carl Nicks was a 6-foot-1, 175-pound shooting guard for the Cavaliers in 1982-83. Signed as a free agent on March 30, 1983, in nine games with Cleveland he averaged seven points, 1.2 assists, 2.9 rebounds, and .7 steals per contest. He scored 22 points in a 101–91 victory over the Bulls on April 5 in Chicago. He was waived on October 25, 1983.

1970 EXPANSION DRAFT CHOICES

Butch Beard (Atlanta)
Len Chappell (Milwaukee)
Johnny Egan (Los Angeles)
Bobby Lewis (San Francisco)
McCoy McLemore (Detroit)
Don Ohl (Atlanta)
Loy Petersen (Chicago)
Luther Rackley (Cincinnati)
Bingo Smith (San Diego)
John Warren (New York)
Walt Wesley (Chicago)

NISSALKE, TOM

Tom Nissalke was Cleveland's head coach from 1982-83 to 1983-84. His teams finished 23-59 and 28-54, respectively. After his second season, he was fired. His overall record as Cavaliers head coach was 51-113.

NOVEMBER

The following are five memorable Cavaliers games that were played in the month of November:

NOVEMBER 2, 1970

Cleveland was destroyed by the Philadelphia 76ers 141–87 to drop to 0-11 in front of 3,022 fans at the Spectrum. The Cavaliers trailed 36–14 after one quarter, 68–36 at the half, and 104–64 after three quarters. John Johnson led the Cavs with 20 points. The 76ers were led by Archie Clark's 21 points.

NOVEMBER 6, 1973

The Cavaliers came out of the gate like gangbusters, outscoring the Los Angeles Lakers 40–16 in the first quarter and cruising to a 115–96 shocker in front of 3,124 fans at the Cleveland Arena. Bingo Smith's 22 points paced the Cavs, while Austin Carr scored 20 and Lenny Wilkens had 18. Jerry West led the Lakers with 21 points.

NOVEMBER 19, 1977

The Cavaliers were pounded by the Portland Trail Blazers 109–67 before 12,666 fans at the Memorial Coliseum. It was all Portland from the start. The Cavs trailed by 12 points after the first quarter, by 26 at halftime, and by 39 after three periods. Campy Russell and Jim Chones both led Cleveland with 12 points. Leading Portland with 17 points each were Tom Owens and Larry Steele.

NOVEMBER 9, 1981

The Cavaliers defeated the Chicago Bulls 102–101 before 10,514 fans at The Coliseum when Bobby Wilkerson hit a layup with just seconds to go, giving the Cavs a 3-2 record, the only time they would be above the .500 mark in what turned out to be a horrible season. James Edwards led Cleveland with 22 points. Kenny Carr scored 19 and Wilkerson had 18. James Wilkes and Reggie Theus each led Chicago with 20 points.

NOVEMBER 12, 1992

After trailing by 11 points after the first quarter, the Cavaliers recovered and defeated the Golden State Warriors 126–122 in double overtime before a crowd of 15,025 at the Oakland-Alameda County Coliseum Arena. The Cavs cut the margin to four points by halftime and caught Golden State at 106 after regulation. The score was 112–112 after the first overtime. Leading the way for Cleveland were Mark Price and John Williams with 21 points each. Tim Hardaway led the Warriors with 35 points.

NUMBER ONE OVERALL DRAFT CHOICES

Austin Carr (1971)
Brad Daugherty (1986)
LeBron James (2003)
Kyrie Irving (2011)
Anthony Bennett (2013)
Andrew Wiggins (2014)

O

OCIEPKA, BOB

Bob Ociepka was a Cavaliers assistant coach from 1999-2000 to 2000-01.

OCTOBER

The following are five memorable Cavaliers games that were played in the month of October:

OCTOBER 14, 1970

In their first game ever, the Cavaliers fell to the Buffalo Braves, also playing their first game ever, 107–92 in front of 7,129 fans at the Buffalo Memorial Auditorium. It was all Braves from the start. They led by 11 points after one quarter, by 14 at halftime, and by 23 after three quarters. Bingo Smith led the Cavs with 21 points. Don May led Buffalo with 24 points.

OCTOBER 18, 1974

The Cavaliers lost their season opener to the Portland Trail Blazers 131–129 in four overtimes before 11,409 fans at the Memorial Coliseum. The game was tied at 97 after regulation. Both teams scored eight points in each of the first three overtime periods before the Blazers outscored the Cavs 10–8 in the fourth overtime period. Leading the way for Cleveland were Austin Carr with 34 points, Dick Snyder with 25, and Bingo Smith with 20. Former Cavalier John Johnson and Sidney Wicks each scored 29 for Portland.

OCTOBER 25, 1977

The Cavaliers won an overtime thriller against the New York Knicks 117–112 before 19,694 fans at Madison Square Garden. The score was 21–21 after the first quarter and 49–49 at the half. Cleveland was up 81–75 after three quarters, then New York tied the score at 105 after regulation. Leading the Cavs with 28 points each were former Knicks great Walt Frazier and Campy Russell. Bob McAdoo led New York with 29 points.

OCTOBER 25, 1985

Cleveland lost a thrilling season opener to the Chicago Bulls 116–115 in overtime before 11,124 fans at Chicago Stadium. The game was tight from start to finish. World B. Free led the Cavaliers with 27 points. Roy Hinson had 21. Orlando Woolridge was tops on the Bulls with 35 points.

OCTOBER 29, 2003

In his first game as a Cavalier, LeBron James scored a team-best 25 points and had six rebounds, nine assists, and four steals, but the Cavs lost to the Sacramento Kings 106–92 before 17,317 fans at ARCO Arena. The Cavaliers trailed by 13 points at the half but cut the margin to five entering the fourth quarter before the Kings took control again. Peja Stojakovic led Sacramento with 22 points.

OLIVER, GERALD

Gerald Oliver was a Cavaliers assistant coach from 1980-81 to 1981-82.

OLIVER, JIMMY

Jimmy Oliver was a 6-foot-5, 205-pound shooting guard for the Cavaliers in 1991-92. A second-round draft pick in 1991 out of Purdue University, he averaged 3.6 points, .7 assists, one rebound, .3 steals, and .1 blocked shots per game in his one season with Cleveland. He scored 11 points twice—in a 148–80 victory over Miami on December 17 at The Coliseum and in a 119–115 overtime triumph against Indiana on January 22, again at The Coliseum. He became a free agent on July 1, 1992, and was not re-signed.

OLLIE, KEVIN

Kevin Ollie was a 6-foot-4, 195-pound point guard for the Cavaliers in 2003-04. Signed as a free agent on July 17, 2003, in his one season with the Cavs he averaged 4.2 points, 2.9 assists, 2.1 rebounds, .6 steals, and .1 blocked shots per game. He scored 12 points twice—in a 106–95 defeat to the Wizards on November 19 at Washington and in a 107–96 victory over New York on January 6 at Gund Arena. He was traded to Philadelphia on July 20, 2004.

O'NEAL, SHAQUILLE

Shaquille O'Neal was a 7-foot-1, 325-pound center for the Cavaliers in 2009-10. Traded from the Suns on June 26, 2009, in his one season with the Cavs he averaged 12 points, 6.7 rebounds, 1.5 assists, .3 steals, and 1.2 blocked shots per game. He scored 22 points twice—in a 100–99 victory over the Thunder on January 23 at Quicken Loans Arena and in a 94–73 win over the Pacers on January 29 at Indiana. He scored 21 points in a 120–88 playoff loss to the Celtics on May 11 at Quicken Loans Arena. He became a free agent on July 1, 2010, and was not re-signed. He was inducted into the Naismith Memorial Basketball Hall of Fame in 2016.

ONUAKU, ARINZE

Arinze Onuaku was a 6-foot-9, 275-pound power forward for the Cavaliers in 2013-14. He signed the first of two 10-day contracts on February 22, 2014, and played two games with Cleveland. He was waived on March 12, 2014.

OPENERS

Please see Team Statistics on page 215.

OPENING-GAME STARTING LINEUPS

1970-71	Johnny Egan, John Warren, Luther Rackley, Bingo Smith, McCoy McLemore
1971-72	Charlie Davis, Bingo Smith, Walt Wesley, John Johnson, Dave Sorenson
1972-73	Jim Cleamons, Austin Carr, Rick Roberson, John Johnson, Dave Sorenson
1973-74	Lenny Wilkens, Austin Carr, Bob Rule, Bingo Smith, Dwight Davis
1974-75	Jim Cleamons, Austin Carr, Steve Patterson, Bingo Smith, Dwight Davis
1975-76	Jim Cleamons, Dick Snyder, Jim Chones, Bingo Smith, Jim Brewer

1976-77	Jim Cleamons, Dick Snyder, Jim Chones, Bingo Smith, Jim Brewer
1977-78	Foots Walker, Walt Frazier, Jim Chones, Campy Russell, Jim Brewer
1978-79	Foots Walker, Walt Frazier, Jim Chones, Campy Russell, Jim Brewer
1979-80	Randy Smith, Austin Carr, John Lambert, Mike Mitchell, Campy Russell
1980-81	Randy Smith, Roger Phegley, Dave Robisch, Mike Mitchell, Kenny Carr
1981-82	James Silas, Bobby Wilkerson, Bill Laimbeer, Mike Mitchell, Richard Washington
1982-83	Geoff Huston, Ron Brewer, James Edwards, Scott Wedman, Cliff Robinson
1983-84	Geoff Huston, World B. Free, Cliff Robinson, Roy Hinson, Lonnie Shelton
1984-85	John Bagley, World B. Free, Melvin Turpin, Ron Anderson, Jeff Cook
1985-86	John Bagley, World B. Free, Mark West, Phil Hubbard, Roy Hinson
1986-87	John Bagley, Ron Harper, Brad Daugherty, John Williams, Mark West
1987-88	Mark Price, Ron Harper, Brad Daugherty, Phil Hubbard, Mark West
1988-89	Mark Price, Ron Harper, Brad Daugherty, Mike Sanders, Larry Nance
1989-90	Steve Kerr, Ron Harper, Tree Rollins, Randolph Keys, John Williams
1990-91	Mark Price, Craig Ehlo, Brad Daugherty, Chucky Brown, John Williams
1991-92	Terrell Brandon, Craig Ehlo, Brad Daugherty, Larry Nance, John Williams
1992-93	Mark Price, Craig Ehlo, Brad Daugherty, Mike Sanders, Larry Nance
1993-94	Mark Price, Gerald Wilkins, Brad Daugherty, Larry Nance, John Williams
1994-95	Mark Price, Bobby Phills, John Williams, Chris Mills, Tyrone Hill

1995-96	Terrell Brandon, Bobby Phills, John Amaechi, Chris Mills, Tyrone Hill
1996-97	Terrell Brandon, Bob Sura, Mark West, Chris Mills, Tyrone Hill
1997-98	Bob Sura, Derek Anderson, Zydrunas Ilgauskas, Wesley Person, Danny Ferry
1998-99	Brevin Knight, Wesley Person, Zydrunas Ilgauskas, Cedric Henderson, Shawn Kemp
1999-2000	Brevin Knight, Bob Sura, Andrew DeClercq, Cedric Henderson, Shawn Kemp
2000-01	Andre Miller, Matt Harpring, Zydrunas Ilgauskas, Lamond Murray, Clarence Weatherspoon
2001-02	Andre Miller, Wesley Person, Michael Doleac, Lamond Murray, Chris Mihm
2002-03	Bimbo Coles, Ricky Davis, DeSagana Diop, Darius Miles, Tyrone Hill
2003-04	LeBron James, Ricky Davis, Zydrunas Ilgauskas, Darius Miles, Carlos Boozer
2004-05	Jeff McInnis, Lucious Harris, Zydrunas Ilgauskas, LeBron James, Drew Gooden
2005-06	Eric Snow, Larry Hughes, Zydrunas Ilgauskas, LeBron James, Drew Gooden
2006-07	Eric Snow, Larry Hughes, Zydrunas Ilgauskas, LeBron James, Drew Gooden
2007-08	Daniel Gibson, Larry Hughes, Zydrunas Ilgauskas, LeBron James, Drew Gooden
2008-09	Mo Williams, Delonte West, Zydrunas Ilgauskas, LeBron James, Ben Wallace
2009-10	Mo Williams, Anthony Parker, Shaquille O'Neal, LeBron James, Anderson Varejao
2010-11	Ramon Sessions, Anthony Parker, Anderson Varejao, Jamario Moon, J. J. Hickson
2011-12	Kyrie Irving, Anthony Parker, Anderson Varejao, Omri Casspi, Antawn Jamison
2012-13	Kyrie Irving, Dion Waiters, Anderson Varejao, Alonzo Gee, Tristan Thompson
2013-14	Kyrie Irving, Dion Waiters, Anderson Varejao, Earl Clark, Tristan Thompson

2014-15	Kyrie Irving, Dion Waiters, Anderson Varejao, LeBron James, Kevin Love
2015-16	Mo Williams, J.R. Smith, Timofey Mozgov, LeBron James, Kevin Love

OSOWSKI, MARK

Mark Osowski was a Cavaliers assistant coach in 2003-04.

OVERTIME GAMES (POSTSEASON)

Please see Team Statistics on page 215.

OVERTIME GAMES (REGULAR SEASON)

Please see Team Statistics on page 215.

OWNERS (MAJORITY)

Nick Mileti (1970-71 to 1979-80)
Ted Stepien (1980-81 to 1982-83)
George Gund/Gordon Gund (1983-84 to 2004-05)
Dan Gilbert (2004-05 to present)

P

PADDIO, GERALD

Gerald Paddio was a 6-foot-7, 205-pound small forward for the Cavaliers in 1990-91. Signed as a free agent on September 27, 1990, in his one season with Cleveland he averaged 7.2 points, 1.7 rebounds, 1.3 assists, .3 steals, and .1 blocked shots per game. He scored 24 points in a 102–97 loss to the Knicks in New York on March 20. He was released on July 1, 1991.

PALACIO, MILT

Milt Palacio was a 6-foot-3, 195-pound point guard for the Cavaliers in 2002-03. Traded from Phoenix on September 17, 2002, in his one season with Cleveland he averaged five points, 3.2 assists, 2.9 rebounds, .9 steals, and .2 blocked shots per game. He scored 20 points in a 122–95 victory over Utah on March 16 at Gund Arena. He became a free agent on July 1, 2003, and was not re-signed.

PARGO, JEREMY

Jeremy Pargo was a 6-foot-2, 219-pound point guard for the Cavaliers in 2012-13. He was traded from Memphis on July 25, 2012. In his one season with the Cavs he averaged 7.8 points, 2.6 assists, 1.3 rebounds, .5 steals, and .1 blocked shots per game. He scored 28 points in a 92–83 victory over the 76ers on November 21 at Quicken Loans Arena. He was waived on January 22, 2013.

PARKER, ANTHONY

Anthony Parker was a 6-foot-6, 215-pound small forward and shooting guard for the Cavaliers from 2009-10 to 2011-12. Signed as a free agent on July 13, 2009, he averaged 7.7 points, 2.9 rebounds, 2.4 assists, .8 steals, and .2 blocked shots per game in his three seasons with Cleveland. His best season as a Cavalier was 2010-11 when he averaged 8.3 points, three rebounds, three assists, .9 steals, and .1 blocked shots per contest.

Parker scored 27 points in a 107–98 loss to the Bucks in Milwaukee on April 4, 2012. He scored 14 points in a 120–88 playoff defeat to Boston on May 11, 2010, at Quicken Loans Arena. He retired on June 27, 2012.

PARKER, SMUSH

William "Smush" Parker was a 6-foot-4, 190-pound point guard for the Cavaliers in 2002-03. Signed as a free agent on September 26, 2002, he averaged 6.2 points, 2.5 assists, 1.8 rebounds, .7 steals, and .2 blocked shots per game in his one season with Cleveland. He scored 21 points in a 113–108 defeat to the Magic on January 29 at Orlando. He became a free agent again on July 1, 2003, and was not re-signed.

PATTERSON, STEVE

Steve Patterson was a 6-foot-9, 225-pound center for the Cavaliers from 1971-72 to 1975-76. A second-round draft choice in 1971 out of UCLA, he averaged 4.7 points, 4.8 rebounds, 1.2 assists, .4 steals, and .5 blocked shots per game in his five seasons with Cleveland. His best season as a Cavalier was 1973-74 when he averaged 7.8 points, 8.1 rebounds, 2.2 assists, .6 steals, and .8 blocked shots per contest. He scored 23 points in a 100–98 loss to the Pistons on January 19, 1975, at Detroit. He was traded to Chicago on November 27, 1975.

PAVLOVIC, SASHA

Sasha Pavlovic was a 6-foot-8, 220-pound shooting guard and small forward for the Cavaliers from 2004-05 to 2008-09. Traded from the Bobcats on June 23, 2004, in his five seasons with Cleveland he averaged 6.1 points, 1.1 assists, 1.9 rebounds, .5 steals, and .2 blocked shots per game. His best season as a Cavalier was 2006-07 when he averaged nine points, 1.6 assists, 2.4 rebounds, .8 steals, and .3 blocked shots per contest.

Pavlovic scored 25 points in a 124–100 victory over Sacramento on March 13, 2007, at Quicken Loans Arena. He scored 17 points in a 102–92 playoff win over New Jersey on May 8, 2007, again at Quicken Loans Arena. He was traded to Phoenix on June 26, 2009.

PAXSON, JIM

Jim Paxson was the Cavaliers' general manager from 1999-2000 to 2004-05.

PERKINS, KENDRICK

Kendrick Perkins was a 6-foot-10, 270-pound center for the Cavaliers in 2014-15. Signed as a free agent on February 24, 2015, in 17 games with Cleveland he averaged 2.6 points, 2.4 rebounds, .5 assists, .1 steals, and .2 blocked shots per contest. He scored seven points in a 113–108 overtime win against Washington on April 15 at Quicken Loans Arena. He scored three points in the playoffs twice—in a 101–93 victory over the Celtics on April 26 in Boston and in a 118–88 triumph over Atlanta on May 26 at Quicken Loans Arena. He became a free agent again on July 1, 2015, and was not re-signed.

PERSON, WESLEY

Wesley Person was a 6-foot-6, 195-pound shooting guard for the Cavaliers from 1997-98 to 2001-02. Traded from Phoenix on October 1, 1997, in his five seasons with Cleveland he averaged 12 points, two assists, 3.6 rebounds, .9 steals, and .4 blocked shots per game. His best season as a Cavalier was 1997-98 when he averaged 14.7 points, 2.3 assists, 4.4 rebounds, 1.6 steals, and .6 blocked shots per contest.

Person scored 33 points on three occasions. He scored 15 points in an 80–74 playoff defeat to Indiana on April 30, 1998, at Gund Arena. He was traded to Memphis on June 26, 2002.

PHEGLEY, ROGER

Roger Phegley was a 6-foot-6, 205-pound shooting guard for the Cavaliers from 1980-81 to 1981-82. Traded from New Jersey on September 24, 1980, in his two seasons with the Cavs he averaged 13.1 points, 2.2 assists, 2.9 rebounds, .7 steals, and .2 blocked shots per game. His best season as a Cavalier was 1980-81 when he averaged 14.4 points, 2.2 assists, three rebounds, .8 steals, and .2 blocked shots per contest. He scored 30 points in a 126–106 loss to the Suns on March 4, 1981, at Phoenix. He was traded to San Antonio on December 23, 1981.

PHELPS, JEFF

Jeff Phelps was a Cavaliers local television studio host from 2003-04 to 2009-10 and has been since 2012-13. He was the Cavs' local television sideline reporter from 2010-11 to 2011-12.

PHILLS, BOBBY

Bobby Phills was a 6-foot-5, 210-pound shooting guard for the Cavaliers from 1991-92 to 1996-97. He signed a 10-day contract on March 19, 1992, and on March 29, 1992, signed a contract for the rest of the 1991-92 season. He became a free agent again on July 1, 1992. He was re-signed as a free agent again on August 1, 1992.

In his six seasons with the Cavs Phills averaged 10.5 points, 2.5 assists, three rebounds, 1.2 steals, and .3 blocked shots per game. His best season as a Cavalier was 1995-96 when he averaged 14.6 points, 3.8 assists, 3.6 rebounds, 1.4 steals, and .4 blocked shots per contest. He scored 43 points in a 124–121 double-overtime victory against Portland on December 30, 1995, at Gund Arena. He scored 21 points in a 90–84 playoff win over the Knicks on April 29, 1995, at New York. He became a free agent again on July 1, 1997, and was not re-signed.

PLAYERS ON ROSTER BY SEASON

1970-71 – 16
1971-72 – 14
1972-73 – 15
1973-74 – 13
1974-75 – 12
1975-76 – 15
1976-77 – 15
1977-78 – 12
1978-79 – 14
1979-80 – 15
1980-81 – 18
1981-82 – 23
1982-83 – 18
1983-84 – 13
1984-85 – 19
1985-86 – 17
1986-87 – 15
1987-88 – 17
1988-89 – 12
1989-90 – 17
1990-91 – 16
1991-92 – 16
1992-93 – 14
1993-94 – 17
1994-95 – 15
1995-96 – 15
1996-97 – 13
1997-98 – 16
1998-99 – 17
1999-2000 – 20

2000-01 – 20	2008-09 – 16
2001-02 – 15	2009-10 – 18
2002-03 – 14	2010-11 – 19
2003-04 – 21	2011-12 – 21
2004-05 – 16	2012-13 – 19
2005-06 – 17	2013-14 – 21
2006-07 – 15	2014-15 – 20
2007-08 – 23	2015-16 – 18

POLLARD, SCOT

Scot Pollard was a 6-foot-11, 265-pound center for the Cavaliers in 2006-07. Signed as a free agent on August 18, 2006, in his one season with Cleveland he averaged one point, 1.3 rebounds, .1 assists, and .2 steals per game. He scored four points three times. He became a free agent again on July 1, 2007, and was not re-signed.

POQUETTE, BEN

Ben Poquette was a 6-foot-9, 235-pound power forward for the Cavaliers from 1983-84 to 1986-87. Traded from the Jazz on October 14, 1983, in his four seasons with Cleveland he averaged five points, 4.5 rebounds, .9 assists, .4 steals, and .6 blocked shots per game. His best season as a Cavalier was 1984-85 when he averaged 6.7 points, six rebounds, one assist, .6 steals, and .7 blocked shots per contest.

Poquette scored 22 points in a 144–127 defeat to the Nuggets in Denver on January 26, 1985. He scored 10 points in the playoffs twice—in a 126–123 loss to the Celtics at Boston on April 18, 1985, and in a 108–106 defeat to the Celtics again on April 20, 1985, likewise at Boston. He was traded to Chicago on February 15, 1987.

PORTER, PAUL

Paul Porter was the Cavaliers' local radio broadcaster from 1981-82 to 1982-83.

POSEY, JAMES

James Posey has been a Cavaliers assistant coach since 2014-15.

POSTSEASON SERIES THE CAVALIERS LOST AND WHO THEY WOULD HAVE PLAYED HAD THEY WON

(Does not include the NBA Finals, since there would not have been a next opponent)

Boston defeated Cleveland four games to two in the 1975-76 Eastern Conference Finals. Had the Cavs won . . . vs. Phoenix in the NBA Finals.

Washington defeated Cleveland two games to one in the 1976-77 Eastern Conference First Round. Had the Cavs won . . . vs. Philadelphia in the Eastern Conference Semifinals.

New York defeated Cleveland two games to none in the 1977-78 Eastern Conference First Round. Had the Cavs won . . . vs. Philadelphia in the Eastern Conference Semifinals.

Boston defeated Cleveland three games to one in the 1984-85 Eastern Conference First Round. Had the Cavs won . . . vs. Detroit in the Eastern Conference Semifinals.

Chicago defeated Cleveland three games to two in the 1987-88 Eastern Conference First Round. Had the Cavs won . . . vs. Detroit in the Eastern Conference Semifinals.

Chicago defeated Cleveland three games to two in the 1988-89 Eastern Conference First Round. Had the Cavs won . . . vs. New York in the Eastern Conference Semifinals.

Philadelphia defeated Cleveland three games to two in the 1989-90 Eastern Conference First Round. Had the Cavs won . . . vs. Chicago in the Eastern Conference Semifinals.

Chicago defeated Cleveland four games to two in the 1991-92 Eastern Conference Finals. Had the Cavs won . . . vs. Portland in the NBA Finals.

Chicago defeated Cleveland four games to none in the 1992-93 Eastern Conference Semifinals. Had the Cavs won . . . vs. New York in the Eastern Conference Finals.

Chicago defeated Cleveland three games to none in the 1993-94 Eastern Conference First Round. Had the Cavs won . . . vs. New York in the Eastern Conference Semifinals.

New York defeated Cleveland three games to one in the 1994-95 Eastern Conference First Round. Had the Cavs won . . . vs. Indiana in the Eastern Conference Semifinals.

New York defeated Cleveland three games to none in the 1995-96 Eastern Conference First Round. Had the Cavs won . . . vs. Chicago in the Eastern Conference Semifinals.

Indiana defeated Cleveland three games to one in the 1997-98 Eastern Conference First Round. Had the Cavs won . . . vs. New York in the Eastern Conference Semifinals.

Detroit defeated Cleveland four games to three in the 2005-06 Eastern Conference Semifinals. Had the Cavs won . . . vs. Miami in the Eastern Conference Finals.

Boston defeated Cleveland four games to three in the 2007-08 Eastern Conference Semifinals. Had the Cavs won . . . vs. Detroit in the Eastern Conference Finals.

Orlando defeated Cleveland four games to two in the 2008-09 Eastern Conference Finals. Had the Cavs won . . . vs. L.A. Lakers in the NBA Finals.

Boston defeated Cleveland four games to two in the 2009-10 Eastern Conference Semifinals. Had the Cavs won . . . vs. Orlando in the Eastern Conference Finals.

POTAPENKO, VITALY

Vitaly Potapenko was a 6-foot-10, 280-pound center for the Cavaliers from 1996-97 to 1998-99. A first-round draft pick in 1996 out of Wright State University, he averaged 6.7 points, 3.5 rebounds, .6 assists, .4 steals, and .4 blocked shots per game in his three seasons with the Cavs. His best season as a Cavalier was 1998-99 when he averaged 8.4 points, 5.5 rebounds, .9 assists, .6 steals, and .9 blocked shots per contest.

Potapenko scored 22 points in a 98–96 overtime victory against the Bullets on November 2, 1996, at Washington. He scored eight points in a 92–86 playoff loss to the Pacers on April 25, 1998, at Indiana. He was traded to Boston on March 11, 1999.

POWE, LEON

Leon Powe was a 6-foot-8, 240-pound small forward and power forward for the Cavaliers from 2009-10 to 2010-11. Signed as a free agent on August 12, 2009, in his two seasons with Cleveland he averaged 4.4 points, 2.9 rebounds, .1 assists, .4 steals, and .1 blocked shots per game. His best season as a Cavalier was 2010-11 when he averaged five points, 2.7 rebounds, .1 assists, .5 steals, and .2 blocked shots per contest. He scored 16 points in a 104–79 win over the Pistons on March 21, 2010, at Quicken Loans Arena. He scored four points in a 124–95 playoff victory over the Celtics in Boston on May 7, 2010. He was waived on February 24, 2011.

PRESIDENTS

Nick Mileti (1970-71 to 1979-80)
Ted Stepien (1980-81 to 1981-82)
Harry Weltman (1982-83)
Gordon Gund (1983-84)
Thaxter Trafton (1985-86 to 1987-88)
Tom Chestnut (1990-91 to 1994-95)
Jim Boland (1997-98 to 2001-02)
Len Komoroski (2002-03 to 2004-05, 2009-10 to 2010-11)

PRESSEY, PAUL

Paul Pressey was a Cavaliers assistant coach from 2010-11 to 2012-13.

PRICE, A. J.

A. J. Price was a 6-foot-2, 181-pound point guard for the Cavaliers in 2014-15. He was signed as a free agent on September 26, 2014, and was waived on November 1, 2014. He was re-signed on waivers from Indiana on November 30, 2014. In 11 games with Cleveland he averaged two points, 1.2 assists, 1.4 rebounds, and .3 steals per contest. He scored six points twice—in a 109–90 defeat to Dallas on January 4 at Quicken Loans Arena and in a 95–92 loss to the 76ers on January 5 at Philadelphia. He was waived again on January 7, 2015.

PRICE, MARK

Mark Price was a 6-foot, 170-pound point guard for the Cavaliers from 1986-87 to 1994-95. Traded from Dallas on June 17, 1986, he averaged 16.4 points, 7.2 assists, 2.6 rebounds, 1.3 steals, and .1 blocked shots per game in his nine seasons with Cleveland. His best season as a Cavalier was 1989-90 when he averaged 19.6 points, 9.1 assists, 3.4 rebounds, 1.6 steals, and .1 blocked shots per contest. The season before, Price averaged 18.9 points, 8.4 assists, three rebounds, 1.5 steals, and .1 blocked shots per game. In 1992-93, he averaged 18.2 points, eight assists, 2.7 rebounds, 1.2 steals, and .1 blocked shots per contest.

Mark Price, 1991-92.
(AndersonsClevelandDesign.com)

Price scored 39 points in a 97–93 victory over Seattle on December 12, 1992, at The Coliseum. He scored 37 points twice—in a 120–114 loss to the Warriors on March 9, 1989, at Golden State and in a 133–131 overtime defeat to Indiana on February 14, 1990, at The Coliseum. He had 35 points in a 120–113 playoff win over the Nets on April 23, 1992, again at The Coliseum. He was an All-Star in 1988-89 and from 1991-92 to 1993-94. He was traded to Washington on September 27, 1995. His jersey number 25 was retired by the team on November 13, 1999.

Price was a Cavaliers local television broadcaster in 2004-05.

PRUNTY, JOE

Joe Prunty was a Cavaliers assistant coach from 2010-11 to 2012-13.

Q

QUICKEN LOANS ARENA

Quicken Loans Arena, or "The Q" as it is also known, has been the Cavaliers' home since 1994-95. It was known as Gund Arena through 2004-05. Its seating capacity is 20,562.

QUINN, CHRIS

Chris Quinn was a 6-foot-2, 185-pound shooting guard for the Cavaliers in 2012-13. He was signed as a free agent on March 20, 2013. In seven games with the Cavs he averaged 1.4 points, 1.3 assists, .3 rebounds, and .4 steals per contest. He scored four points in a 116–78 loss to the Rockets in Houston on March 22. He was waived on July 19, 2013.

R

RACKLEY, LUTHER

Luther Rackley was a 6-foot-10, 220-pound center for the Cavaliers from 1970-71 to 1971-72. He was chosen from Cincinnati in the 1970 Expansion Draft. In his two seasons with Cleveland he averaged seven points, five rebounds, and .8 assists per game. His best season as a Cavalier was 1970-71 when he averaged 7.6 points, 5.3 rebounds, and .9 assists per contest. He scored 26 points in a 128–108 loss to the Warriors on October 17, 1970, in San Francisco. He was traded to the Knicks on November 15, 1971.

RADIO BROADCASTS

The following are the Cavaliers' local radio broadcasters and the flagship stations on which Cavs games have been aired:

1970-71	Bob Brown (WERE-AM 1300)
	Joe Tait (WERE-AM 1300)
1971-72 to 1972-73	Joe Tait (WERE-AM 1300)
1973-74 to 1980-81	Joe Tait (WWWE-AM 1100)
1981-82 to 1982-83	Paul Porter (WBBG-AM 1260)
1983-84	Joe Tait (WBBG-AM 1260)
1984-85 to 1987-88	Joe Tait (WWWE-AM 1100)
1988-89	Joe Tait (WRMR-AM 850)
	Howard Kelleman (WRMR-AM 850)
1989-90	Joe Tait (WRMR-AM 850)
	Jim Johnson (WRMR-AM 850)
1990-91	Joe Tait (WWWE-AM 1100)
	Jim Johnson (WWWE-AM 1100)
1991-92	Joe Tait (WWWE-AM 1100)
	Jim Johnson (WWWE-AM 1100)
1992-93 to 1995-96	Joe Tait/Mike Snyder (studio host) (WWWE-AM 1100)

1996-97 to 2009-10	Joe Tait/Mike Snyder (studio host) (WTAM-AM 1100)
2010-11	Joe Tait and Jim Chones/Mike Snyder (studio host) (WTAM-AM 1100) Mike Snyder and Jim Chones/Mike Snyder (studio host) (WTAM-AM 1100)
2011-12 to 2013-14	John Michael and Jim Chones/Mike Snyder (studio host) (WTAM-AM 1100)
2014-15 to present	John Michael and Jim Chones/Mike Snyder (studio host) (WTAM-AM 1100) Rafael Hernandez Brito (WLFM-LP) (FM 87.7) (Spanish)

RAY, CLIFFORD

Clifford Ray was a Cavaliers assistant coach in 2002-03.

REGHI, MICHAEL

Michael Reghi was a Cavaliers local television broadcaster from 1994-95 to 2005-06.

REID, J. R.

J. R. Reid was a 6-foot-9, 247-pound power forward for the Cavaliers in 2000-01. Traded from Milwaukee on June 27, 2000, in six games with Cleveland he averaged 1.7 points, 1.3 rebounds, .2 assists, .3 steals, and .2 blocked shots per contest. He scored five points in a 107–89 loss to the Bucks on December 28 at Gund Arena. He was waived on January 2, 2001.

RESTANI, KEVIN

Kevin Restani was a 6-foot-9, 225-pound power forward for the Cavaliers in 1981-82. He was chosen in the third round of the 1974 draft from the University of San Francisco and on June 10, 1974, was traded to Milwaukee. He was re-signed on waivers from the Spurs on December 23, 1981. In his one season with the Cavs he averaged 1.6 points, 2.3 rebounds, .4 assists, .3 steals, and .2 blocked shots per game. He scored 10 points in a 117–114 defeat to New York on April 10 at The Coliseum. He became a free agent on July 1, 1982, and was not re-signed.

RESULTS (POSTSEASON)

Please see Team Statistics on page 215.

RETIRED JERSEY NUMBERS

42	Nate Thurmond (December 18, 1977)
7	Bingo Smith (December 4, 1979)
34	Austin Carr (January 3, 1981)
22	Larry Nance (January 30, 1995)
43	Brad Daugherty (March 1, 1997)
25	Mark Price (November 13, 1999)
11	Zydrunas Ilgauskas (March 8, 2014)

RIDGLE, JACKIE

Jackie Ridgle was a 6-foot-4, 195-pound shooting guard for the Cavaliers in 1971-72. A third-round draft pick in 1971 out of the University of California, Berkeley, he averaged 1.8 points, .2 assists, and .5 rebounds per game in his one season with the Cavs. He scored eight points on two occasions—in a 104–84 defeat to the Knicks on December 18 in New York and in a 125–102 loss to the Trail Blazers on January 8 at Portland. He became a free agent on July 1, 1972, and was not re-signed.

ROBERSON, RICK

Rick Roberson was a 6-foot-9, 231-pound power forward and center for the Cavaliers from 1971-72 to 1972-73. Traded from Los Angeles on October 13, 1971, in his two seasons with Cleveland he averaged 12.8 points, 12 rebounds, and 1.9 assists per game. His best season as a Cavalier was 1971-72 when he averaged 13.1 points, 12.7 rebounds, and 1.7 assists per contest. He scored 29 points in a 124–120 victory over the Lakers on March 22, 1972, at the Cleveland Arena. He was traded to Portland on April 24, 1973.

ROBERTS, FRED

Fred Roberts was a 6-foot-10, 218-pound small forward for the Cavaliers in 1994-95. He signed the first of two 10-day contracts on February 23, 1995, and on March 16, 1995, signed a contract for the rest of the 1994-95 season. In his one season with the Cavs he averaged 3.8 points, 1.6 rebounds, .4 assists, .3 steals, and .1 blocked shots per game. He scored 14 points in a 105–102 victory over New Jersey on February 25 at Gund Arena. He scored six points in a 103–79 playoff defeat to the Knicks on April 27 at New York. He became a free agent again on July 1, 1995, and was not re-signed.

ROBINSON, CLIFF

Cliff Robinson was a 6-foot-9, 220-pound power forward and center for the Cavaliers from 1981-82 to 1983-84. Traded from Kansas City on February 16, 1982, in his three seasons with Cleveland he averaged 17.7 points, 10.5 rebounds, 2.1 assists, .9 steals, and .7 blocked shots per game. His best season as a Cavalier was 1982-83 when he averaged 18 points, 11.1 rebounds, 1.9 assists, .8 steals, and .8 blocked shots per contest.

Robinson scored 40 points in a 132–124 overtime victory against the Pacers on April 15, 1983, at Indiana. He scored 36 points in a 110–107 triumph over the Clippers on February 6, 1983, at The Coliseum. He was traded to Washington on June 19, 1984.

ROBINSON, LARRY

Larry Robinson was a 6-foot-3, 180-pound shooting guard for the Cavaliers in 2000-01. Traded from Atlanta on January 2, 2001, he played one game with Cleveland. He was waived on January 5, 2001.

ROBINZINE, BILL

Bill Robinzine was a 6-foot-7, 230-pound power forward for Cleveland in 1980-81. Traded from the Kings on September 25, 1980, in eight games with the Cavs he averaged 4.1 points, 1.6 rebounds, .6 assists, and .5 steals per contest. He scored 10 points in a 126–112 win over the Nets in New Jersey on October 24. He was traded to Dallas on October 30, 1980.

ROBISCH, DAVE

Dave Robisch was a 6-foot-10, 235-pound center for the Cavaliers from 1979-80 to 1980-81. Traded from the Lakers on October 5, 1979, in his two seasons with Cleveland he averaged 14.6 points, eight rebounds, 2.5 assists, .6 steals, and .6 blocked shots per game. His best season as a Cavalier was 1979-80 when he averaged 15.3 points, eight rebounds, 2.3 assists, .6 steals, and .6 blocked shots per contest. He scored 36 points in a 116–112 victory over the Spurs on January 17, 1980, at The Coliseum. He was traded to Denver on October 31, 1980.

RODGERS, JIMMY

Jimmy Rodgers was the Cavaliers' assistant coach from 1971-72 to 1978-79.

ROGERS, JOHNNY

Johnny Rogers was a 6-foot-10, 225-pound power forward for the Cavaliers in 1987-88. Signed as a free agent on November 10, 1987, in his one season with Cleveland he averaged 2.6 points, 1.1 rebounds, .1 assists, .2 steals, and .1 blocked shots per game. He scored 11 points in a 109–88 victory over Boston on November 17 at The Coliseum. He became a free agent again on July 1, 1988, and was not re-signed.

ROLLINS, TREE

Wayne "Tree" Rollins was a 7-foot-1, 235-pound center for the Cavaliers from 1988-89 to 1989-90. He was signed as a free agent on August 2, 1988. In his two seasons with the Cavs he averaged 2.4 points, 2.7 rebounds, .4 assists, .2 steals, and .8 blocked shots per game. His best season as a Cavalier was 1989-90 when he averaged 2.6 points, 3.2 rebounds, .5 assists, .3 steals, and 1.1 blocked shots per contest.

Rollins scored 10 points in a 100–92 defeat to the Bullets on November 10, 1989, at Washington. He scored nine points in a 101–94 playoff loss to the Bulls on May 3, 1989, at Chicago. He became a free agent again on July 1, 1990, and was not re-signed.

ROOKIE OF THE YEAR

LeBron James (2003-04)
Kyrie Irving (2011-12)

ROTHSTEIN, RON

Ron Rothstein was a Cavaliers assistant coach from 1993-94 to 1998-99.

RULE, BOB

Bob Rule was a 6-foot-9, 220-pound center for the Cavaliers from 1972-73 to 1973-74. Traded from Philadelphia on November 10, 1972, in his two seasons with the Cavs he averaged 4.3 points, 2.8 rebounds, 1.1 assists, .5 steals, and .4 blocked shots per game. His best season as a Cavalier was 1973-74 when he averaged 7.2 points, four rebounds, 1.8 assists, .5 steals, and .4 blocked shots per contest. He scored 22 points in a 115–110 loss to Atlanta on November 4, 1973, at the Cleveland Arena. He was waived on December 1, 1973.

RUSSELL, CAMPY

Michael "Campy" Russell was a 6-foot-8, 215-pound small forward for the Cavaliers from 1974-75 to 1979-80 and in 1984-85. He was chosen in the first round of the 1974 draft from the University of Michigan. He was traded to New York on September 25, 1980. He was traded back from the Knicks on September 29, 1984.

In his seven seasons with Cleveland, Russell averaged 16.1 points, 5.1 rebounds, 2.8 assists, one steal, and .2 blocked shots per game. His best season as a Cavalier was 1978-79, when he averaged 21.9 points, 6.8 rebounds, 4.7 assists, 1.3 steals, and .3 blocked shots per contest. The season before, he averaged 19.4 points, 6.4 rebounds, 3.9 assists, 1.2 steals, and .2 blocked shots per game. The season before that, he averaged 16.5 points, six rebounds, 2.7 assists, one steal, and .3 blocked shots per contest.

Russell scored 41 points in a 124–120 loss to Phoenix on March 13, 1979, at The Coliseum. He scored 38 points in a 129–116 defeat to the 76ers on December 17, 1977, at Philadelphia. He had 32 points in a 109–107 playoff loss to the Knicks in New York on April 14, 1978. He was an All-Star in 1978-79. He was waived on November 5, 1984.

Russell has been a Cavaliers local television studio host since 2004-05.

S

SAMUELS, SAMARDO

Samardo Samuels was a 6-foot-9, 260-pound center and power forward for the Cavaliers from 2010-11 to 2012-13. Signed as a free agent on July 21, 2010, in his three seasons with Cleveland he averaged 5.9 points, 3.4 rebounds, .4 assists, .3 steals, and .4 blocked shots per game. His best season as a Cavalier was 2010-11 when he averaged 7.8 points, 4.3 rebounds, .5 assists, .4 steals, and .5 blocked shots per contest. He scored 23 points in a 109–99 loss to San Antonio on March 2, 2011, at Quicken Loans Arena. He was waived on January 6, 2013.

SANDERS, MIKE

Mike Sanders was a 6-foot-6, 210-pound small forward for the Cavaliers from 1987-88 to 1988-89 and 1991-92 to 1992-93. He was traded from the Suns on February 25, 1988. He became a free agent on July 1, 1989. He was re-signed to a 10-day contract on March 12, 1992, and on March 22, 1992, signed as a free agent again.

In his four seasons with the Cavs Sanders averaged 8.7 points, 3.4 rebounds, 1.5 assists, .9 steals, and .4 blocked shots per game. His best season as a Cavalier was 1991-92 when he averaged 9.2 points, 4.2 rebounds, two assists, one steal, and .4 blocked shots per contest. He scored 30 points in a 125–109 loss to the Knicks in New York on February 2, 1989. He scored 18 points in a 104–93 playoff defeat to the Bulls on April 28, 1988, at Chicago. He became a free agent again on July 1, 1993, and was not re-signed.

SCHREINER, DENNY

Denny Schreiner was a Cavaliers local television broadcaster from 1989-90 to 1993-94.

SCOTT, BYRON

Byron Scott was the Cavaliers' head coach from 2010-11 to 2012-13. His Cavs teams went 19-63, 21-45, and 24-58, respectively. His 2010-11 team lost 26 consecutive games, tying the 1976-77 Tampa Bay Buccaneers for the longest losing streak by a U.S. major professional sports team. He was fired after the 2012-13 season. His overall record as Cleveland's head coach was 64-166.

SCOTT, SHAWNELLE

Shawnelle Scott was a 6-foot-10, 250-pound center for the Cavaliers from 1996-97 to 1997-98. He was signed as a free agent on September 6, 1996. In his two seasons with the Cavs he averaged 1.1 points, 1.3 rebounds, .1 assists, .1 steals, and .2 blocked shots per game. His best season as a Cavalier was 1997-98 when he averaged 1.1 points, 1.4 rebounds, .2 assists, .1 steals, and .2 blocked shots per contest. He scored five points on three occasions. He scored two points in a 106–77 playoff defeat to the Pacers on April 23, 1998, at Indiana. He was waived on June 29, 1998.

SEASON WIN-LOSS RECORDS

Please see Team Statistics on page 215.

SESSIONS, RAMON

Ramon Sessions was a 6-foot-3, 190-pound point guard for the Cavaliers from 2010-11 to 2011-12. Traded on July 26, 2010, from the Timberwolves, in his two seasons with Cleveland he averaged 12.3 points, 5.2 assists, 3.1 rebounds, .7 steals, and .1 blocked shots per game. His best season as a Cavalier was 2010-11 when he averaged 13.3 points, 5.2 assists, 3.1 rebounds, .7 steals, and .1 blocked shots per contest. He scored 32 points in a 104–99 win over the Lakers on February 16, 2011, at Quicken Loans Arena. He was traded to the Lakers on March 15, 2012.

SHANLEY, GIB

Gib Shanley was a Cavaliers local television broadcaster from 1970-71 to 1975-76.

SHELTON, LONNIE

Lonnie Shelton was a 6-foot-8, 240-pound power forward for the Cavaliers from 1983-84 to 1985-86. Traded from Seattle on June 27, 1983, in his three seasons with the Cavs he averaged 7.9 points, 4.4 rebounds, 1.9 assists, .8 steals, and .4 blocked shots per game. His best season as a Cavalier was 1983-84 when he averaged 10.8 points, 4.8 rebounds, 2.3 assists, one steal, and .7 blocked shots per contest.

Shelton scored 33 points in a 120–119 overtime loss to the Pacers on March 31, 1984, at The Coliseum. He scored 14 points in a 105–98 playoff victory over Boston on April 23, 1985, again at The Coliseum. He became a free agent on July 1, 1986, and was not re-signed.

SHUMPERT, IMAN

Iman Shumpert has been a 6-foot-5, 220-pound shooting guard for the Cavaliers since 2014-15. Traded from New York on January 5, 2015, in his two seasons with Cleveland he has averaged 6.3 points, 1.6 assists, 3.8 rebounds, 1.1 steals, and .3 blocked shots per game. His best season as a Cavalier has been 2014-15 when he averaged 7.2 points, 1.5 assists, 3.8 rebounds, 1.3 steals, and .3 blocked shots per contest. He scored 23 points in a 125–99 victory over the Timberwolves in Minnesota on January 8, 2016. He scored 22 points in a 99–92 playoff loss to the Bulls on May 4, 2015, at Quicken Loans Arena.

SILAS, JAMES

James Silas was a 6-foot-1, 180-pound shooting guard for the Cavaliers in 1981-82. Traded from the Spurs on June 16, 1981, in his one season with Cleveland he averaged 11.2 points, 3.3 assists, 1.6 rebounds, .6 steals, and .1 blocked shots per game. He scored 31 points three times. He became a free agent on July 1, 1982, and was not re-signed.

SILAS, PAUL

Paul Silas was the Cavaliers' head coach in 2003-04 and a Cavs head coach in 2004-05. His 2003-04 team barely missed the playoffs with a 35-47 record. He was fired the next season with the Cavs' record at 34-30. Silas, the father of ex-Cavaliers assistant coach Stephen Silas, had an overall record as Cleveland's head coach of 69-77.

SILAS, STEPHEN

Stephen Silas was a Cavaliers assistant coach from 2003-04 to 2004-05. He is the son of ex-Cavs head coach Paul Silas.

SIMMONS, CEDRIC

Cedric Simmons was a 6-foot-9, 235-pound power forward for the Cavaliers in 2007-08. Traded from New Orleans on September 29, 2007, in seven games with Cleveland he averaged .6 points, 2.1 rebounds, .3 steals, and .7 blocked shots per game. He scored two points twice—in a 122–100 loss to the Nuggets on November 12 at Denver and in a 113–83 defeat to the Nuggets again on February 10 at Quicken Loans Arena. He was traded to Chicago on February 21, 2008.

SIMS, HENRY

Henry Sims was a 6-foot-10, 248-pound center for the Cavaliers in 2013-14. Signed as a free agent on September 30, 2013, in his one season with the Cavs he averaged 2.2 points, 2.8 rebounds, .3 assists, .3 steals, and .4 blocked shots per game. He scored seven points on three occasions. He was traded to Philadelphia on February 20, 2014.

SKINNER, BRIAN

Brian Skinner was a 6-foot-9, 255-pound power forward for the Cavaliers in 2001-02. Traded from Toronto on October 26, 2001, in his one season with Cleveland he averaged 3.4 points, 4.3 rebounds, .3 assists, .4 steals, and .9 blocked shots per game. He scored 11 points twice—in a 114–81 loss to Minnesota on January 29 at Gund Arena and in a 94–80 defeat to the Raptors on March 22, again at Gund Arena. He became a free agent on July 1, 2002, and was not re-signed.

SLOAN, DONALD

Donald Sloan was a 6-foot-3, 205-pound point guard and shooting guard for the Cavaliers from 2011-12 to 2012-13. Signed as a free agent on March 16, 2012, he averaged 5.5 points, 2.9 assists, 1.9 rebounds, .3 steals, and .1 blocked shots per game in his two seasons with Cleveland. His best season as a Cavalier was 2011-12 when he averaged 6.6 points, 3.7 assists, 2.4 rebounds, .4 steals, and .1 blocked shots per contest. He scored 15 points in a 100–84 loss to Orlando on April 15, 2012, at Quicken Loans Arena. He was waived on December 25, 2012.

SMART, KEITH

Keith Smart was a Cavaliers head coach in 2002-03. He had a 9-31 record after taking over for John Lucas with the team at 8-34 for a final mark of 17-65. He was a Cavs assistant coach from 2000-01 to 2002-03.

SMITH, BINGO

Bobby "Bingo" Smith was a 6-foot-5, 195-pound shooting guard and small forward for the Cavaliers from 1970-71 to 1979-80. He was selected from San Diego in the 1970 Expansion Draft. In his 10 seasons with Cleveland he averaged 13.2 points, 2.2 assists, 4.2 rebounds, .8 steals, and .3 blocked shots per game. His best season as a Cavalier was 1974-75 when he averaged 15.9 points, 2.8 assists, five rebounds, one steal, and .3 blocked shots per contest. In his first season with the team he averaged 15.2 points, 3.4 assists, and 5.6 rebounds per game. The next season, he averaged 15 points, three assists, and 6.1 rebounds per contest.

Bingo Smith prepares to shoot against the Bucks, February 13, 1976. (AndersonsCleveland Design.com)

Smith scored 41 points in a 107–99 victory over the Bullets on November 6, 1974, at Washington. He scored 37 points in a 108–103 triumph over San Francisco on March 16, 1971, at the Cleveland Arena. He had 27 points in a 106–87 playoff win over Boston on May 14, 1976, at The Coliseum. He was traded to the Clippers on October 27, 1979. His jersey number 7 was retired by the Cavaliers on December 4, 1979.

SMITH, ELMORE

Elmore Smith was a 7-foot, 250-pound center for the Cavaliers from 1976-77 to 1978-79. Traded from Milwaukee on January 13, 1977, in his three seasons with Cleveland he averaged 10.5 points, 7.2 rebounds, .6 assists, .5 steals, and 1.9 blocked shots per game. His best season as a Cavalier was 1977-78 when he averaged 12.5 points, 8.4 rebounds, .7 assists, .6 steals, and 2.2 blocked shots per contest.

Smith scored 32 points in a 110–93 victory over Washington on February 2, 1978, at The Coliseum. He scored 20 points in a 104–98 playoff defeat to the Bullets on April 17, 1977, at Washington. He became a free agent on July 1, 1979, and was not re-signed.

SMITH, JOE

Joe Smith was a 6-foot-10, 225-pound power forward and center for the Cavaliers from 2007-08 to 2008-09. He was traded from Chicago on February 21, 2008. He was traded to Oklahoma City on August 13, 2008. He was re-signed as a free agent on March 4, 2009.

In his two seasons with the Cavs Smith averaged 7.4 points, 4.9 rebounds, .7 assists, .3 steals, and .6 blocked shots per game. His best season as a Cavalier was 2007-08 when he averaged 8.1 points, five rebounds, .7 assists, .3 steals, and .6 blocked shots per contest. He scored 20 points in a 100–95 loss to the Bulls on April 11, 2008, at Chicago. He scored 19 points in a 79–68 playoff win over the Pistons on April 24, 2009, at Detroit. He became a free agent again on July 1, 2009, and was not re-signed.

SMITH, J. R.

J. R. Smith has been a 6-foot-6, 225-pound shooting guard for the Cavaliers since 2014-15. Traded from the Knicks on January 5, 2015, in his two seasons with Cleveland he has averaged 12.5 points, two assists, 3.1 rebounds, 1.2 steals, and .3 blocked shots per game. His best season as a Cavalier has been 2014-15 when he averaged 12.7 points, 2.5 assists, 3.5 rebounds, 1.4 steals, and .4 blocked shots per contest. The next season, he averaged 12.4 points, 1.7 assists, 2.8 rebounds, 1.1 steals, and .3 blocked shots per game. He scored 29 points in a 107–100 loss to the Suns on January 13, 2015, in Phoenix. He scored 28 points in a 97–89 playoff win over the Hawks on May 20, 2015, at Atlanta.

J. R. Smith, 2014-15. **(*AndersonsClevelandDesign.com*)**

SMITH, RANDY

Randy Smith was a 6-foot-3, 180-pound shooting guard for the Cavaliers from 1979-80 to 1980-81. Traded from San Diego on September 21, 1979, in his two seasons with the Cavs he averaged 16.1 points, 4.4 assists, 2.7 rebounds, 1.5 steals, and .1 blocked shots per game. His best season as a Cavalier was 1979-80 when he averaged 17.6 points, 4.4 assists, 3.1 rebounds, 1.5 steals, and .1 blocked shots per contest. He scored 36 points in a 116–109 loss to the Spurs on January 11, 1980, at San Antonio. He was traded to the Knicks on May 20, 1981.

SMITH, ROBERT

Robert Smith was a 5-foot-11, 165-pound point guard for the Cavaliers in 1980-81 and 1984-85. He was signed as a free agent on October 1, 1980, and was waived on October 14, 1980. He was re-signed as a free agent again on September 27, 1984. In his two seasons with Cleveland he averaged three points, 1.3 assists, .9 rebounds, and .3 steals per game. His best season as a Cavalier was 1980-81 when, in one game, a 130–103 defeat to the Celtics in Boston on October 10, he scored eight points and had three assists and three rebounds. He was waived again on November 26, 1984.

SMITH, WILLIE

Willie Smith was a 6-foot-2, 170-pound point guard for Cleveland in 1979-80. Traded from Portland on August 24, 1979, in his one season with the Cavs he averaged 4.8 points, 4.2 assists, two rebounds, and 1.2 steals per game. He scored 14 points twice—in a 122–119 victory over New Jersey on March 11 at The Coliseum and in a 130–122 defeat to the Celtics on March 28 at Boston. He became a free agent on July 1, 1980, and was not re-signed.

SNOW, ERIC

Eric Snow was a 6-foot-3, 190-pound point guard and shooting guard for the Cavaliers from 2004-05 to 2007-08. Traded from the 76ers on July 20, 2004, in his four seasons with Cleveland he averaged four points, 3.9 assists, 2.1 rebounds, .8 steals, and .2 blocked shots per game. His best season as a Cavalier was 2005-06 when he averaged 4.8 points, 4.2 assists, 2.4 rebounds, .9 steals, and .2 blocked shots per contest.

Snow scored 18 points in a 104–92 victory over the Clippers on January 13, 2007, at Los Angeles. He also scored 18 points in a 121–120 overtime playoff win against the Wizards on May 3, 2006, at Quicken Loans Arena. He won the J. Walter Kennedy Citizenship Award in 2004-05. He was released on April 5, 2009.

SNYDER, DICK

Dick Snyder was a 6-foot-5, 207-pound shooting guard for the Cavaliers from 1974-75 to 1977-78. Traded from Seattle on May 28, 1974, in his four seasons with the Cavs he averaged 10.6 points, 2.4 assists, 2.1 rebounds, .6 steals, and .4 blocked shots per game. His best season as a Cavalier was

1974-75 when he averaged 14.2 points, 3.4 assists, 2.9 rebounds, .8 steals, and .5 blocked shots per contest. The next season, he averaged 12.6 points, 2.7 assists, 2.4 rebounds, .7 steals, and .4 blocked shots per game. The season after that, he averaged 9.3 points, two assists, 1.8 rebounds, .5 steals, and .4 blocked shots per contest.

Snyder scored 36 points in a 111–88 victory over Buffalo on December 28, 1975, at The Coliseum. He scored 26 points in a 92–91 playoff win over Washington on April 22, 1976, again at The Coliseum. He became a free agent on July 1, 1978, and was not re-signed.

SNYDER, MIKE

Mike Snyder has been the Cavaliers' local radio studio host since 1992-93. He was also a Cavs local radio broadcaster in 2010-11.

SORENSON, DAVE

Dave Sorenson was a 6-foot-8, 225-pound power forward for the Cavaliers from 1970-71 to 1972-73. A second-round draft pick in 1970 out of Ohio State University, he averaged 8.8 points, five rebounds, and 1.5 assists per game in his three seasons with Cleveland. His best season as a Cavalier was 1970-71 when he averaged 11.3 points, 6.2 rebounds, and 2.1 assists per contest. He scored 34 points in a 123–112 victory over the Braves on December 19, 1970, at the Cleveland Arena. He was traded to Philadelphia on November 10, 1972.

SPEIGHTS, MARREESE

Marreese Speights was a 6-foot-10, 255-pound center for the Cavaliers in 2012-13. Traded from Memphis on January 22, 2013, in his one season with Cleveland he averaged 10.2 points, 5.1 rebounds, .7 assists, .4 steals, and .7 blocked shots per game. He scored 23 points twice—in a 102–97 loss to New York on March 4 at Quicken Loans Arena and in a 102–94 defeat to the Hawks on April 1 at Atlanta. He became a free agent on July 1, 2013, and was not re-signed.

SPICUZZA, PAUL

Paul Spicuzza was Cleveland's head trainer in 1980-81.

SPIRO, STEPHEN

Stephen Spiro has been the Cavaliers' head trainer since 2013-14.

SPORTSCHANNEL OHIO

Sportschannel Ohio was a Cavaliers local television station from 1989-90 to 1997-98.

SPORTSMANSHIP AWARD

Terrell Brandon (1996-97)

STACK, RYAN

Ryan Stack was a 6-foot-11, 215-pound power forward for the Cavaliers from 1998-99 to 1999-2000. A second-round draft choice in 1998 out of the University of South Carolina, he averaged 2.3 points, 1.8 rebounds, .2 assists, .1 steals, and .5 blocked shots per game in his two seasons with the Cavs. His best season as a Cavalier was 1998-99 when he averaged 2.6 points, 1.9 rebounds, .3 assists, .1 steals, and .6 blocked shots per contest. He scored 11 points in a 93–80 loss to the Heat in Miami on April 21, 1999. He became a free agent on July 1, 2000, and was not re-signed.

STEPIEN, TED

Ted Stepien was the Cavaliers' majority owner from 1980-81 to 1982-83. His tenure was marred by numerous horrible trades that sent first-round draft choices in exchange for players who were average at best. He came to be known around town as "Terrible Ted," and his god-awful basketball team came to be known as the "Cadavers." Toward the end of his ownership, he came extremely close to relocating the Cavaliers to Toronto. He doubled as team president in his first two seasons as owner. He sold the Cavs in 1983 to an ownership team headed by brothers Gordon and George Gund.

STEWART, MICHAEL

Michael Stewart was a 6-foot-10, 230-pound power forward for the Cavaliers from 2002-03 to 2003-04. Traded from the Raptors on September 25, 2002, in his two seasons with Cleveland he averaged .8 points, 1.3

rebounds, .1 assists, .1 steals, and .4 blocked shots per game. His best season as a Cavalier was 2003-04 when he averaged one point, 2.3 rebounds, .1 steals, and one blocked shot per contest. He scored six points in a 92–88 defeat to the Pistons on November 28, 2003, at Detroit. He was traded to Boston on December 15, 2003.

STITH, BRYANT

Bryant Stith was a 6-foot-5, 208-pound shooting guard for the Cavaliers in 2001-02. Signed as a free agent on August 13, 2001, in his one season with Cleveland he averaged 4.2 points, .8 assists, 1.7 rebounds, .6 steals, and .1 blocked shots per game. He scored 20 points in a 108–101 loss to the Celtics on January 26 at Gund Arena. He was traded to the Clippers on July 30, 2002.

STRASSER, CHARLIE

Charlie Strasser was the Cavaliers' trainer or head trainer from 1974-75 to 1979-80.

STREAKS

Please see Team Statistics on page 215.

SUITER, GARY

Gary Suiter was a 6-foot-9, 225-pound center and forward for the Cavaliers in 1970-71. He was signed as a free agent on September 29, 1970. In his one season with the Cavs he averaged 1.4 points, 1.4 rebounds, and .1 assists per game. He scored six points in a 118–95 loss to the Rockets on December 13 at the Cleveland Arena.

Suiter was known for his wacky ways, including walking up to the press box and telling the beat writers that, had head coach Bill Fitch played him more, he could have led the team, which finished 15-67, to the NBA title. In the middle of a game, he was found at a concession stand in uniform and warmups. Not surprisingly, he was waived on January 4, 1971.

SUNDOV, BRUNO

Bruno Sundov was a 7-foot-2, 220-pound center for the Cavaliers in 2003-04. Traded from Boston on July 29, 2003, he played four games with Cleveland. He was waived on January 15, 2004.

SURA, BOB

Bob Sura was a 6-foot-5, 200-pound shooting guard and point guard for Cleveland from 1995-96 to 1999-2000. He was a first-round draft choice in 1995 from Florida State University. In his five seasons with the Cavs he averaged 8.1 points, 3.7 assists, 2.8 rebounds, one steal, and .3 blocked shots per game. His best season as a Cavalier was 1999-2000 when he averaged 13.8 points, 3.9 assists, 3.9 rebounds, 1.2 steals, and .3 blocked shots per contest.

Sura scored 31 points in a 116–107 overtime triumph against the Pistons on January 25, 2000, at Gund Arena. He scored four points in the playoffs twice—in an 81–76 loss to the Knicks on May 1, 1996, at New York and in a 106–77 defeat to the Pacers on April 23, 1998, at Indiana. He was traded to the Warriors on April 23, 1998.

SZCZERBIAK, WALLY

Wally Szczerbiak was a 6-foot-7, 244-pound small forward for the Cavaliers from 2007-08 to 2008-09. Traded from Seattle on February 21, 2008, in his two seasons with Cleveland he averaged 7.3 points, 3.2 rebounds, 1.2 assists, .4 steals, and .2 blocked shots per game. His best season as a Cavalier was 2007-08 when he averaged 8.2 points, 3.2 rebounds, 1.4 assists, .4 steals, and .3 blocked shots per contest.

Szczerbiak scored 21 points in a 111–110 overtime loss to the 76ers on April 15, 2009, at Quicken Loans Arena. He scored 26 points in a 105–88 playoff win over the Wizards on May 2, 2008, at Washington. He became a free agent on July 1, 2009, and was not re-signed.

T

TAIT, JOE

Joe Tait was a Cavaliers local radio broadcaster in 1970-71, from 1988-89 to 1991-92, and in 2010-11. He was the Cavs' local radio broadcaster from 1971-72 to 1980-81, 1983-84 to 1987-88, and 1992-93 to 2009-10.

Tait's distaste for team majority owner Ted Stepien, who was destroying the franchise, came to a head toward the end of the 1980-81 season and resulted in Tait leaving his post after the season. The Cavs honored their living legend with Joe Tait Night in their final home game of the season against Philadelphia. Remarkably, more than 20,000 fans showed up at The Coliseum for a bad basketball team, proving that he would be missed in a big way. The angry crowd not only showed support for its worshipped broadcaster but also voiced its discontent over the fact that Stepien was staying behind to run the team.

With Stepien gone, having sold the Cavaliers to brothers Gordon and George Gund, Tait returned to the team in 1983-84. On March 26, 2008, he announced his 3,000th game for the Cavaliers, against the New Orleans Hornets. The radio broadcast location at Quicken Loans Arena, in section C126, has been forever renamed "The Joe Tait Perch" in honor of that achievement.

Some three years later, on April 8, 2011, in a game against Chicago, the team honored Tait with Joe Tait Appreciation Night and by raising a commemorative banner with his name, his years as a Cavaliers broadcaster, and a microphone next to the Cavs' retired numbers. His final game was the April 13 contest between the Cavaliers and Washington Wizards. The team sent him out a winner, defeating Washington 100–93. As the final minute played out, Frank Sinatra's "My Way" blared throughout The Q as cameras focused on his final call as a Cavs broadcaster.

Tait was a Cavaliers local television broadcaster when he wasn't calling the games on radio from 1988-89 to 1991-92.

Joe Tait (left) and Cleveland sports talk radio legend Pete Franklin circa 1976. (AndersonsClevelandDesign.com)

TATUM, EARL

Earl Tatum was a 6-foot-5, 185-pound shooting guard for Cleveland in 1979-80. Traded from Detroit on February 15, 1979, in his one season with the Cavs he averaged 2.6 points, .6 assists, .8 rebounds, .5 steals, and .2 blocked shots per game. He scored 11 points in a 137–117 victory over the Pistons on October 16 at The Coliseum. He became a free agent on July 1, 1980, and was not re-signed.

TEAM NAME

With the help of a name-the-team contest in the *Plain Dealer* in the spring of 1970 that drew more than 14,000 entries, owner Nick Mileti made the final call on what Cleveland's NBA expansion team would be called—the "Cavaliers."

TEDDY BEARS, THE

The Teddy Bears were the Cavaliers' dance team from 1980-81 to 1982-83.

TELEVISION BROADCASTS

The following are the Cavaliers' local television broadcasters and the stations on which Cavs games have been aired:

1970-71	Gib Shanley, Hal Lebovitz, and Bob Brown (WEWS-TV Channel 5)
1971-72 to 1974-75	Gib Shanley and Hal Lebovitz (WEWS-TV Channel 5)
1975-76	Gib Shanley and Jim Lessig (WEWS-TV Channel 5)
1976-77	Harry Jones and Jim Mueller (WJW-Channel 8)
1977-78 to 1978-79	Harry Jones and Jim Mueller (WJKW-Channel 8)
1979-80	Fred McLeod and Jim Mueller (WJKW-Channel 8)
1980-81	Bruce Drennan (WUAB-Channel 43)
1981-82	Bruce Drennan and Austin Carr (WUAB-Channel 43)
1982-83 to 1983-84	Nev Chandler and Austin Carr (WUAB-Channel 43)
1984-85	Nev Chandler and Jack Corrigan (WUAB-Channel 43)
1985-86 to 1986-87	Jim Brinson and Jack Corrigan (WUAB-Channel 43)
1987-88	Jack Corrigan and Jim Chones (WUAB-Channel 43)
1988-89	Joe Tait and Jim Chones (WOIO-Channel 19)
1989-90 to 1991-92	Denny Schreiner and Jim Chones (Sportschannel Ohio)
	Joe Tait and Jim Chones (WOIO-Channel 19)
1992-93	Denny Schreiner and Jim Chones (Sportschannel Ohio)
	Greg Gumbel and Jim Chones (WOIO-Channel 19)
1993-94	Denny Schreiner and Jim Chones (Sportschannel Ohio)
	Denny Schreiner and Jim Chones (WOIO-Channel 19)
1994-95 to 1996-97	Michael Reghi and Jim Chones (Sportschannel Ohio)
	Michael Reghi and Quinn Buckner (WUAB-Channel 43)
1997-98	Michael Reghi and Matt Guokas (Sportschannel Ohio)
	Michael Reghi and Brad Daugherty (WUAB-Channel 43)

1998-99 to 1999-2000	Michael Reghi and Austin Carr (Fox Sports Ohio)
	Michael Reghi and Austin Carr (WUAB-Channel 43)
	Michael Reghi and Matt Guokas (Fox Sports Ohio)
	Michael Reghi and Matt Guokas (WUAB-Channel 43)
2000-01 to 2003-04	Michael Reghi and Austin Carr (Fox Sports Net Ohio)
	Michael Reghi and Austin Carr (WUAB-Channel 43)
	Michael Reghi and Matt Guokas (Fox Sports Net Ohio)
	Michael Reghi and Matt Guokas (WUAB-Channel 43)
2004-05	Michael Reghi and Austin Carr (FSN Ohio)
	Michael Reghi and Austin Carr (WUAB-Channel 43)
	Michael Reghi and Mark Price (FSN Ohio)
	Michael Reghi and Mark Price (WUAB-Channel 43)
2005-06	Michael Reghi and Austin Carr (FSN Ohio)
	Michael Reghi and Austin Carr (WUAB-Channel 43)
	Michael Reghi and Scott Williams (FSN Ohio)
	Michael Reghi and Scott Williams (WUAB-Channel 43)
2006-07 to 2007-08	Fred McLeod and Austin Carr (FSN Ohio)
	Fred McLeod and Austin Carr (WUAB-Channel 43) (select simulcasts)
2008-09 to 2009-10	Fred McLeod and Austin Carr (Fox Sports Ohio)
	Fred McLeod and Austin Carr (WUAB-Channel 43) (select simulcasts)
2010-11 to 2011-12	Fred McLeod and Austin Carr/Jeff Phelps (sideline reporter) (Fox Sports Ohio)
	Fred McLeod and Austin Carr/Jeff Phelps (sideline reporter) (WUAB-Channel 43) (select simulcasts)
2012-13 to present	Fred McLeod and Austin Carr/Allie Clifton (sideline reporter) (Fox Sports Ohio)
	Fred McLeod and Austin Carr/Allie Clifton (sideline reporter) (WUAB-Channel 43) (select simulcasts)

TELFAIR, SEBASTIAN

Sebastian Telfair was a 6-foot, 165-pound point guard for the Cavaliers in 2009-10. Traded from the Clippers on February 17, 2010, in four games with Cleveland he averaged 9.8 points, three assists, one rebound, and .5 steals per contest. He scored 21 points in a 116–113 loss to the Pacers on April 9 at Quicken Loans Arena. He was traded to Minnesota on July 26, 2010.

TEN HIGHEST/LOWEST-SCORING GAMES

Please see Team Statistics on page 215.

TEN MOST ONE-SIDED GAMES

Please see Team Statistics on page 215.

THOMAS, BILLY

Billy Thomas was a 6-foot-4, 208-pound small forward for the Cavaliers in 2007-08. He signed the first of two 10-day contracts on February 22, 2008, and became a free agent on March 13, 2008. He was re-signed as a free agent again on April 16, 2008. In seven games with Cleveland he averaged 1.7 points, .3 rebounds, and .1 steals per contest. He scored nine points in a 90–89 victory over Washington on February 22 at Quicken Loans Arena. He scored three points in a 116–86 playoff win over the Wizards again on April 21, likewise at Quicken Loans Arena. He was waived on September 8, 2008.

THOMAS, CARL

Carl Thomas was a 6-foot-4, 175-pound shooting guard for the Cavaliers from 1996-97 to 1997-98. He was signed as a free agent on September 23, 1996. He became a free agent again on July 1, 1997. He was re-signed to the first of two 10-day contracts on February 2, 1998, and on February 22, 1998, signed a contract for the rest of the 1997-98 season.

In his two seasons with Cleveland Thomas averaged two points, .4 assists, one rebound, .4 steals, and .1 blocked shots per game. His best season as a Cavalier was 1997-98 when he averaged 2.7 points, .3 assists, 1.3 rebounds, .6 steals, and .2 blocked shots per contest. He scored 13 points in a 106–101 win over Vancouver on February 25, 1998, at Gund Arena. He scored two points in a 106–77 playoff loss to the Pacers on April 23, 1998, at Indiana. He became a free agent again on July 1, 1998, and was not re-signed.

THOMPSON, MYCHEL

Mychel Thompson was a 6-foot-6, 211-pound shooting guard for the Cavaliers in 2011-12. Signed as a free agent on December 15, 2011, in five games with Cleveland he averaged 3.6 points, 1.4 assists, one rebound, .4 steals, and .2 blocked shots per contest. He scored eight points in a 93–90 loss to Boston on January 31 at Quicken Loans Arena. He was waived on February 6, 2012.

THOMPSON, PAUL

Paul Thompson was a 6-foot-6, 210-pound small forward for the Cavaliers from 1983-84 to 1984-85. He was selected in the third round of the 1983 draft from Tulane University. In his two seasons with the Cavs he averaged 9.5 points, 3.7 rebounds, 1.6 assists, one steal, and .5 blocked shots per game. His best season as a Cavalier was 1984-85 when he averaged 10.5 points, 3.5 rebounds, 1.8 assists, 1.2 steals, and .6 blocked shots per contest. He scored 26 points in a 114–106 victory over San Antonio on November 27, 1983, at The Coliseum. He was traded to Milwaukee on February 12, 1985.

THOMPSON, TRISTAN

Tristan Thompson has been a 6-foot-9, 238-pound power forward for the Cavaliers since 2011-12. A first-round draft pick in 2011 out of the University of Texas, he has averaged 9.7 points, 8.5 rebounds, .8 assists, .5 steals, and .7 blocked shots per game in his five seasons with Cleveland. His best season as a Cavalier has been 2012-13 when he averaged 11.7 points, 9.4 rebounds, 1.3 assists, .7 steals, and .9 blocked shots per contest. The next season, he averaged 11.7 points, 9.2 rebounds, .9 assists, .5 steals, and .4 blocked shots per game. In 2015-16, he averaged 7.8 points, nine rebounds, .8 assists, .5 steals, and .6 blocked shots per contest.

Thompson scored 29 points in a 97–91 triumph over the Celtics in Boston on April 5, 2013. He scored 19 points in a 104–91 Finals loss to the Warriors on June 14, 2015, at Golden State.

THURMOND, NATE

Nate Thurmond was a 6-foot-11, 225-pound center for the Cavaliers from 1975-76 to 1976-77. Traded from the Bulls on November 27, 1975, in his two seasons with Cleveland he averaged five points, 6.3 rebounds, 1.3 assists, .3

Tristan Thompson slams one home against the Lakers with Kyrie Irving looking on, February 8, 2015. (*AndersonsClevelandDesign.com*)

steals, and 1.5 blocked shots per game. His best season as a Cavalier was 1976-77, when he averaged 5.5 points, 7.6 rebounds, 1.7 assists, .3 steals, and 1.7 blocked shots per contest. In 1975-76, he averaged 4.6 points, 5.3 rebounds, one assist, .3 steals, and 1.3 blocked shots per game.

Thurmond scored 15 points in a 108–93 defeat to the Rockets on January 28, 1976, at Houston. He scored 13 points twice in the playoffs—in a 99–94 loss to the Celtics in Boston on May 16, 1976, and in a 94–87 defeat to the Celtics again on May 18, 1976, at The Coliseum. He was a driving force behind the success of the 1975-76 Miracle of Richfield Cavaliers who nearly advanced to the Finals. He became a free agent on July 1, 1977, and was not re signed. His jersey number 42 was retired by the Cavaliers on December 18, 1977. He was inducted into the Naismith Memorial Basketball Hall of Fame in 1985.

TIBBETTS, NATE

Nate Tibbetts was a Cavaliers assistant coach from 2011-12 to 2012-13.

TILLIS, DARREN

Darren Tillis was a 6-foot-11, 215-pound center for the Cavaliers in 1982-83. Traded from Boston on January 14, 1983, in his one season with the Cavs he averaged 4.1 points, 3.3 rebounds, .4 assists, .2 steals, and .8 blocked shots per game. He scored 22 points in a 117–94 loss to the Kings on March 22 in Kansas City. He was traded to Golden State on August 16, 1983.

TONEY, SEDRIC

Sedric Toney was a 6-foot-2, 178-pound point guard for the Cavaliers in 1993-94. Signed as a free agent on November 9, 1993, he averaged .5 points, .9 assists, and .3 rebounds per contest in 12 games with Cleveland. He scored two points on three occasions. He was waived on December 21, 1993.

TOP TENS (CAREER) (POSTSEASON)

Please see Individual Statistics on page 185.

TOP TENS (CAREER) (REGULAR SEASON)

Please see Individual Statistics on page 185.

TOP TENS (SEASON)

Please see Individual Statistics on page 185.

TRADES

The following are 10 notable Cavaliers trades:

May 28, 1974 – 1974 first-round draft pick (Tom Burleson) to Seattle for Dick Snyder and 1974 first-round draft pick (Campy Russell)

November 27, 1975 – Steve Patterson and Eric Fernsten to Chicago for Nate Thurmond and Rowland Garrett

February 15, 1980 – Butch Lee and 1982 first-round draft pick (James Worthy) to Los Angeles for 1980 first-round draft pick (Chad Kinch)

December 15, 1982 – Ron Brewer to Golden State for World B. Free

June 16, 1986 – Roy Hinson to Philadelphia for 1986 first-round draft pick (Brad Daugherty)

February 25, 1988 – Kevin Johnson, Tyrone Corbin, Mark West, 1988 first-round draft pick (Dan Majerle), 1988 second-round draft pick (Dean Garrett), and 1989 second-round draft pick (Greg Grant) to Phoenix for Larry Nance, Mike Sanders, and 1988 first-round draft pick (Randolph Keys)

November 16, 1989 – Ron Harper, 1990 first-round draft pick (Loy Vaught), 1991 second-round draft pick (Joe Wylie), and 1992 first-round draft pick (Elmore Spencer) to L.A. Clippers for Danny Ferry and Reggie Williams

March 11, 1999 – Vitaly Potapenko to Boston for Andrew DeClerq and 1999 first-round draft pick (Andre Miller)

February 24, 2011 – Mo Williams and Jamario Moon to L.A. Clippers for Baron Davis and 2011 first-round draft pick (Kyrie Irving)

August 23, 2014 – As part of a three-team trade, Andrew Wiggins, Anthony Bennett, and trade exception to Minnesota for Kevin Love; 2015 first-round draft pick to Philadelphia

TRAFTON, THAXTER

Thaxter Trafton was the Cavaliers' president from 1985-86 to 1987-88.

TRAINERS/HEAD TRAINERS

Ron Culp (1970-71 to 1973-74)
Charlie Strasser (1974-75 to 1979-80)

Paul Spicuzza (1980-81)
Gary Briggs (1981-82 to 1999-2000)
Max Benton (2001-02 to 2012-13)
Stephen Spiro (2013-14 to present)

TRAYLOR, ROBERT

Robert Traylor was a 6-foot-8, 284-pound center for the Cavaliers in 2000-01 and 2004-05. He was traded from the Bucks on June 27, 2000. He was traded to Philadelphia on August 3, 2001. He was re-signed on August 5, 2004, as a free agent.

In his two seasons with Cleveland Traylor averaged 5.6 points, 4.4 rebounds, .9 assists, .7 steals, and .9 blocked shots per game. His best season as a Cavalier was 2000-01 when he averaged 5.7 points, 4.3 rebounds, .9 assists, .7 steals, and 1.1 blocked shots per contest. He scored 22 points in a 100–86 win over Boston on April 19, 2005, at Gund Arena. He became a free agent again on July 1, 2005, and was not re-signed.

TREPAGNIER, JEFF

Jeff Trepagnier was a 6-foot-4, 200-pound shooting guard for Cleveland in 2001-02. He was a second-round draft pick in 2001 out of the University of Southern California. In 12 games with the Cavaliers he averaged 1.5 points, one assist, one rebound, .7 steals, and .3 blocked shots per contest. He scored eight points in a 79–68 loss to the 76ers in Philadelphia on November 23. He became a free agent on July 1, 2002, and was not re-signed.

TRIPLE-DOUBLES (POSTSEASON)

Please see Individual Statistics on page 185.

TRIPLE-DOUBLES (REGULAR SEASON)

Please see Individual Statistics on page 185.

TURPIN, MELVIN

Melvin Turpin was a 6-foot-11, 240-pound center for the Cavaliers from 1984-85 to 1986-87. Traded from the Bullets on June 19, 1984, in his three seasons with Cleveland he averaged 10.4 points, 5.4 rebounds, .6 assists, .5 steals, and one blocked shot per game. His best season as a Cavalier was 1985-86 when he averaged 13.7 points, seven rebounds, .7 assists, .8 steals, and 1.3 blocked shots per contest.

Turpin scored 32 points in a 112–107 victory over the Knicks on March 11, 1986, at New York. He scored 10 points in a 105–98 playoff win over Boston on April 23, 1985, at The Coliseum. He was traded to Utah on October 8, 1987.

20-20 CLUB (POSTSEASON)

Please see Individual Statistics on page 185.

20-20 CLUB (REGULAR SEASON)

Please see Individual Statistics on page 185.

***LeBron James with his family in the midst of mayhem in downtown Cleveland as some 1.3 million fans gather for a Cleveland Cavaliers Championship Parade and Rally celebrating the Cavs' 2015-16 NBA title, June 22, 2016.* (*AndersonsClevelandDesign.com*)**

2016 CHAMPIONSHIP PARADE AND RALLY

On June 22, 2016, the city of Cleveland threw a Cleveland Cavaliers Championship Parade and Rally in honor of the 2015-16 Cavs team that had won the franchise's first NBA title three nights earlier by defeating the Golden State Warriors 93–89 in a thrilling Game 7 at Oracle Arena. The celebration featured a 60-plus-unit parade complete with floats, specialty vehicles, the Ohio State University Spring Athletic Band, and of course, the much anticipated appearance of the 2015-16 Cavaliers.

The 1.3-mile ticker-tape parade began outside Quicken Loans Arena and traveled through downtown. Its primary route was East Ninth Street; it concluded more than four hours after it began on East Sixth Street between Mall B and Mall C, where the team congregated on a stage. The rally lasted about an hour and featured a special program of celebration with an array of entertainment, special presentations, and celebrations from the stage, including speeches by all of the players. The parade and rally were broadcast live on local television and radio.

Although the Browns won the NFL Championship in 1964, it was the first championship parade for a major professional Cleveland sports team in 68 years, since the parade celebrating the Indians 1948 World Series win. Some 1.3 million people showed up at the parade and rally to celebrate the Cavs' achievement.

U

UNIFORMS/LOGOS

The Cavaliers' original colors of wine and gold emanated from the hues of owner Nick Mileti's alma mater of John Adams High School. The wine was changed to a "Cavaliers wine" to set the team apart somewhat. The jerseys featured a feathered treatment of the letter "C" in "Cavaliers." The primary color on the home uniform was gold and on the road uniform was wine. The team logo was that of a swashbuckling cavalier with a pointing sword looking left, surrounded by the team name and a basketball.

With the Cavs' move from the Cleveland Arena to The Coliseum came a change to the uniform. The new duds still featured gold home uniforms and wine road uniforms, but they had "Marquette"-style horizontal white, wine and gold stacked piping—a checkerboard pattern—along the sides of both the jersey and shorts.

In 1980-81, the gold shade was altered from yellowish to metallic, and the checkerboard pattern was removed. Two stripes—white and gold—were placed below a newly fonted "CLEVELAND" and, above the uniform number, still the only time in team history in which the city name was featured on both the home and road jerseys.

By 1983-84, the wine-and-gold color scheme was gone. The new colors were burnt orange, white, and royal blue. The team logo was scrapped, replaced by the word "CAVS" in an arched pattern with the letter "V" in the shape of a hoop and a circle above as a basketball. The burnt orange acted as the primary color on the road uniform and the secondary color on the white home uniform. The burnt orange as the primary road color was replaced by the royal blue road uniforms in 1987-88, and the "CAVS" logo was replaced with the block "CLEVELAND" in 1989-90.

With the team's move to Gund Arena (now Quicken Loans Arena) in 1994-95 came another new look, this time pastel blue and black. The home uniform was white, and the road uniform was black, both with a jagged blue splash across the torso and double-lined lettering that said "CAVS" at home and "CLEVELAND" on the road, both outlined in orange. The new

The Cavaliers' logo from 1970-71 to 1982-83. (AndersonsClevelandDesign.com)

logo featured the jagged blue splash partly encompassing a basketball about to fall through the net with the double-lined lettering of "CAVS" beneath it. The look was modified in 1997-98 by losing the torso splash. Instead, the uniforms featured a more streamlined blue and orange piping along the right side of the jerseys and shorts.

After two decades without them, the team's original colors of wine and gold—a "new expression of wine and gold"—returned in 2003-04. They were a crimson-hued wine color and a metallic, almost copper, gold. Dark blue, the secondary color, was a tribute to the Cavaliers teams of the early 1990s. The new primary logo featured a basketball with a diagonal "CLEVELAND CAVALIERS" in front of it and a sword poking through the lettering pointing to the left. Although they still donned the dark blue periodically, the Cavaliers returned to their original wine and gold hues in 2010-11. The primary logo was also tweaked a bit.

UZOH, BEN

Ben Uzoh was a 6-foot-3, 205-pound point guard for the Cavaliers in 2011-12. Signed to a 10-day contract on February 10, 2012, he played two games with the Cavs. He became a free agent again on February 20, 2012, and was not re-signed.

V

VALENTINE, DARNELL

Darnell Valentine was a 6-foot-1, 183-pound shooting guard and point guard for the Cavaliers in 1988-89 and 1990-91. He was traded from Miami on June 23, 1988. He became a free agent on July 1, 1989. He was re-signed as a free agent on December 3, 1990.

In his two seasons with the Cavs Valentine averaged 6.9 points, 3.7 assists, 1.9 rebounds, 1.1 steals, and .1 blocked shots per game. His best season as a Cavalier was 1990-91 when he averaged 9.4 points, 5.4 assists, 2.6 rebounds, 1.5 steals, and .2 blocked shots per contest. He scored 28 points in a 118–114 loss to the Hawks in Atlanta on February 5, 1991. He scored eight points in the playoffs on two occasions—in a 95–88 defeat to the Bulls on April 28, 1989, at The Coliseum and in a 101–94 loss to the Bulls again on May 3, 1989, at Chicago. He became a free agent again on July 1, 1991, and was not re-signed.

VAREJAO, ANDERSON

Anderson Varejao was a 6-foot-10, 273-pound center and power forward for Cleveland from 2004-05 to 2015-16. Traded from the Magic on July 23, 2004, in his 12 seasons with the Cavs he averaged 7.6 points, 7.5 rebounds, 1.2 assists, .9 steals, and .7 blocked shots per game. His best season as a Cavalier was 2012-13 when he averaged 14.1 points, 14.4 rebounds, 3.4 assists, 1.5 steals, and .6 blocked shots per contest. In 2010-11, he averaged 9.1 points, 9.7 rebounds, 1.5 assists, .9 steals, and 1.2 blocked shots per game. The next season he averaged 10.8 points, 11.5 rebounds, 1.7 assists, 1.4 steals, and .7 blocked shots per game.

Varejao scored 35 points in a 114–101 loss to the Nets on November 13, 2012, at Brooklyn. He scored 26 points in a 117–92 win over Chicago on January 2, 2009, at Quicken Loans Arena. He had 16 points in an 86–77 playoff victory over Detroit on May 13, 2006, also at Quicken Loans Arena.

Known for his physical, all-out effort, Varejao dove for many balls and mixed it up underneath with the best of them. He was also known for his unique, floppy hairstyle, which spawned periodic "Wild Thing" Wig Nights in which fans in attendance received a wild head piece that resembled his mop top.

He was traded to Portland on February 18, 2016. He was then immediately waived by Portland and subsequently picked up by Golden State for the veterans minimum.

VOCE, GARY

Gary Voce was a 6-foot-9, 240-pound power forward for the Cavaliers in 1989-90. Signed as a free agent on October 5, 1989, he played one game with Cleveland. He was waived on November 15, 1989.

W

WAGNER, DAJUAN

Dajuan Wagner was a 6-foot-2, 200-pound shooting guard for Cleveland from 2002-03 to 2004-05. He was a first-round draft pick in 2002 out of the University of Memphis. In his three seasons with the Cavs he averaged 9.4 points, 1.9 assists, 1.4 rebounds, .7 steals, and .1 blocked shots per game. His best season as a Cavalier was 2002-03 when he averaged 13.4 points, 2.8 assists, 1.7 rebounds, .8 steals, and .1 blocked shots per contest. He scored 33 points in a 96–83 victory over the Raptors on December 11, 2002, at Gund Arena. He became a free agent on July 1, 2005, and was not re-signed.

WAITERS, DION

Dion Waiters was a 6-foot-4, 225-pound shooting guard for the Cavaliers from 2012-13 to 2014-15. A first-round draft choice in 2012 from Syracuse University, in his three seasons with Cleveland he averaged 14.3 points, 2.8 assists, 2.4 rebounds, one steal, and .3 blocked shots. His best season as a Cavalier was 2013-14 when he averaged 15.9 points, three assists, 2.8 rebounds, .9 steals, and .2 blocked shots per contest. He scored 33 points in a 124–118 loss to the Kings in Sacramento on January 14, 2013. He was traded to the Thunder on January 5, 2015.

WALKER, FOOTS

Clarence "Foots" Walker was a 6-foot, 184-pound point guard for the Cavaliers from 1974-75 to 1979-80. He was a third-round draft choice in 1974 out of State University of West Georgia. In his six seasons with Cleveland he averaged 7.2 points, five assists, three rebounds, 1.7 steals, and .2 blocked shots per game. His best season as a Cavalier was 1979-80 when he averaged 9.4 points, eight assists, 3.8 rebounds, two steals, and .2 blocked shots per contest.

Walker scored 26 points in a 113–111 victory over Los Angeles on October 17, 1978, at The Coliseum. He scored 20 points in the playoffs twice—in a 109–100 loss to the Bullets on April 13, 1977, in Washington and in a 91–83 win over the Bullets on April 15, 1977, at The Coliseum. He was traded to the Nets on September 24, 1980.

WALLACE, BEN

Ben Wallace was a 6-foot-9, 240-pound power forward for the Cavaliers from 2007-08 to 2008-09. Traded from Chicago on February 21, 2008, in his two seasons with the Cavs he averaged 3.3 points, 6.7 rebounds, .7 assists, .9 steals, and 1.4 blocked shots per game. His best season as a Cavalier was 2007-08 when he averaged 4.2 points, 7.4 rebounds, .6 assists, .9 steals, and 1.7 blocked shots per contest.

Wallace scored 13 points in a 117–92 victory over the Bulls on January 2, 2009, at Quicken Loans Arena. He scored nine points in a 108–84 playoff win over the Celtics on May 10, 2008, also at Quicken Loans Arena. He was traded to Phoenix on June 26, 2009.

WALTON, LUKE

Luke Walton was a 6-foot-8, 235-pound power forward for the Cavaliers from 2011-12 to 2012-13. Traded from the Lakers on March 15, 2012, in his two seasons with Cleveland he averaged three points, 2.5 rebounds, 2.8 assists, .6 steals, and .2 blocked shots per game. His best season as a Cavalier was 2012-13 when he averaged 3.4 points, 2.9 rebounds, 3.3 assists, .8 steals, and .3 blocked shots per contest. He scored nine points in a 96–86 loss to the Mavericks on March 15, 2013, in Dallas. He became a free agent on July 1, 2013, and was not re-signed.

WARNER, CORNELL

Cornell Warner was a 6-foot-9, 220-pound center for the Cavaliers from 1972-73 to 1973-74. Signed as a free agent on November 4, 1972, he averaged 5.5 points, 7.2 rebounds, one assist, and .4 blocked shots per game in his two seasons with Cleveland. His best season as a Cavalier was 1972-73 when he averaged 5.7 points, 7.5 rebounds, and one assist per contest. He scored 16 points in a 106–104 win over the Pistons on February 17, 1973, at Detroit. He was waived on October 29, 1973.

WARREN, JOHN

John Warren was a 6-foot-3, 180-pound shooting guard and point guard for the Cavaliers from 1970-71 to 1973-74. He was selected from New York in the 1970 Expansion Draft. In his four seasons with the Cavs he averaged 6.6 points, 2.1 assists, 2.5 rebounds, .4 steals, and .1 blocked shots per game. His best season as a Cavalier was 1970-71 when he averaged 11.5 points, 4.2 assists, and 4.2 rebounds per contest. He scored 27 points in a 111–105 loss to Seattle on November 8, 1970, at the Cleveland Arena.

Little more than a month later, on the evening of December 9, 1970, another home game, Warren did the unthinkable—he scored a basket for the Portland Trail Blazers! Yes, he scored two points for the opposing team. He was waived on October 16, 1974.

WASHINGTON, BOBBY

Bobby Washington was a 5-foot-11, 175-pound point guard for the Cavaliers from 1970-71 to 1971-72. Claimed on waivers from Milwaukee on December 12, 1970, in his two seasons with Cleveland he averaged six points, 3.6 assists, and two rebounds per game. His best season as a Cavalier was 1970-71 when he averaged 7.4 points, four assists, and 2.2 rebounds per contest. He scored 26 points in a 116–111 loss to the Lakers at the Cleveland Arena on February 9, 1971. He became a free agent on July 1, 1972, and was not re-signed.

WASHINGTON, RICHARD

Richard Washington was a 6-foot-11, 220-pound power forward for the Cavaliers from 1980-81 to 1981-82. Traded from the Mavericks on October 30, 1980, he averaged 9.1 points, 5.1 rebounds, 1.5 assists, .6 steals, and .6 blocked shots per game in his two seasons with Cleveland. His best season as a Cavalier was 1980-81 when he averaged 9.9 points, 5.3 rebounds, 1.6 assists, .6 steals, and .8 blocked shots per contest. He scored 24 points on four occasions. He was waived on October 19, 1983.

WBBG-AM 1260

WBBG-AM 1260 was the Cavaliers' flagship radio station from 1981-82 to 1983-84.

WEATHERSPOON, CLARENCE

Clarence Weatherspoon was a 6-foot-6, 240-pound power forward for the Cavaliers in 2000-01. Traded from Miami on August 30, 2000, in his one season with Cleveland he averaged 11.3 points, 9.7 rebounds, 1.3 assists, one steal, and 1.3 blocked shots per game. He scored 24 points in a 107–98 loss to the 76ers on November 15 in Philadelphia. He became a free agent on July 1, 2001, and was not re-signed.

WEDMAN, SCOTT

Scott Wedman was a 6-foot-7, 215-pound small forward for the Cavaliers from 1981-82 to 1982-83. He was acquired as a free agent on June 8, 1981. In his two seasons with the Cavs he averaged 13.8 points, 5.8 rebounds, 2.5 assists, 1.1 steals, and .3 blocked shots per game. His best season as a Cavalier was 1982-83 when he averaged 18.1 points, 5.9 rebounds, 2.5 assists, .7 steals, and .3 blocked shots per contest. He scored 30 points on two occasions—in a 100–97 loss to the Pacers on April 9, 1982, at Indiana and in a 98–82 win over the Bullets on January 8, 1983, at The Coliseum. He was traded to Boston on January 14, 1983.

WELSCH, JIRI

Jiri Welsch was a 6-foot-7, 208-pound small forward for the Cavaliers in 2004-05. Traded from the Celtics on February 24, 2005, in 16 games with the Cavs, he averaged 2.9 points, 1.8 rebounds, 1.2 assists, and .3 steals per contest. He scored six points on three occasions. He was traded to Milwaukee on June 28, 2005.

WELTMAN, HARRY

Harry Weltman was the Cavaliers' president in 1982-83 and was their general manager from 1983-84 to 1985-86.

WERE-AM 1300

WERE-AM 1300 was the Cavaliers' flagship radio station from 1970-71 to 1972-73.

WESLEY, DAVID

David Wesley was a 6-foot, 190-pound shooting guard for Cleveland in 2006-07. He was signed as a free agent on September 5, 2006. In his one season with the Cavs he averaged 2.1 points, 1.1 assists, one rebound, .3 steals, and .1 blocked shots per game. He scored 11 points in a 124–97 victory over Golden State on January 30 at Quicken Loans Arena. He was traded to New Orleans on September 29, 2007.

WESLEY, WALT

Walt Wesley was a 6-foot-11, 220-pound center for the Cavaliers from 1970-71 to 1972-73. Chosen in the 1970 Expansion Draft from Chicago, in his three seasons with Cleveland he averaged 14.3 points, 8.3 rebounds, and .9 assists per game. His best season as a Cavalier was 1970-71 when he averaged 17.7 points, 8.7 rebounds, and one assist per contest. He scored 50 points—a team record that stood for more than 34 years—in a 125–109 victory over Cincinnati on February 19, 1971, at the Cleveland Arena. He was traded to Phoenix on November 22, 1972.

WEST, DELONTE

Delonte West was a 6-foot-4, 180-pound shooting guard and point guard for the Cavaliers from 2007-08 to 2009-10. Traded from the SuperSonics on February 21, 2008, in his three seasons with Cleveland he averaged 10.3 points, 3.6 assists, 3.1 rebounds, 1.2 steals, and .4 blocked shots per game. His best season as a Cavalier was 2008-09 when he averaged 11.7 points, 3.5 assists, 3.2 rebounds, 1.5 steals, and .2 blocked shots per contest.

West scored 27 points in a 92–85 loss to the Bucks on March 6, 2010, at Milwaukee. He scored 22 points in a 103–90 playoff defeat to the Magic on May 30, 2009, in Orlando. He was traded to Minnesota on July 26, 2010.

WEST, MARK

Mark West was a 6-foot-10, 230-pound center for the Cavaliers from 1984-85 to 1987-88 and in 1996-97. He was acquired as a free agent on November 23, 1984. He was traded to the Suns on February 25, 1988. He was re-signed as a free agent again on August 9, 1996.

In his five seasons with Cleveland West averaged 5.2 points, 4.1 rebounds, .4 assists, .3 steals, and one blocked shot per game. His best season as a Cavalier was 1987-88 when he averaged 8.5 points, 5.2 rebounds, .9 assists, .5 steals, and 1.5 blocked shots per contest. He scored 27 points in a 113–106 victory over Washington on November 1, 1986, at The Coliseum. He scored four points twice in the playoffs—in a 108–106 defeat to the Celtics on April 20,

1985, at Boston and in a 117–115 loss to the Celtics again on April 25, 1985, at The Coliseum. He became a free agent again on July 1, 1997, and was not re-signed.

WEWS-TV CHANNEL 5

WEWS-TV Channel 5 was the Cavaliers' local television station from 1970-71 to 1975-76.

WHATLEY, ENNIS

Ennis Whatley was a 6-foot-3, 177-pound point guard for the Cavaliers in 1985-86. Traded from Chicago on June 18, 1985, in eight games with Cleveland he averaged 2.8 points, 1.6 assists, .9 rebounds, and .6 steals per contest. He scored 14 points in a 101–98 loss to the Bullets on November 20 at Washington. He was waived on December 16, 1985.

WHITEHEAD, JEROME

Jerome Whitehead was a 6-foot-10, 220-pound center for the Cavaliers in 1980-81. Traded from Dallas on October 30, 1980, he played three games with Cleveland. He was waived on November 17, 1980.

WILCOX, WES

Wes Wilcox was a Cavaliers assistant coach in 2004-05.

WILKENS, LENNY

Lenny Wilkens was a 6-foot-1, 180-pound point guard for the Cavaliers from 1972-73 to 1973-74. Traded from Seattle on August 23, 1972, in his two seasons with Cleveland he averaged 18.5 points, 7.7 assists, 4.2 rebounds, 1.3 steals, and .2 blocked shots per game. His best season as a Cavalier was 1972-73 when he averaged 20.5 points, 8.4 assists, and 4.6 rebounds per contest. He scored 36 points in a 108–93 victory over Los Angeles on January 6, 1973, at the Cleveland Arena. He was an All-Star in 1972-73. He was traded to Portland on October 7, 1974.

Wilkens was the Cavaliers' head coach from 1986-87 to 1992-93. He led the Cavs to postseason appearances in five of his seven years, including a pair of 57-win seasons in 1988-89 and 1991-92. Both times, they were ousted in the playoffs by Michael Jordan and the Bulls: in the first round in 1988-89—"The Shot"—and in the Eastern Conference Finals in 1991-92. Wilkens was the Eastern Conference head coach in the 1988-89 All-Star Game. He resigned after the 1992-93 season. His overall record as Cleveland's head coach was 316-258. His postseason mark was 18-23. He was inducted into the Naismith Memorial Basketball Hall of Fame as a player in 1989 and as a coach in 1998.

Lenny Wilkens dribbles past the Kings' Nate "Tiny" Archibald, 1973. (AndersonsClevelandDesign.com)

WILKERSON, BOBBY

Bobby Wilkerson was a 6-foot-6, 195-pound small forward for the Cavaliers from 1981-82 to 1982-83. Signed as a free agent on June 20, 1981, he averaged 8.7 points, 3.5 rebounds, three assists, 1.1 steals, and .3 blocked shots per game in his two seasons with Cleveland. His best season as a Cavalier was 1981-82 when he averaged 11 points, 3.8 rebounds, 3.6 assists, 1.4 steals, and .4 blocked shots per contest. He scored 28 points twice—in a 125–110 victory over the Mavericks in Dallas on November 3, 1981, and in a 119–107 defeat to New Jersey on December 19, 1981, at The Coliseum. He was waived on October 19, 1983.

WILKINS, GERALD

Gerald Wilkins was a 6-foot-6, 185-pound shooting guard and small forward for Cleveland from 1992-93 to 1993-94. Signed as a free agent on October 8, 1992, in his two seasons with the Cavs he averaged 12.7 points, 2.7 assists, 3.2 rebounds, 1.1 steals, and .3 blocked shots per game. His best season as a Cavalier was 1993-94 when he averaged 14.3 points, 3.1 assists, 3.7 rebounds, 1.3 steals, and .5 blocked shots per contest.

Wilkins scored 38 points in a 118–109 triumph over the Magic on January 12, 1994, at Orlando. He scored 28 points in a 105–96 playoff defeat to the Bulls on May 1, 1994, at Chicago. He was chosen by Vancouver in the 1995 Expansion Draft.

WILKS, MIKE

Mike Wilks was a 5-foot-10, 185-pound point guard for the Cavaliers in 2005-06. Signed as a free agent on September 27, 2005, in his one season with Cleveland he averaged 1.1 points, .5 assists, .7 rebounds, and .2 steals per game. He scored six points in a 92–84 loss to New York on January 10 at Quicken Loans Arena. He was traded to Seattle on February 23, 2006.

WILLIAMS, CHUCKIE

Chuckie Williams was a 6-foot-3, 180-pound shooting guard for the Cavaliers in 1976-77. Selected in the first round of the 1976 draft, in his one season with Cleveland he averaged 1.7 points, .3 assists, and .2 rebounds per game. He scored six points in a 116–96 loss to the 76ers in Philadelphia on January 7. He was waived on September 26, 1977.

WILLIAMS, ERIC

Eric Williams was a 6-foot-8, 220-pound small forward for the Cavaliers in 2003-04. Traded from Boston on December 15, 2003, in his one season with the Cavs he averaged 9.4 points, 3.8 rebounds, 1.9 assists, one steal, and .2 blocked shots per game. He scored 22 points in a 107–96 victory over the Knicks on January 6 at Gund Arena. He became a free agent on July 1, 2004, and was not re-signed.

WILLIAMS, JAWAD

Jawad Williams was a 6-foot-9, 218-pound small forward and point guard for the Cavaliers from 2008-09 to 2010-11. Signed on September 29, 2008, as a free agent, in his three seasons with the Cavs he averaged 3.8 points, 1.5 rebounds, .6 assists, .2 steals, and .1 blocked shots per game. His best season as a Cavalier was 2010-11 when he averaged four points, 1.8 rebounds, .8 assists, .3 steals, and .1 blocked shots per contest. He scored 17 points in a 104–97 win over the Nets on February 9, 2010, at Quicken Loans Arena. He was waived on December 27, 2010.

WILLIAMS, JOHN

John Williams was a 6-foot-11, 215-pound power forward and center for the Cavaliers from 1986-87 to 1994-95. He was a second-round draft choice in 1985 from Tulane University. In his nine seasons with the Cavs he averaged 12.9 points, 7.1 rebounds, 2.1 assists, .9 steals, and 1.8 blocked shots per game. His best season as a Cavalier was 1989-90 when he averaged 16.8 points, 8.1 rebounds, two assists, one steal, and two blocked shots per contest. In his rookie season with the Cavs he averaged 14.6 points, 7.9 rebounds, 1.9 assists, .7 steals, and 2.1 blocked shots per game. In 1993-94, he averaged 13.7 points, 7.6 rebounds, 2.5 assists, one steal, and 1.7 blocked shots per contest.

Williams scored 33 points in a 100–97 victory over the Pistons on April 8, 1990, at The Coliseum. He scored 32 points in a 120–101 win over the SuperSonics on December 15, 1989, also at The Coliseum. He had 23 points in a 111–106 playoff loss to the 76ers in Philadelphia on April 26, 1990. He was traded to Phoenix on October 7, 1995.

WILLIAMS, KEVIN

Kevin Williams was a 6-foot-2, 175-pound shooting guard for the Cavaliers in 1984-85. He was signed as a free agent on December 20, 1984. In his one season with Cleveland he averaged 3.5 points, 1.3 assists, 1.4 rebounds, .5 steals, and .1 blocked shots per game. He scored 13 points in a 109–108 overtime victory against the Knicks on April 12 at New York. He scored two points in a 117–115 playoff defeat to Boston on April 25 at The Coliseum. He was waived on September 17, 1985.

WILLIAMS, MO

Mo Williams was a 6-foot-1, 198-pound point guard for Cleveland from 2008-09 to 2010-11 and in 2015-16. He was traded from the Bucks on August 13, 2008. He was traded to the Clippers on February 24, 2011. He was re-signed as a free agent on July 10, 2015.

In his four seasons with the Cavs Williams averaged 14.8 points, 4.6 assists, 2.9 rebounds, .8 steals, and .2 blocked shots per game. His best season as a Cavalier was 2008-09 when he averaged 17.8 points, 4.1 assists, 3.4 rebounds, .9 steals, and .1 blocked shots per contest. He scored 44 points in a 109–92 victory over the Suns on February 11, 2009, at Quicken Loans Arena. He scored 24 points in the playoffs twice—in a 99–78 win over the Pistons on April 26, 2009, at Detroit and in a 112–102 triumph over the Magic on May 28, 2009, at Quicken Loans Arena. He was an All-Star in 2008-09. He retired on September 26, 2016.

WILLIAMS, REGGIE

Reggie Williams was a 6-foot-7, 190-pound small forward for the Cavaliers in 1989-90. Traded from the Clippers on November 16, 1989, in his one season with the Cavs he averaged 6.8 points, 1.9 rebounds, 1.2 assists, .7 steals, and .3 blocked shots per game. He scored 17 points in a 115–104 loss to the Hawks on December 25 at Atlanta. He was waived on February 26, 1990.

WILLIAMS, SCOTT

Scott Williams was a 6-foot-10, 230-pound center for the Cavaliers in 2004-05. Signed as a free agent on September 28, 2004, in 19 games with the Cavs he averaged 1.7 points, 1.6 rebounds, .4 assists, .2 steals, and .3 blocked shots per contest. He scored six points in a 92–86 triumph over the Grizzlies on December 13 in Memphis. He became a free agent again on July 1, 2005, and was not re-signed.

Williams was a Cavaliers local television broadcaster in 2005-06.

WILLOUGHBY, BILL

Bill Willoughby was a 6-foot-8, 205-pound small forward for the Cavaliers in 1979-80. Signed as a free agent on September 12, 1979, in his one season with Cleveland he averaged 6.9 points, 4.2 rebounds, .9 assists, .4 steals, and .8 blocked shots per game. He scored 20 points in a 110–103 loss to the Celtics on January 30 at Boston. He became a free agent again on July 1, 1980, and was not re-signed.

WILSON, MIKE

Mike Wilson was a 6-foot-4, 175-pound shooting guard for the Cavaliers in 1984-85. He was a third-round draft pick in 1982 out of Marquette University. He was waived on October 22, 1982. He was re-signed on waivers from Washington on November 16, 1984. In 11 games with the Cavs he averaged seven points, 2.2 assists, 1.6 rebounds, .9 steals, and .3 blocked shots per contest. He scored 13 points in a 107–106 loss to Golden State on November 23 at The Coliseum. He was waived again on December 14, 1984.

WINTERS, BRIAN

Brian Winters was a Cavaliers assistant coach from 1986-87 to 1992-93.

WITTE, LUKE

Luke Witte was a 7-foot, 235-pound center for the Cavaliers from 1973-74 to 1975-76. He was a fourth-round draft pick in 1973 from Ohio State University. In his three seasons with the Cavs he averaged 3.2 points, three rebounds, .5 assists, .1 steals, and .4 blocked shots per game. His best season as a Cavalier was 1973-74 when he averaged 4.5 points, four rebounds, .7 assists, .1 steals, and .4 blocked shots per contest.

Witte scored 17 points in a 111–110 overtime win against the Lakers on January 22, 1974, at Los Angeles. He scored six points in a 106–87 playoff victory over Boston on May 14, 1976, at The Coliseum. He became a free agent on July 1, 1976, and was not re-signed.

WITTMAN, RANDY

Randy Wittman was the Cavaliers' head coach from 1999-2000 to 2000-01. His 1999-2000 team began the season 11-9 but finished 32-50. His

2000-01 team started 15-7 but wound up 30-52. He was fired after the season. His overall record as Cleveland's head coach was 62-102.

WJKW-CHANNEL 8

WJKW-Channel 8 was the Cavaliers' local television station from 1977-78 to 1979-80.

WJW-CHANNEL 8

WJW-Channel 8 was the Cavaliers' local television station in 1976-77.

WLFM-LP FM 87.7

WLFM-LP FM 87.7 has been the Cavaliers' Spanish flagship radio station since 2014-15.

WOIO-CHANNEL 19

WOIO-Channel 19 was the Cavaliers' local television station in 1988-89 and a Cavs local television station from 1989-90 to 1993-94.

WOODSON, MIKE

Mike Woodson was a 6-foot-5, 195-pound shooting guard for the Cavaliers in 1990-91. Signed on December 13, 1990, as a free agent, he played four games with the Cavs. He was waived on December 24, 1990.

Woodson was a Cavaliers assistant coach from 1999-2000 to 2000-01.

WRIGHT, LORENZEN

Lorenzen Wright was a 6-foot-11, 225-pound center for the Cavaliers in 2008-09. Signed as a free agent on September 5, 2008, he averaged 1.4 points, 1.5 rebounds, .2 assists, .2 steals, and .3 blocked shots per contest in 17 games with Cleveland. He scored seven points in a 102–93 overtime defeat to the Bulls on January 15 at Chicago. He became a free agent again on July 1, 2009, and was not re-signed.

WRMR-AM 850

WRMR-AM 850 was the Cavaliers' flagship radio station from 1988-89 to 1989-90.

WRONG-WAY BASKET

Six years after Jim Marshall's infamous "wrong-way" 66-yard run that resulted in a safety for the San Francisco 49ers rather than a touchdown for Marshall's Minnesota Vikings, the Cavaliers' John Warren "accomplished" basketball's version of a wrong-way score. During a 109–102 loss to Portland on December 9, 1970, at the Cleveland Arena, Warren scored a basket for the Trail Blazers!

It happened at the beginning of the fourth quarter off the jump ball at center floor that was customary at the start of each quarter back then. Warren's teammate, Bobby Lewis, got possession of the ball and passed it up court to Warren, who went in for a layup . . . but in the Trail Blazers' basket! And Portland's Leroy Ellis tried to block the shot! Ellis got credit for the points. Even more amusing was that, while Warren went in for the layup, teammate Bingo Smith was standing in the corner begging for the ball! Those four or five seconds some 46 years ago in Portland, Oregon, will go down as perhaps the most embarrassing in Cavs history.

WTAM-AM 1100

WTAM-AM 1100 has been the Cavaliers' flagship radio station since 1996-97.

WUAB-CHANNEL 43

WUAB-Channel 43 was the Cavaliers' local television station from 1980-81 to 1987-88 and a Cavs local television station since 1994-95.

WWWE-AM 1100

WWWE-AM 1100 was the Cavaliers' flagship radio station from 1973-74 to 1980-81, 1984-85 to 1987-88, and 1990-91 to 1995-96.

X

X-RAYS

The following are five notable injuries to Cavaliers players:

Austin Carr (1974-75) – Some two months into the season, Carr suffered a right knee injury that sidelined him for about half the schedule, which likely cost the Cavs a postseason berth. It also kept him from perhaps attaining true greatness in the NBA.

Jim Chones (1975-76) – In a practice session two days before the Cavaliers' opening game of their Eastern Conference Finals series against Boston, Chones broke his right foot, which ended his season. Many observers opine that, had the injury not occurred, Cleveland would have won the NBA Championship.

Campy Russell (1979-80) – About halfway through the schedule, Russell suffered a season-ending injury, which likely kept the Cavs out of the playoffs.

Jeff McInnis (2003-04) – A late-season injury to McInnis headed the red-hot Cavs on a downhill slide. They barely missed the playoffs.

Kevin Love (2014-15) – Love suffered a dislocated left shoulder early in Cleveland's Game 4 matchup with the Celtics in the first round of the playoffs. Many observers believe that his injury was a huge factor in the Cavaliers' falling just short of the NBA title.

Y

YULETIDE CHEER (CAVS ON CHRISTMAS)

Please see Team Statistics on page 215.

Z

ZELLER, TYLER

Tyler Zeller was a 7-foot, 253-pound center for the Cavaliers from 2012-13 to 2013-14. Traded from Dallas on June 29, 2012, in his two seasons with the Cavs he averaged 6.9 points, 4.9 rebounds, .9 assists, .4 steals, and .7 blocked shots per game. His best season as a Cavalier was 2012-13 when he averaged 7.9 points, 5.7 rebounds, 1.2 assists, .5 steals, and .9 blocked shots per contest. He scored 23 points in a 118–111 loss to Houston on March 22, 2014, at Quicken Loans Arena. He was traded to the Celtics on July 10, 2014.

INDIVIDUAL STATISTICS

REGULAR SEASON

TOP TENS (SEASON)

MINUTES

1. LeBron James	3,388	(2004-05)
2. LeBron James	3,361	(2005-06)
3. Wesley Person	3,198	(1997-98)
4. Mike Mitchell	3,194	(1980-81)
5. LeBron James	3,190	(2006-07)
6. Chris Mills	3,167	(1996-97)
7. Ricky Davis	3,131	(2002-03)
8. LeBron James	3,122	(2003-04)
9. Austin Carr	3,100	(1973-74)
10. Austin Carr	3,097	(1972-73)

POINTS

1. LeBron James	2,478	(2005-06)
2. LeBron James	2,304	(2008-09)
3. LeBron James	2,258	(2009-10)
4. LeBron James	2,250	(2007-08)
5. LeBron James	2,175	(2004-05)
6. LeBron James	2,132	(2006-07)
7. Mike Mitchell	2,012	(1980-81)
8. LeBron James	1,920	(2015-16)
9. Ron Harper	1,874	(1986-87)
10. Mike Mitchell	1,820	(1979-80)

SCORING AVERAGE

1. LeBron James	31.4	(2005-06)
2. LeBron James	30	(2007-08)
3. LeBron James	29.7	(2009-10)
4. LeBron James	28.4	(2008-09)
5. LeBron James	27.3	(2006-07)
6. LeBron James	27.2	(2004-05)
7. LeBron James	25.3	(2014-15)
8. LeBron James	25.3	(2015-16)
9. Mike Mitchell	24.5	(1980-81)
10. World B. Free	24.2	(1982-83)

FIELD GOALS

1. LeBron James	875	(2005-06)
2. Mike Mitchell	853	(1980-81)
3. LeBron James	795	(2004-05)
4. LeBron James	794	(2007-08)
5. LeBron James	789	(2008-09)
6. Mike Mitchell	775	(1979-80)
7. LeBron James	772	(2006-07)
8. LeBron James	768	(2009-10)
9. Austin Carr	748	(1973-74)
10. LeBron James	737	(2015-16)

FIELD GOAL ATTEMPTS

1. LeBron James	1,823	(2005-06)
2. Mike Mitchell	1,791	(1980-81)
3. LeBron James	1,684	(2004-05)
4. Austin Carr	1,682	(1973-74)
5. LeBron James	1,642	(2007-08)

6. LeBron James	1,621	(2006-07)
7. Ron Harper	1,614	(1986-87)
8. LeBron James	1,613	(2008-09)
9. Austin Carr	1,575	(1972-73)
10. LeBron James	1,528	(2009-10)

FIELD GOAL PERCENTAGE (MINIMUM 200 FIELD GOALS MADE)

1. Tyrone Hill	.600	(1996-97)
2. Tristan Thompson	.588	(2015-16)
3. Anderson Varejao	.572	(2009-10)
4. Brad Daugherty	.571	(1992-93)
5. Brad Daugherty	.570	(1991-92)
6. Shaquille O'Neal	.566	(2009-10)
7. Timofey Mozgov	.565	(2015-16)
8. Michael Cage	.556	(1995-96)
9. J. J. Hickson	.554	(2009-10)
10. Larry Nance	.549	(1992-93)

FREE THROWS MADE

1. LeBron James	601	(2005-06)
2. LeBron James	594	(2008-09)
3. LeBron James	593	(2009-10)
4. LeBron James	549	(2007-08)
5. Shawn Kemp	493	(1999-2000)
6. LeBron James	489	(2006-07)
7. LeBron James	477	(2004-05)
8. Brad Daugherty	435	(1990-91)
9. Campy Russell	417	(1978-79)
10. Brad Daugherty	414	(1991-92)

FREE THROW ATTEMPTS

1. LeBron James	814	(2005-06)
2. LeBron James	773	(2009-10)
3. LeBron James	771	(2007-08)
4. LeBron James	762	(2008-09)
5. LeBron James	701	(2006-07)
6. LeBron James	636	(2004-05)
7. Shawn Kemp	635	(1999-2000)
8. Brad Daugherty	579	(1990-91)
9. Ron Harper	564	(1986-87)
10. Shawn Kemp	556	(1997-98)

FREE THROW PERCENTAGE (MINIMUM 100 FREE THROWS MADE)

1. Mark Price	.948	(1992-93)
2. Mark Price	.947	(1991-92)
3. Mark Price	.914	(1994-95)
4. Mo Williams	.912	(2008-09)
5. Terrell Brandon	.902	(1996-97)
6. Mark Price	.901	(1988-89)
7. Mo Williams	.894	(2009-10)
8. Mark Price	.888	(1989-90)
9. Mark Price	.888	(1993-94)
10. Terrell Brandon	.887	(1995-96)

THREE-POINT FIELD GOALS

1. J. R. Smith	204	(2015-16)
2. Wesley Person	192	(1997-98)
3. Mo Williams	183	(2008-09)
4. Mo Williams	159	(2009-10)
5. Kevin Love	158	(2015-16)
6. Kyrie Irving	157	(2014-15)
7. Mark Price	152	(1989-90)
8. Dan Majerle	146	(1995-96)
9. Kevin Love	144	(2014-15)
10. Danny Ferry	143	(1995-96)
11. Wesley Person	143	(2001-02)

THREE-POINT FIELD GOAL ATTEMPTS

1. J. R. Smith	510	(2015-16)
2. Wesley Person	447	(1997-98)
3. Kevin Love	439	(2015-16)
4. Mo Williams	420	(2008-09)
5. Dan Majerle	414	(1995-96)
6. Donyell Marshall	395	(2005-06)
7. Kevin Love	392	(2014-15)
8. LeBron James	387	(2009-10)
9. LeBron James	384	(2008-09)
10. LeBron James	379	(2005-06)

THREE-POINT FIELD GOAL PERCENTAGE (MINIMUM 25 THREE-POINT FIELD GOALS MADE)

1. Steve Kerr	.507	(1989-90)
2. Mark Price	.486	(1987-88)
3. Daniel Gibson	.477	(2009-10)
4. Steve Kerr	.452	(1990-91)
5. Spencer Hawes	.448	(2013-14)
6. Wesley Person	.444	(2001-02)
7. Mark Price	.441	(1988-89)
8. Bobby Phills	.441	(1995-96)
9. Danny Ferry	.440	(1999-2000)
10. Daniel Gibson	.440	(2007-08)

REBOUNDS

1. Jim Brewer	891	(1975-76)
2. Carlos Boozer	857	(2003-04)
3. Cliff Robinson	856	(1982-83)
4. Jim Chones	844	(1977-78)
5. Jim Chones	842	(1978-79)
6. Kenny Carr	835	(1980-81)
7. Brad Daugherty	830	(1990-91)
8. Rick Roberson	801	(1971-72)
9. Clarence Weatherspoon	796	(2000-01)
10. Tristan Thompson	773	(2012-13)

DEFENSIVE REBOUNDS

1. Cliff Robinson	666	(1982-83)
2. Brad Daugherty	653	(1990-91)
3. Carlos Boozer	627	(2003-04)
4. Jim Chones	625	(1977-78)
5. Kevin Love	613	(2015-16)
6. Cliff Robinson	597	(1983-84)
7. Jim Brewer	593	(1975-76)
8. Kevin Love	589	(2014-15)
9. Jim Chones	582	(1978-79)
10. Kenny Carr	575	(1980-81)

OFFENSIVE REBOUNDS

1. Tristan Thompson	306	(2012-13)
2. Zydrunas Ilgauskas	299	(2004-05)
3. Jim Brewer	298	(1975-76)
4. Michael Cage	288	(1995-96)
5. Zydrunas Ilgauskas	279	(1997-98)
6. Zydrunas Ilgauskas	279	(2003-04)
7. Jim Brewer	275	(1976-77)
8. Tristan Thompson	274	(2014-15)
9. Tyrone Hill	269	(1994-95)
10. Tristan Thompson	269	(2013-14)

REBOUNDING AVERAGE (MINIMUM 800 REBOUNDS OR 70 GAMES)

1. Rick Roberson	12.7	(1971-72)
2. Carlos Boozer	11.4	(2003-04)
3. Cliff Robinson	11.1	(1982-83)
4. Jim Brewer	10.9	(1975-76)
5. Brad Daugherty	10.9	(1990-91)
6. Tyrone Hill	10.9	(1994-95)
7. Brad Daugherty	10.4	(1991-92)
8. Jim Chones	10.3	(1977-78)
9. Jim Chones	10.3	(1978-79)
10. Kenny Carr	10.3	(1980-81)
11. Cliff Robinson	10.3	(1983-84)

FOULS

1. Shawn Kemp	371	(1999-2000)
2. James Edwards	347	(1981-82)
3. Bill Laimbeer	332	(1980-81)
4. Roy Hinson	316	(1985-86)
5. Zydrunas Ilgauskas	313	(2004-05)
6. Roy Hinson	311	(1984-85)
7. Shawn Kemp	310	(1997-98)
8. Roy Hinson	306	(1983-84)
9. John Warren	299	(1970-71)
10. Dwight Davis	297	(1972-73)

DISQUALIFICATIONS

1. James Edwards	17	(1981-82)
2. Shawn Kemp	15	(1997-98)
3. Bill Laimbeer	14	(1980-81)
4. John Warren	13	(1970-71)
5. Roy Hinson	13	(1984-85)
6. Shawn Kemp	13	(1999-2000)
7. Phil Hubbard	11	(1982-83)
8. Roy Hinson	11	(1983-84)
9. Steve Hayes	9	(1982-83)
10. Lonnie Shelton	9	(1983-84)
11. Keith Lee	9	(1985-86)

ASSISTS

1. Andre Miller	882	(2001-02)
2. John Bagley	735	(1985-86)
3. John Bagley	697	(1984-85)
4. Mark Price	666	(1989-90)
5. Andre Miller	657	(2000-01)
6. Brevin Knight	656	(1997-98)
7. LeBron James	651	(2009-10)
8. Mark Price	631	(1988-89)
9. Lenny Wilkens	628	(1972-73)
10. Foots Walker	607	(1979-80)

STEALS

1. Ron Harper	209	(1986-87)
2. Brevin Knight	196	(1997-98)
3. Ron Harper	185	(1988-89)
4. LeBron James	177	(2004-05)
5. Foots Walker	176	(1977-78)
6. Foots Walker	155	(1979-80)
7. Terrell Brandon	138	(1996-97)
8. LeBron James	138	(2007-08)
9. LeBron James	137	(2008-09)
10. Mike Bratz	136	(1980-81)

BLOCKED SHOTS

1. Larry Nance	243	(1991-92)
2. Larry Nance	206	(1988-89)
3. Zydrunas Ilgauskas	201	(2003-04)
4. Larry Nance	200	(1990-91)
5. Larry Nance	198	(1992-93)
6. John Williams	182	(1991-92)

7. Elmore Smith	176 (1977-78)
8. Roy Hinson	173 (1984-85)
9. John Williams	167 (1986-87)
10. John Williams	167 (1989-90)

TURNOVERS

1. Ron Harper	345 (1986-87)
2. Shawn Kemp	291 (1999-2000)
3. Ricky Davis	277 (2002-03)
4. LeBron James	273 (2003-04)
5. LeBron James	272 (2014-15)
6. Shawn Kemp	271 (1997-98)
7. Brad Daugherty	267 (1987-88)
8. Andre Miller	265 (2000-01)
9. LeBron James	262 (2004-05)
10. LeBron James	261 (2009-10)

TOP TENS (CAREER)

SEASONS PLAYED

1. Zydrunas Ilgauskas	12
2. Anderson Varejao	12
3. Danny Ferry	10
4. Bingo Smith	10
5. Austin Carr	9
6. LeBron James	9
7. Mark Price	9
8. John Williams	9
9. Brad Daugherty	8
10. Phil Hubbard	8

GAMES PLAYED

1. Zydrunas Ilgauskas	771
2. Danny Ferry	723
3. Bingo Smith	720
4. LeBron James	693
5. John Williams	661
6. Austin Carr	635
7. Anderson Varejao	591
8. Mark Price	582
9. Brad Daugherty	548
10. Craig Ehlo	513

POINTS

1. LeBron James	18,914
2. Zydrunas Ilgauskas	10,616
3. Brad Daugherty	10,389
4. Austin Carr	10,265
5. Mark Price	9,543
6. Bingo Smith	9,513
7. John Williams	8,504
8. Larry Nance	7,257
9. Campy Russell	6,588
10. Kyrie Irving	6,416

SCORING AVERAGE (MINIMUM 120 GAMES)

1. LeBron James	27.3
2. World B. Free	23
3. Kyrie Irving	20.8
4. Ron Harper	19.4
5. Mike Mitchell	19.3
6. Brad Daugherty	19
7. Shawn Kemp	18.5
8. Lenny Wilkens	18.5
9. Cliff Robinson	17.7
10. Antawn Jamison	17.3

FIELD GOALS

1. LeBron James	6,776
2. Austin Carr	4,272
3. Bingo Smith	4,182
4. Zydrunas Ilgauskas	4,045
5. Brad Daugherty	3,823
6. Mark Price	3,429
7. John Williams	3,198
8. Larry Nance	2,945
9. Campy Russell	2,480
10. Jim Chones	2,456

FIELD GOAL ATTEMPTS

1. LeBron James	14,098
2. Austin Carr	9,480
3. Bingo Smith	9,256
4. Zydrunas Ilgauskas	8,523
5. Brad Daugherty	7,189
6. Mark Price	7,165
7. John Williams	6,633
8. Larry Nance	5,559
9. Campy Russell	5,444
10. Jim Chones	5,332

FIELD GOAL PERCENTAGE (MINIMUM TWO SEASONS AND 600 FIELD GOALS)

1. Mark West	.553
2. Brad Daugherty	.532
3. Larry Nance	.530
4. Carlos Boozer	.528
5. Tyrone Hill	.521
6. Roy Hinson	.516
7. Melvin Turpin	.516
8. Anderson Varejao	.512
9. James Edwards	.508
10. Kenny Carr	.506

FREE THROWS MADE

1. LeBron James	4,384
2. Brad Daugherty	2,741
3. Zydrunas Ilgauskas	2,495
4. John Williams	2,106
5. Mark Price	1,883
6. Austin Carr	1,719
7. Campy Russell	1,627
8. World B. Free	1,406
9. Larry Nance	1,364
10. Phil Hubbard	1,318

FREE THROW ATTEMPTS

1. LeBron James	5,936
2. Brad Daugherty	3,670
3. Zydrunas Ilgauskas	3,197
4. John Williams	2,884
5. Austin Carr	2,127
6. Campy Russell	2,113
7. Mark Price	2,078
8. Phil Hubbard	1,858
9. World B. Free	1,835
10. Larry Nance	1,696

FREE THROW PERCENTAGE (MINIMUM 150 FREE THROWS MADE)

1. Mark Price	.906
2. Mo Williams	.891
3. Terrell Brandon	.868
4. Kyrie Irving	.865
5. C. J. Miles	.863
6. Derek Anderson	.860
7. James Silas	.860

8.	Terry Furlow	.853
9.	Steve Kerr	.852
10.	Johnny Davis	.850

THREE-POINT FIELD GOALS

1.	LeBron James	978
2.	Mark Price	802
3.	Daniel Gibson	578
4.	Wesley Person	550
5.	Kyrie Irving	546
6.	Danny Ferry	543
7.	Mo Williams	414
8.	Craig Ehlo	381
9.	Damon Jones	344
10.	J. R. Smith	335

THREE-POINT FIELD GOAL ATTEMPTS

1.	LeBron James	2,965
2.	Mark Price	1,960
3.	Kyrie Irving	1,445
4.	Daniel Gibson	1,419
5.	Danny Ferry	1,409
6.	Wesley Person	1,303
7.	Mo Williams	1,029
8.	Craig Ehlo	1,001
9.	Damon Jones	878
10.	J. R. Smith	846

THREE-POINT FIELD GOAL PERCENTAGE (MINIMUM 50 THREE-POINT FIELD GOALS)

1.	Steve Kerr	.472
2.	Wesley Person	.422
3.	Mark Price	.409
4.	Daniel Gibson	.407
5.	Mo Williams	.402
6.	Wally Szczerbiak	.400
7.	Bobby Phills	.399
8.	Matthew Dellavedova	.398
9.	Trajan Langdon	.396
10.	J. R. Smith	.396

REBOUNDS

1.	Zydrunas Ilgauskas	5,904
2.	Brad Daugherty	5,227
3.	LeBron James	4,842
4.	John Williams	4,669
5.	Anderson Varejao	4,434
6.	Jim Chones	3,790
7.	Larry Nance	3,561
8.	Jim Brewer	3,551
9.	Tristan Thompson	3,311
10.	Bingo Smith	3,057

DEFENSIVE REBOUNDS

1.	Brad Daugherty	4,020
2.	LeBron James	4,002
3.	Zydrunas Ilgauskas	3,568
4.	John Williams	3,049
5.	Anderson Varejao	2,955
6.	Jim Chones	2,750
7.	Larry Nance	2,494
8.	Jim Brewer	2,259
9.	Tristan Thompson	2,007
10.	Tyrone Hill	1,830

OFFENSIVE REBOUNDS

1.	Zydrunas Ilgauskas	2,336
2.	John Williams	1,620

3. Anderson Varejao	1,479
4. Tristan Thompson	1,304
5. Jim Brewer	1,292
6. Brad Daugherty	1,207
7. Larry Nance	1,067
8. Phil Hubbard	1,051
9. Jim Chones	1,040
10. Tyrone Hill	955

ASSISTS

1. LeBron James	4,835
2. Mark Price	4,206
3. John Bagley	2,311
4. Terrell Brandon	2,235
5. Foots Walker	2,115
6. Brad Daugherty	2,028
7. Andre Miller	2,015
8. Austin Carr	1,820
9. Craig Ehlo	1,803
10. Kyrie Irving	1,696

FOULS

1. Zydrunas Ilgauskas	2,591
2. Bingo Smith	1,752
3. John Williams	1,720
4. Danny Ferry	1,670
5. Anderson Varejao	1,579
6. Brad Daugherty	1,466
7. Phil Hubbard	1,378
8. LeBron James	1,348
9. Austin Carr	1,341
10. Jim Chones	1,259

DISQUALIFICATIONS

1. Zydrunas Ilgauskas	37
2. Phil Hubbard	33
3. Roy Hinson	31
4. Shawn Kemp	30
5. Tyrone Hill	25
6. James Edwards	20
7. Mark West	20
8. Jim Chones	18
9. Bingo Smith	18
10. Bill Laimbeer	17

STEALS

1. LeBron James	1,168
2. Mark Price	734
3. Foots Walker	722
4. Craig Ehlo	661
5. Terrell Brandon	621
6. John Williams	587
7. Ron Harper	530
8. Anderson Varejao	529
9. John Bagley	474
10. Brad Daugherty	422

BLOCKED SHOTS

1. Zydrunas Ilgauskas	1,269
2. John Williams	1,200
3. Larry Nance	1,087
4. LeBron James	580
5. Jim Chones	450
6. Roy Hinson	430
7. Brad Daugherty	397
8. Anderson Varejao	397
9. Jim Brewer	353
10. Mark West	325

MINUTES

1.	LeBron James	27,310
2.	Zydrunas Ilgauskas	21,820
3.	John Williams	20,802
4.	Brad Daugherty	20,029
5.	Bingo Smith	19,221
6.	Austin Carr	19,003
7.	Mark Price	18,127
8.	Danny Ferry	15,045
9.	Larry Nance	14,966
10.	Anderson Varejao	14,773

TURNOVERS

1.	LeBron James	2,323
2.	Brad Daugherty	1,511
3.	Zydrunas Ilgauskas	1,457
4.	Mark Price	1,457
5.	John Williams	1,038
6.	John Bagley	897
7.	Phil Hubbard	862
8.	Kyrie Irving	851
9.	Craig Ehlo	833
10.	Terrell Brandon	818

SEASON LEADERS

GAMES

1970-71 – John Warren, Walt Wesley (82)
1971-72 – Three tied (82)
1972-73 – Austin Carr, John Johnson (82)
1973-74 – Jim Brewer, Bingo Smith (82)
1974-75 – Three tied (82)
1975-76 – Five tied (82)
1976-77 – Three tied (82)
1977-78 – Three tied (82)
1978-79 – Austin Carr, Jim Chones (82)
1979-80 – Three tied (82)
1980-81 – Three tied (82)
1981-82 – Geoff Huston (78)
1982-83 – Phil Hubbard (82)
1983-84 – Paul Thompson (82)
1984-85 – John Bagley (81)
1985-86 – Roy Hinson (82)
1986-87 – Ron Harper (82)
1987-88 – Mark Price (80)
1988-89 – Four tied (82)
1989-90 – John Williams (82)
1990-91 – Craig Ehlo (82)
1991-92 – Terrell Brandon (82)
1992-93 – Terrell Brandon, Craig Ehlo (82)
1993-94 – Gerald Wilkins (82)
1994-95 – Michael Cage, Danny Ferry (82)
1995-96 – Three tied (82)
1996-97 – Danny Ferry, Bob Sura (82)
1997-98 – Three tied (82)
1998-99 – Four tied (50)
1999-2000 – Three tied (82)
2000-01 – Andre Miller, Clarence Weatherspoon (82)
2001-02 – Ricky Davis (82)
2002-03 – Carlos Boozer, Zydrunas Ilgauskas (81)
2003-04 – Kevin Ollie (82)
2004-05 – Drew Gooden (82)
2005-06 – Damon Jones, Eric Snow (82)

2006-07 – Eric Snow (82)
2007-08 – Devin Brown (78)
2008-09 – Three tied (82)
2009-10 – J. J. Hickson, Anthony Parker (81)
2010-11 – Ramon Sessions (81)
2011-12 – Omri Casspi, Antawn Jamison (65)
2012-13 – Alonzo Gee, Tristan Thompson (82)
2013-14 – Tristan Thompson (82)
2014-15 – Tristan Thompson (82)
2015-16 – Tristan Thompson (82)

MINUTES

1970-71 – John Warren (2,610)
1971-72 – John Johnson (3,041)
1972-73 – Austin Carr (3,097)
1973-74 – Austin Carr (3,100)
1974-75 – Jim Cleamons (2,691)
1975-76 – Jim Brewer (2,913)
1976-77 – Jim Brewer (2,672)
1977-78 – Jim Chones (2,906)
1978-79 – Campy Russell (2,859)
1979-80 – Mike Mitchell (2,802)
1980-81 – Mike Mitchell (3,194)
1981-82 – James Edwards (2,539)
1982-83 – Geoff Huston (2,716)
1983-84 – Cliff Robinson (2,402)
1984-85 – John Bagley (2,401)
1985-86 – Roy Hinson (2,834)
1986-87 – Ron Harper (3,064)
1987-88 – Brad Daugherty (2,957)
1988-89 – Ron Harper (2,851)
1989-90 – Craig Ehlo (2,894)
1990-91 – Brad Daugherty (2,946)
1991-92 – Larry Nance (2,880)
1992-93 – Larry Nance (2,753)
1993-94 – Gerald Wilkins (2,768)
1994-95 – Chris Mills (2,814)
1995-96 – Chris Mills (3,060)
1996-97 – Chris Mills (3,167)
1997-98 – Wesley Person (3,198)
1998-99 – Cedric Henderson (1,517)
1999-2000 – Shawn Kemp (2,492)
2000-01 – Andre Miller (2,848)
2001-02 – Andre Miller (3,023)
2002-03 – Ricky Davis (3,131)
2003-04 – LeBron James (3,122)
2004-05 – LeBron James (3,388)
2005-06 – LeBron James (3,361)
2006-07 – LeBron James (3,190)
2007-08 – LeBron James (3,027)
2008-09 – LeBron James (3,054)
2009-10 – LeBron James (2,966)
2010-11 – J. J. Hickson (2,256)
2011-12 – Antawn Jamison (2,149)
2012-13 – Tristan Thompson (2,564)
2013-14 – Tristan Thompson (2,594)
2014-15 – Kyrie Irving (2,730)
2015-16 – LeBron James (2,709)

FIELD GOALS

1970-71 – Walt Wesley (565)
1971-72 – John Johnson (557)
1972-73 – Austin Carr (702)
1973-74 – Austin Carr (748)
1974-75 – Bingo Smith (585)
1975-76 – Jim Chones (563)
1976-77 – Austin Carr (558)
1977-78 – Jim Chones (525)
1978-79 – Campy Russell (603)
1979-80 – Mike Mitchell (775)
1980-81 – Mike Mitchell (853)
1981-82 – James Edwards (528)
1982-83 – Cliff Robinson (587)

1983-84 – World B. Free (626)
1984-85 – World B. Free (609)
1985-86 – World B. Free (652)
1986-87 – Ron Harper (734)
1987-88 – Brad Daugherty (551)
1988-89 – Ron Harper (587)
1989-90 – John Williams (528)
1990-91 – Larry Nance (635)
1991-92 – Brad Daugherty (576)
1992-93 – Larry Nance (533)
1993-94 – Mark Price (480)
1994-95 – John Williams (366)
1995-96 – Terrell Brandon (510)
1996-97 – Terrell Brandon (575)
1997-98 – Shawn Kemp (518)
1998-99 – Shawn Kemp (277)
1999-2000 – Shawn Kemp (484)
2000-01 – Andre Miller (452)
2001-02 – Andre Miller (474)
2002-03 – Ricky Davis (602)
2003-04 – LeBron James (622)
2004-05 – LeBron James (795)
2005-06 – LeBron James (875)
2006-07 – LeBron James (772)
2007-08 – LeBron James (794)
2008-09 – LeBron James (789)
2009-10 – LeBron James (768)
2010-11 – J. J. Hickson (429)
2011-12 – Antawn Jamison (421)
2012-13 – Kyrie Irving (484)
2013-14 – Kyrie Irving (532)
2014-15 – LeBron James (624)
2015-16 – LeBron James (737)

FIELD GOAL ATTEMPTS

1970-71 – Walt Wesley (1,241)
1971-72 – John Johnson (1,286)
1972-73 – Austin Carr (1,575)
1973-74 – Austin Carr (1,682)
1974-75 – Bingo Smith (1,212)
1975-76 – Jim Chones (1,258)
1976-77 – Austin Carr (1,221)
1977-78 – Campy Russell (1,168)
1978-79 – Campy Russell (1,268)
1979-80 – Mike Mitchell (1,482)
1980-81 – Mike Mitchell (1,741)
1981-82 – James Edwards (1,033)
1982-83 – Cliff Robinson (1,230)
1983-84 – World B. Free (1,407)
1984-85 – World B. Free (1,328)
1985-86 – World B. Free (1,433)
1986-87 – Ron Harper (1,614)
1987-88 – Brad Daugherty (1,081)
1988-89 – Ron Harper (1,149)
1989-90 – John Williams (1,070)
1990-91 – Larry Nance (1,211)
1991-92 – Brad Daugherty (1,010)
1992-93 – Mark Price (986)
1993-94 – Mark Price (1,005)
1994-95 – Chris Mills (855)
1995-96 – Terrell Brandon (1,096)
1996-97 – Terrell Brandon (1,313)
1997-98 – Shawn Kemp (1,164)
1998-99 – Shawn Kemp (575)
1999-2000 – Shawn Kemp (1,160)
2000-01 – Andre Miller (999)
2001-02 – Andre Miller (1,045)
2002-03 – Ricky Davis (1,470)
2003-04 – LeBron James (1,492)
2004-05 – LeBron James (1,684)
2005-06 – LeBron James (1,823)
2006-07 – LeBron James (1,621)
2007-08 – LeBron James (1,642)
2008-09 – LeBron James (1,613)
2009-10 – LeBron James (1,528)
2010-11 – J. J. Hickson (936)
2011-12 – Antawn Jamison (1,044)

2012-13 – Kyrie Irving (1,070)
2013-14 – Kyrie Irving (1,237)
2014-15 – LeBron James (1,279)
2015-16 – LeBron James (1,416)

FIELD GOAL PERCENTAGE

1970-71 – Walt Wesley (.455)
1971-72 – Butch Beard (.464)
1972-73 – Lenny Wilkens (.449)
1973-74 – Lenny Wilkens (.465)
1974-75 – Dick Snyder (.504)
1975-76 – Dick Snyder (.501)
1976-77 – Jim Chones (.463)
1977-78 – Elmore Smith (.497)
1978-79 – Mike Mitchell (.513)
1979-80 – Mike Mitchell (.523)
1980-81 – Kenny Carr (.511)
1981-82 – James Edwards (.511)
1982-83 – Phil Hubbard (.482)
1983-84 – Phil Hubbard (.511)
1984-85 – Melvin Turpin (.511)
1985-86 – Melvin Turpin (.544)
1986-87 – Mark West (.543)
1987-88 – Brad Daugherty (.510)
1988-89 – Larry Nance (.539)
1989-90 – Larry Nance (.511)
1990-91 – Larry Nance (.524)
1991-92 – Brad Daugherty (.570)
1992-93 – Brad Daugherty (.571)
1993-94 – Tyrone Hill (.543)
1994-95 – Tyrone Hill (.504)
1995-96 – Michael Cage (.556)
1996-97 – Tyrone Hill (.600)
1997-98 – Zydrunas Ilgauskas (.518)
1998-99 – Shawn Kemp (.482)
1999-2000 – Andrew DeClercq (.508)
2000-01 – Clarence Weatherspoon (.501)
2001-02 – Wesley Person (.495)
2002-03 – Carlos Boozer (.536)
2003-04 – Carlos Boozer (.523)
2004-05 – Anderson Varejao (.513)
2005-06 – Drew Gooden (.512)
2006-07 – Zydrunas Ilgauskas (.485)
2007-08 – LeBron James (.484)
2008-09 – Anderson Varejao (.536)
2009-10 – Anderson Varejao (.572)
2010-11 – Ryan Hollins (.598)
2011-12 – Semih Erden (.527)
2012-13 – Shaun Livingston (.507)
2013-14 – Tyler Zeller (.538)
2014-15 – Timofey Mozgov (.590)
2015-16 – Tristan Thompson (.588)

THREE-POINT FIELD GOALS

1979-80 – Willie Smith (17)
1980-81 – Mike Bratz (57)
1981-82 – Ron Brewer, Scott Wedman (5)
1982-83 – World B. Free (15)
1983-84 – World B. Free (22)
1984-85 – World B. Free (71)
1985-86 – World B. Free (71)
1986-87 – John Bagley (31)
1987-88 – Mark Price (72)
1988-89 – Mark Price (93)
1989-90 – Mark Price (152)
1990-91 – Craig Ehlo (49)
1991-92 – Mark Price (101)
1992-93 – Mark Price (122)
1993-94 – Mark Price (118)
1994-95 – Mark Price (103)
1995-96 – Dan Majerle (146)
1996-97 – Danny Ferry (114)
1997-98 – Wesley Person (192)
1998-99 – Wesley Person (75)

1999-2000 – Bob Sura (122)
2000-01 – Lamond Murray (61)
2001-02 – Wesley Person (143)
2002-03 – Jumaine Jones (111)
2003-04 – LeBron James (63)
2004-05 – LeBron James (108)
2005-06 – Damon Jones (140)
2006-07 – LeBron James (99)
2007-08 – Daniel Gibson (118)
2008-09 – Mo Williams (183)
2009-10 – Mo Williams (159)
2010-11 – Daniel Gibson (118)
2011-12 – Antawn Jamison (91)
2012-13 – C. J. Miles (126)
2013-14 – Kyrie Irving (123)
2014-15 – Kyrie Irving (157)
2015-16 – J. R. Smith (204)

THREE-POINT FIELD GOAL ATTEMPTS

1979-80 – Willie Smith (71)
1980-81 – Mike Bratz (169)
1981-82 – Scott Wedman (23)
1982-83 – World B. Free (42)
1983-84 – World B. Free (69)
1984-85 – World B. Free (193)
1985-86 – World B. Free (169)
1986-87 – John Bagley (103)
1987-88 – Mark Price (148)
1988-89 – Mark Price (211)
1989-90 – Mark Price (374)
1990-91 – Craig Ehlo (149)
1991-92 – Mark Price (261)
1992-93 – Mark Price (293)
1993-94 – Mark Price (297)
1994-95 – Mark Price (253)
1995-96 – Dan Majerle (414)
1996-97 – Danny Ferry (284)
1997-98 – Wesley Person (447)
1998-99 – Wesley Person (200)
1999-2000 – Bob Sura (332)
2000-01 – Lamond Murray (165)
2001-02 – Wesley Person (322)
2002-03 – Jumaine Jones (314)
2003-04 – LeBron James (217)
2004-05 – LeBron James (308)
2005-06 – Donyell Marshall (395)
2006-07 – LeBron James (310)
2007-08 – LeBron James (359)
2008-09 – Mo Williams (420)
2009-10 – LeBron James (387)
2010-11 – Daniel Gibson (293)
2011-12 – Antawn Jamison (267)
2012-13 – C. J. Miles (328)
2013-14 – Kyrie Irving (344)
2014-15 – Kevin Love (392)
2015-16 – J. R. Smith (510)

THREE-POINT FIELD GOAL PERCENTAGE (MINIMUM 25 THREE-POINT FIELD GOALS MADE)

1980-81 – Mike Bratz (.337)
1984-85 – World B. Free (.368)
1985-86 – World B. Free (.420)
1986-87 – John Bagley (.301)
1987-88 – Mark Price (.486)
1988-89 – Mark Price (.411)
1989-90 – Steve Kerr (.507)
1990-91 – Steve Kerr (.452)
1991-92 – Steve Kerr (.432)
1992-93 – Mark Price (.416)
1993-94 – Mark Price (.397)
1994-95 – Mark Price (.407)
1995-96 – Bobby Phills (.441)
1996-97 – Danny Ferry (.401)

1997-98 – Wesley Person (.430)
1998-99 – Danny Ferry (.392)
1999-2000 – Danny Ferry (.440)
2000-01 – Trajan Langdon (.411)
2001-02 – Wesley Person (.444)
2002-03 – Ricky Davis (.363)
2003-04 – Kedrick Brown, Jeff McInnis (.388)
2004-05 – Sasha Pavlovic (.385)
2005-06 – Damon Jones (.377)
2006-07 – Daniel Gibson (.419)
2007-08 – Daniel Gibson (.440)
2008-09 – Mo Williams (.436)
2009-10 – Daniel Gibson (.477)
2010-11 – Daniel Gibson (.403)
2011-12 – Ramon Sessions (.419)
2012-13 – Kyrie Irving (.391)
2013-14 – Spencer Hawes (.448)
2014-15 – Kyrie Irving (.415)
2015-16 – Matthew Dellavedova (.410)

FREE THROWS MADE

1970-71 – Walt Wesley (325)
1971-72 – John Johnson (277)
1972-73 – Lenny Wilkens (394)
1973-74 – Lenny Wilkens (289)
1974-75 – Dwight Davis (176)
1975-76 – Campy Russell (266)
1976-77 – Campy Russell (288)
1977-78 – Campy Russell (352)
1978-79 – Campy Russell (417)
1979-80 – Dave Robisch (277)
1980-81 – Mike Mitchell (302)
1981-82 – James Edwards (246)
1982-83 – World B. Free (324)
1983-84 – World B. Free (395)
1984-85 – Phil Hubbard (371)
1985-86 – World B. Free (379)
1986-87 – Ron Harper (386)
1987-88 – Brad Daugherty (378)
1988-89 – Brad Daugherty (386)
1989-90 – John Williams (325)
1990-91 – Brad Daugherty (435)
1991-92 – Brad Daugherty (414)
1992-93 – Brad Daugherty (391)
1993-94 – Brad Daugherty (256)
1994-95 – Tyrone Hill (263)
1995-96 – Terrell Brandon (338)
1996-97 – Terrell Brandon (268)
1997-98 – Shawn Kemp (404)
1998-99 – Shawn Kemp (307)
1999-2000 – Shawn Kemp (493)
2000-01 – Andre Miller (375)
2001-02 – Andre Miller (365)
2002-03 – Zydrunas Ilgauskas (400)
2003-04 – LeBron James (347)
2004-05 – LeBron James (477)
2005-06 – LeBron James (601)
2006-07 – LeBron James (489)
2007-08 – LeBron James (549)
2008-09 – LeBron James (594)
2009-10 – LeBron James (593)
2010-11 – Ramon Sessions (348)
2011-12 – Antawn Jamison (185)
2012-13 – Kyrie Irving (248)
2013-14 – Kyrie Irving (291)
2014-15 – LeBron James (375)
2015-16 – LeBron James (359)

FREE THROW ATTEMPTS

1970-71 – Walt Wesley (473)
1971-72 – Rick Roberson (366)
1972-73 – Lenny Wilkens (476)
1973-74 – Lenny Wilkens (361)
1974-75 – Dwight Davis (245)

1975-76 – Campy Russell (344)
1976-77 – Campy Russell (370)
1977-78 – Campy Russell (469)
1978-79 – Campy Russell (523)
1979-80 – Mike Mitchell (343)
1980-81 – Kenny Carr (409)
1981-82 – James Edwards (339)
1982-83 – World B. Free (434)
1983-84 – World B. Free (504)
1984-85 – Phil Hubbard (494)
1985-86 – Roy Hinson (506)
1986-87 – Ron Harper (564)
1987-88 – Brad Daugherty (528)
1988-89 – Brad Daugherty (524)
1989-90 – John Williams (440)
1990-91 – Brad Daugherty (579)
1991-92 – Brad Daugherty (533)
1992-93 – Brad Daugherty (492)
1993-94 – Brad Daugherty (326)
1994-95 – Tyrone Hill (397)
1995-96 – Terrell Brandon (381)
1996-97 – Tyrone Hill (381)
1997-98 – Shawn Kemp (556)
1998-99 – Shawn Kemp (389)
1999-2000 – Shawn Kemp (635)
2000-01 – Andre Miller (450)
2001-02 – Andre Miller (447)
2002-03 – Zydrunas Ilgauskas (512)
2003-04 – LeBron James (460)
2004-05 – LeBron James (636)
2005-06 – LeBron James (814)
2006-07 – LeBron James (701)
2007-08 – LeBron James (771)
2008-09 – LeBron James (762)
2009-10 – LeBron James (773)
2010-11 – Ramon Sessions (423)
2011-12 – Antawn Jamison (271)
2012-13 – Tristan Thompson (291)
2013-14 – Tristan Thompson (339)
2014-15 – LeBron James (528)
2015-16 – LeBron James (491)

FREE THROW PERCENTAGE

1970-71 – John Warren (.829)
1971-72 – Charlie Davis (.840)
1972-73 – Lenny Wilkens (.828)
1973-74 – Austin Carr (.856)
1974-75 – Dick Snyder (.846)
1975-76 – Dick Snyder (.824)
1976-77 – Dick Snyder (.852)
1977-78 – Walt Frazier (.850)
1978-79 – Austin Carr (.816)
1979-80 – Dave Robisch (.842)
1980-81 – Roger Phegley (.839)
1981-82 – James Silas (.860)
1982-83 – World B. Free (.747)
1983-84 – John Bagley (.793)
1984-85 – Johnny Davis (.850)
1985-86 – Melvin Turpin (.811)
1986-87 – John Bagley (.831)
1987-88 – Mark Price (.877)
1988-89 – Mark Price (.901)
1989-90 – Mark Price (.888)
1990-91 – Darnell Valentine (.831)
1991-92 – Mark Price (.947)
1992-93 – Mark Price (.948)
1993-94 – Mark Price (.888)
1994-95 – Mark Price (.914)
1995-96 – Terrell Brandon (.887)
1996-97 – Terrell Brandon (.902)
1997-98 – Derek Anderson (.873)
1998-99 – Derek Anderson (.836)
1999-2000 – Shawn Kemp (.776)
2000-01 – Andre Miller (.833)
2001-02 – Lamond Murray (.817)
2002-03 – Dajuan Wagner (.800)
2003-04 – Kevin Ollie (.835)

2004-05 – Jeff McInnis (.813)
2005-06 – Zydrunas Ilgauskas (.834)
2006-07 – Zydrunas Ilgauskas (.807)
2007-08 – Zydrunas Ilgauskas (.802)
2008-09 – Mo Williams (.912)
2009-10 – Mo Williams (.894)
2010-11 – Ramon Sessions (.823)
2011-12 – Kyrie Irving (.872)
2012-13 – Kyrie Irving (.855)
2013-14 – Kyrie Irving (.861)
2014-15 – Kyrie Irving (.863)
2015-16 – Mo Williams (.905)

REBOUNDS

1970-71 – Walt Wesley (713)
1971-72 – Rick Roberson (801)
1972-73 – Rick Roberson (693)
1973-74 – Dwight Davis (644)
1974-75 – Jim Chones (677)
1975-76 – Jim Brewer (891)
1976-77 – Jim Brewer (762)
1977-78 – Jim Chones (844)
1978-79 – Jim Chones (842)
1979-80 – Dave Robisch (658)
1980-81 – Kenny Carr (835)
1981-82 – James Edwards (581)
1982-83 – Cliff Robinson (856)
1983-84 – Cliff Robinson (753)
1984-85 – Roy Hinson (596)
1985-86 – Roy Hinson (639)
1986-87 – Brad Daugherty (647)
1987-88 – Brad Daugherty (665)
1988-89 – Brad Daugherty (718)
1989-90 – John Williams (663)
1990-91 – Brad Daugherty (830)
1991-92 – Brad Daugherty (760)
1992-93 – Brad Daugherty (726)
1993-94 – John Williams (575)
1994-95 – Tyrone Hill (765)
1995-96 – Michael Cage (729)
1996-97 – Tyrone Hill (736)
1997-98 – Shawn Kemp (745)
1998-99 – Shawn Kemp (388)
1999-2000 – Shawn Kemp (725)
2000-01 – Clarence Weatherspoon (796)
2001-02 – Jumaine Jones (490)
2002-03 – Zydrunas Ilgauskas (611)
2003-04 – Carlos Boozer (857)
2004-05 – Drew Gooden (753)
2005-06 – Drew Gooden (665)
2006-07 – Drew Gooden (681)
2007-08 – Zydrunas Ilgauskas (682)
2008-09 – LeBron James (613)
2009-10 – Anderson Varejao (578)
2010-11 – J. J. Hickson (695)
2011-12 – Antawn Jamison (408)
2012-13 – Tristan Thompson (773)
2013-14 – Tristan Thompson (754)
2014-15 – Kevin Love (731)
2015-16 – Kevin Love (762)

DEFENSIVE REBOUNDS

1973-74 – Dwight Davis (470)
1974-75 – Jim Chones (521)
1975-76 – Jim Brewer (593)
1976-77 – Jim Brewer (487)
1977-78 – Jim Chones (625)
1978-79 – Jim Chones (582)
1979-80 – Dave Robisch (433)
1980-81 – Kenny Carr (575)
1981-82 – James Edwards (392)
1982-83 – Cliff Robinson (666)
1983-84 – Cliff Robinson (597)
1984-85 – Roy Hinson (410)
1985-86 – Roy Hinson (472)

1986-87 – Brad Daugherty (495)
1987-88 – Brad Daugherty (514)
1988-89 – Brad Daugherty (551)
1989-90 – John Williams (443)
1990-91 – Brad Daugherty (653)
1991-92 – Brad Daugherty (569)
1992-93 – Brad Daugherty (562)
1993-94 – Brad Daugherty (380)
1994-95 – Tyrone Hill (496)
1995-96 – Michael Cage (441)
1996-97 – Tyrone Hill (477)
1997-98 – Shawn Kemp (526)
1998-99 – Shawn Kemp (257)
1999-2000 – Shawn Kemp (494)
2000-01 – Clarence Weatherspoon (573)
2001-02 – Jumaine Jones (365)
2002-03 – Carlos Boozer (407)
2003-04 – Carlos Boozer (627)
2004-05 – Drew Gooden (546)
2005-06 – LeBron James (481)
2006-07 – LeBron James (443)
2007-08 – LeBron James (459)
2008-09 – LeBron James (507)
2009-10 – LeBron James (483)
2010-11 – J. J. Hickson (478)
2011-12 – Antawn Jamison (285)
2012-13 – Tristan Thompson (467)
2013-14 – Tristan Thompson (485)
2014-15 – Kevin Love (589)
2015-16 – Kevin Love (613)

OFFENSIVE REBOUNDS

1973-74 – Steve Patterson (223)
1974-75 – Jim Brewer (205)
1975-76 – Jim Brewer (298)
1976-77 – Jim Brewer (275)
1977-78 – Jim Chones (219)
1978-79 – Jim Chones (260)
1979-80 – Dave Robisch (225)
1980-81 – Bill Laimbeer (266)
1981-82 – James Edwards (189)
1982-83 – Phil Hubbard (222)
1983-84 – Roy Hinson (175)
1984-85 – Phil Hubbard (214)
1985-86 – Melvin Turpin (182)
1986-87 – John Williams (222)
1987-88 – John Williams (159)
1988-89 – John Williams (173)
1989-90 – John Williams (220)
1990-91 – Larry Nance (201)
1991-92 – John Williams (228)
1992-93 – Larry Nance (184)
1993-94 – John Williams (207)
1994-95 – Tyrone Hill (269)
1995-96 – Michael Cage (288)
1996-97 – Tyrone Hill (259)
1997-98 – Zydrunas Ilgauskas (279)
1998-99 – Shawn Kemp (131)
1999-2000 – Shawn Kemp (231)
2000-01 – Clarence Weatherspoon (223)
2001-02 – Zydrunas Ilgauskas (136)
2002-03 – Zydrunas Ilgauskas (240)
2003-04 – Zydrunas Ilgauskas (279)
2004-05 – Zydrunas Ilgauskas (299)
2005-06 – Zydrunas Ilgauskas (245)
2006-07 – Drew Gooden (263)
2007-08 – Zydrunas Ilgauskas (263)
2008-09 – Anderson Varejao (166)
2009-10 – Anderson Varejao (189)
2010-11 – J. J. Hickson (217)
2011-12 – Tristan Thompson (187)
2012-13 – Tristan Thompson (306)
2013-14 – Tristan Thompson (269)
2014-15 – Tristan Thompson (274)
2015-16 – Tristan Thompson (268)

ASSISTS

1970-71 – John Warren (347)
1971-72 – Butch Beard (456)
1972-73 – Lenny Wilkens (628)
1973-74 – Lenny Wilkens (522)
1974-75 – Jim Cleamons (381)
1975-76 – Jim Cleamons (428)
1976-77 – Jim Cleamons (308)
1977-78 – Foots Walker (453)
1978-79 – Campy Russell (348)
1979-80 – Foots Walker (607)
1980-81 – Mike Bratz (452)
1981-82 – Geoff Huston (590)
1982-83 – Geoff Huston (487)
1983-84 – Geoff Huston (413)
1984-85 – John Bagley (697)
1985-86 – John Bagley (735)
1986-87 – Ron Harper (394)
1987-88 – Mark Price (480)
1988-89 – Mark Price (631)
1989-90 – Mark Price (666)
1990-91 – Craig Ehlo (376)
1991-92 – Mark Price (535)
1992-93 – Mark Price (602)
1993-94 – Mark Price (589)
1994-95 – Terrell Brandon (363)
1995-96 – Terrell Brandon (487)
1996-97 – Terrell Brandon (490)
1997-98 – Brevin Knight (656)
1998-99 – Brevin Knight (302)
1999-2000 – Andre Miller (476)
2000-01 – Andre Miller (657)
2001-02 – Andre Miller (882)
2002-03 – Ricky Davis (436)
2003-04 – LeBron James (465)
2004-05 – LeBron James (577)
2005-06 – LeBron James (521)
2006-07 – LeBron James (470)
2007-08 – LeBron James (539)
2008-09 – LeBron James (587)
2009-10 – LeBron James (651)
2010-11 – Ramon Sessions (419)
2011-12 – Kyrie Irving (275)
2012-13 – Kyrie Irving (350)
2013-14 – Kyrie Irving (433)
2014-15 – LeBron James (511)
2015-16 – LeBron James (514)

FOULS

1970-71 – John Warren (299)
1971-72 – John Johnson (268)
1972-73 – Dwight Davis (297)
1973-74 – Dwight Davis (291)
1974-75 – Dwight Davis (254)
1975-76 – Jim Chones (241)
1976-77 – Jim Chones (258)
1977-78 – Elmore Smith (241)
1978-79 – Jim Chones (278)
1979-80 – Mike Mitchell (259)
1980-81 – Bill Laimbeer (332)
1981-82 – James Edwards (347)
1982-83 – Cliff Robinson (272)
1983-84 – Roy Hinson (306)
1984-85 – Roy Hinson (311)
1985-86 – Roy Hinson (316)
1986-87 – Brad Daugherty (248)
1987-88 – Brad Daugherty (235)
1988-89 – Mike Sanders (230)
1989-90 – Craig Ehlo (226)
1990-91 – Danny Ferry (230)
1991-92 – Larry Nance (200)
1992-93 – Larry Nance (223)
1993-94 – Chris Mills (232)
1994-95 – Tyrone Hill (245)

1995-96 – Chris Mills (241)
1996-97 – Tyrone Hill (268)
1997-98 – Shawn Kemp (310)
1998-99 – Shawn Kemp (159)
1999-2000 – Shawn Kemp (371)
2000-01 – Andre Miller (229)
2001-02 – Chris Mihm (260)
2002-03 – Zydrunas Ilgauskas (274)
2003-04 – Zydrunas Ilgauskas (277)
2004-05 – Zydrunas Ilgauskas (313)
2005-06 – Zydrunas Ilgauskas (280)
2006-07 – Anderson Varejao (269)
2007-08 – Zydrunas Ilgauskas (247)
2008-09 – Anderson Varejao (239)
2009-10 – Anderson Varejao (223)
2010-11 – J. J. Hickson (215)
2011-12 – Antawn Jamison (164)
2012-13 – Tyler Zeller (251)
2013-14 – Tristan Thompson (188)
2014-15 – Tristan Thompson (189)
2015-16 – J. R. Smith (204)

DISQUALIFICATIONS

1970-71 – John Warren (13)
1971-72 – Rick Roberson (7)
1972-73 – Dwight Davis, Rick Roberson (5)
1973-74 – Dwight Davis (6)
1974-75 – Jim Chones (5)
1975-76 – Campy Russell (5)
1976-77 – Five tied (3)
1977-78 – Jim Chones, Elmore Smith (4)
1978-79 – Mike Mitchell (4)
1979-80 – John Lambert, Mike Mitchell (4)
1980-81 – Bill Laimbeer (14)
1981-82 – James Edwards (17)
1982-83 – Phil Hubbard (11)
1983-84 – Roy Hinson (11)
1984-85 – Roy Hinson (13)
1985-86 – Keith Lee (9)
1986-87 – Phil Hubbard (6)
1987-88 – Ron Harper, Larry Nance (3)
1988-89 – Mike Sanders (2)
1989-90 – Larry Nance, Tree Rollins (3)
1990-91 – Larry Nance (3)
1991-92 – Larry Nance, John Williams (2)
1992-93 – Larry Nance (3)
1993-94 – Tyrone Hill (5)
1994-95 – Tyrone Hill (4)
1995-96 – Three tied (3)
1996-97 – Tyrone Hill (6)
1997-98 – Shawn Kemp (15)
1998-99 – Five tied (2)
1999-2000 – Shawn Kemp (13)
2000-01 – Robert Traylor (3)
2001-02 – Chris Mihm (7)
2002-03 – Three tied (4)
2003-04 – Three tied (2)
2004-05 – Zydrunas Ilgauskas (7)
2005-06 – Zydrunas Ilgauskas (5)
2006-07 – Zydrunas Ilgauskas (4)
2007-08 – Zydrunas Ilgauskas (4)
2008-09 – Sasha Pavlovic (4)
2009-10 – Anderson Varejao (2)
2010-11 – Daniel Gibson, Ryan Hollins (3)
2011-12 – Samardo Samuels (2)
2012-13 – Tyler Zeller (5)
2013-14 – Anderson Varejao (2)
2014-15 – Four tied (1)
2015-16 – Four tied (1)

STEALS

1973-74 – Lenny Wilkens (97)
1974-75 – Jim Cleamons (84)
1975-76 – Jim Cleamons (124)
1976-77 – Jim Brewer (94)
1977-78 – Foots Walker (176)
1978-79 – Foots Walker (130)
1979-80 – Foots Walker (155)
1980-81 – Mike Bratz (136)
1981-82 – Bobby Wilkerson (92)
1982-83 – Phil Hubbard (87)
1983-84 – World B. Free (94)
1984-85 – John Bagley (129)
1985-86 – John Bagley (122)
1986-87 – Ron Harper (209)
1987-88 – Ron Harper (122)
1988-89 – Ron Harper (185)
1989-90 – Craig Ehlo (126)
1990-91 – Craig Ehlo (121)
1991-92 – Mark Price (94)
1992-93 – Craig Ehlo (104)
1993-94 – Gerald Wilkins (105)
1994-95 – Bobby Phills (115)
1995-96 – Terrell Brandon (132)
1996-97 – Terrell Brandon (138)
1997-98 – Brevin Knight (196)
1998-99 – Brevin Knight (70)
1999-2000 – Brevin Knight (107)
2000-01 – Andre Miller (119)
2001-02 – Andre Miller (126)
2002-03 – Ricky Davis (125)
2003-04 – LeBron James (130)
2004-05 – LeBron James (177)
2005-06 – LeBron James (123)
2006-07 – LeBron James (125)
2007-08 – LeBron James (138)
2008-09 – LeBron James (137)
2009-10 – LeBron James (125)
2010-11 – Anthony Parker (67)
2011-12 – Alonzo Gee (83)
2012-13 – Alonzo Gee (107)
2013-14 – Kyrie Irving (108)
2014-15 – Kyrie Irving (114)
2015-16 – LeBron James (104)

TURNOVERS

1977-78 – Campy Russell (206)
1978-79 – Campy Russell (259)
1979-80 – Randy Smith (200)
1980-81 – Kenny Carr (236)
1981-82 – Geoff Huston (172)
1982-83 – Cliff Robinson (223)
1983-84 – Cliff Robinson (187)
1984-85 – John Bagley (207)
1985-86 – John Bagley (239)
1986-87 – Ron Harper (345)
1987-88 – Brad Daugherty (267)
1988-89 – Brad Daugherty, Ron Harper (230)
1989-90 – Mark Price (214)
1990-91 – Brad Daugherty (211)
1991-92 – Brad Daugherty (185)
1992-93 – Mark Price (196)
1993-94 – Mark Price (189)
1994-95 – Tyrone Hill (151)
1995-96 – Terrell Brandon (142)
1996-97 – Bob Sura (181)
1997-98 – Shawn Kemp (271)
1998-99 – Shawn Kemp (127)
1999-2000 – Shawn Kemp (291)
2000-01 – Andre Miller (265)
2001-02 – Andre Miller (245)
2002-03 – Ricky Davis (277)
2003-04 – LeBron James (273)
2004-05 – LeBron James (262)

2005-06 – LeBron James (260)
2006-07 – LeBron James (250)
2007-08 – LeBron James (255)
2008-09 – LeBron James (241)
2009-10 – LeBron James (261)
2010-11 – Ramon Sessions (178)
2011-12 – Kyrie Irving (160)
2012-13 – Kyrie Irving (191)
2013-14 – Kyrie Irving (190)
2014-15 – LeBron James (272)
2015-16 – LeBron James (249)

BLOCKED SHOTS

1973-74 – Dwight Davis (74)
1974-75 – Jim Chones (120)
1975-76 – Jim Chones (93)
1976-77 – Jim Brewer (82)
1977-78 – Elmore Smith (176)
1978-79 – Jim Chones (102)
1979-80 – Mike Mitchell (77)
1980-81 – Bill Laimbeer (78)
1981-82 – James Edwards (117)
1982-83 – Cliff Robinson (58)
1983-84 – Roy Hinson (145)
1984-85 – Roy Hinson (173)
1985-86 – Roy Hinson (112)
1986-87 – John Williams (167)
1987-88 – John Williams (145)
1988-89 – Larry Nance (206)
1989-90 – John Williams (167)
1990-91 – Larry Nance (200)
1991-92 – Larry Nance (243)
1992-93 – Larry Nance (198)
1993-94 – John Williams (130)
1994-95 – John Williams (101)
1995-96 – Michael Cage (79)
1996-97 – Mark West (55)
1997-98 – Zydrunas Ilgauskas (135)
1998-99 – Shawn Kemp (45)
1999-2000 – Shawn Kemp (96)
2000-01 – Clarence Weatherspoon (105)
2001-02 – Chris Mihm (89)
2002-03 – Zydrunas Ilgauskas (152)
2003-04 – Zydrunas Ilgauskas (201)
2004-05 – Zydrunas Ilgauskas (165)
2005-06 – Zydrunas Ilgauskas (136)
2006-07 – Zydrunas Ilgauskas (98)
2007-08 – Zydrunas Ilgauskas (120)
2008-09 – LeBron James (93)
2009-10 – LeBron James (77)
2010-11 – J. J. Hickson (54)
2011-12 – Tristan Thompson (62)
2012-13 – Tristan Thompson (71)
2013-14 – Anderson Varejao (39)
2014-15 – Tristan Thompson (61)
2015-16 – Timofey Mozgov (57)

POINTS

1970-71 – Walt Wesley (1,455)
1971-72 – John Johnson (1,391)
1972-73 – Austin Carr (1,685)
1973-74 – Austin Carr (1,775)
1974-75 – Bingo Smith (1,302)
1975-76 – Jim Chones (1,298)
1976-77 – Austin Carr (1,329)
1977-78 – Campy Russell (1,398)
1978-79 – Campy Russell (1,623)
1979-80 – Mike Mitchell (1,820)
1980-81 – Mike Mitchell (2,012)
1981-82 – James Edwards (1,288)
1982-83 – Cliff Robinson (1,387)
1983-84 – World B. Free (1,669)
1984-85 – World B. Free (1,597)
1985-86 – World B. Free (1,754)
1986-87 – Ron Harper (1,874)

1987-88 – Brad Daugherty (1,480)
1988-89 – Ron Harper (1,526)
1989-90 – Mark Price (1,430)
1990-91 – Brad Daugherty (1,645)
1991-92 – Brad Daugherty (1,566)
1992-93 – Brad Daugherty (1,432)
1993-94 – Mark Price (1,316)
1994-95 – Chris Mills (986)
1995-96 – Terrell Brandon (1,449)
1996-97 – Terrell Brandon (1,519)
1997-98 – Shawn Kemp (1,442)
1998-99 – Shawn Kemp (862)
1999-2000 – Shawn Kemp (1,463)
2000-01 – Andre Miller (1,296)
2001-02 – Andre Miller (1,335)
2002-03 – Ricky Davis (1,626)
2003-04 – LeBron James (1,654)
2004-05 – LeBron James (2,175)
2005-06 – LeBron James (2,478)
2006-07 – LeBron James (2,132)
2007-08 – LeBron James (2,250)
2008-09 – LeBron James (2,304)
2009-10 – LeBron James (2,258)
2010-11 – J. J. Hickson (1,105)
2011-12 – Antawn Jamison (1,118)
2012-13 – Kyrie Irving (1,325)
2013-14 – Kyrie Irving (1,478)
2014-15 – LeBron James (1,743)
2015-16 – LeBron James (1,920)

SCORING AVERAGE

1970-71 – Walt Wesley (17.7)
1971-72 – John Johnson (17)
1972-73 – Austin Carr (20.5)
1973-74 – Austin Carr (21.9)
1974-75 – Bingo Smith (15.9)
1975-76 – Jim Chones (15.8)
1976-77 – Campy Russell (16.5)
1977-78 – Campy Russell (19.4)
1978-79 – Campy Russell (21.9)
1979-80 – Mike Mitchell (22.2)
1980-81 – Mike Mitchell (24.5)
1981-82 – Ron Brewer (19.4)
1982-83 – World B. Free (24.2)
1983-84 – World B. Free (22.3)
1984-85 – World B. Free (22.5)
1985-86 – World B. Free (22.9)
1986-87 – Ron Harper (22.9)
1987-88 – Brad Daugherty (18.9)
1988-89 – Brad Daugherty (18.9)
1989-90 – Mark Price (19.6)
1990-91 – Brad Daugherty (21.6)
1991-92 – Brad Daugherty (21.5)
1992-93 – Brad Daugherty (20.2)
1993-94 – Mark Price (17.3)
1994-95 – Mark Price (15.8)
1995-96 – Terrell Brandon (19.3)
1996-97 – Terrell Brandon (19.5)
1997-98 – Shawn Kemp (18)
1998-99 – Shawn Kemp (20.5)
1999-2000 – Shawn Kemp (17.8)
2000-01 – Andre Miller (15.8)
2001-02 – Lamond Murray (16.6)
2002-03 – Ricky Davis (20.6)
2003-04 – LeBron James (20.9)
2004-05 – LeBron James (27.2)
2005-06 – LeBron James (31.4)
2006-07 – LeBron James (27.3)
2007-08 – LeBron James (30)
2008-09 – LeBron James (28.4)
2009-10 – LeBron James (29.7)
2010-11 – Antawn Jamison (18)
2011-12 – Kyrie Irving (18.5)
2012-13 – Kyrie Irving (22.5)
2013-14 – Kyrie Irving (20.8)
2014-15 – LeBron James (25.3)
2015-16 – LeBron James (25.3)

BEST/HIGHEST SEASON PERFORMANCES

Points – 2,478 (LeBron James, 2005-06)
Minutes – 3,388 (LeBron James, 2004-05)
Field Goal Attempts – 1,823 (LeBron James, 2005-06)
Field Goals – 875 (LeBron James, 2005-06)
Field Goal Percentage – 60 (Tyrone Hill, 1996-97)
Free Throw Attempts – 814 (LeBron James, 2005-06)
Free Throws Made – 601 (LeBron James, 2005-06)
Free Throw Percentage – 94.8 (Mark Price, 1992-93)
Three-Point Field Goal Attempts – 510 (J. R. Smith, 2015-16)
Three-Point Field Goals – 204 (J. R. Smith, 2015-16)
Three-Point Field Goal Percentage – 50.7 (Steve Kerr, 1989-90)
Rebounds – 891 (Jim Brewer, 1975-76)
Defensive Rebounds – 666 (Cliff Robinson, 1982-83)
Offensive Rebounds – 306 (Tristan Thompson, 2012-13)
Assists – 882 (Andre Miller, 2001-02)
Steals – 209 (Ron Harper, 1986-87)
Blocked Shots – 243 (Larry Nance, 1991-92)
Fouls – 371 (Shawn Kemp, 1999-2000)
Disqualifications – 17 (James Edwards, 1981-82)
Turnovers – 345 (Ron Harper, 1986-87)
Scoring Average – 31.4 (LeBron James, 2005-06)

TRIPLE-DOUBLES

John Johnson (December 26, 1970, vs. Buffalo) – 33 points/12 rebounds/12 assists
John Johnson (October 29, 1971, vs. Atlanta) – 22 points/10 rebounds/10 assists
John Johnson (November 12, 1971, at Portland) – 18 points/12 rebounds/11 assists
John Johnson (February 23, 1972, vs. Boston) – 23 points/14 rebounds/11 assists
John Johnson (March 16, 1972, vs. Baltimore) – 19 points/10 rebounds/10 assists
Foots Walker (February 23, 1975, vs. Atlanta) – 18 points/12 rebounds/11 assists
Foots Walker (December 2, 1979, vs. Atlanta) – 15 points/10 rebounds/11 assists
John Bagley (February 6, 1985, at Boston) – 10 points/11 rebounds/16 assists
John Bagley (December 28, 1985, vs. Milwaukee) – 18 points/11 rebounds/13 assists
Brad Daugherty (December 19, 1986, vs. Utah) – 19 points/10 rebounds/11 assists
Brad Daugherty (February 3, 1988, at Washington) – 20 points/10 rebounds/11 assists
Ron Harper (January 31, 1989, vs. Philadelphia) – 25 points/10 rebounds/10 assists

Mark Price (January 15, 1990, vs. San Antonio) – 25 points/11 rebounds/12 assists
Brad Daugherty (March 24, 1992, vs. Indiana) – 32 points/11 rebounds/11 assists
Larry Nance (April 9, 1992, vs. Charlotte) – 26 points/10 rebounds/14 assists
Brad Daugherty (December 12, 1992, vs. Seattle) – 11 points/12 rebounds/11 assists
Bobby Phills (April 19, 1995, vs. Miami) – 11 points/11 rebounds/10 assists
Andre Miller (February 5, 2000, vs. Atlanta) – 28 points/10 rebounds/12 assists
Andre Miller (November 2, 2001, at Miami) – 30 points/10 rebounds/12 assists
Andre Miller (January 26, 2002, vs. Boston) – 25 points/10 rebounds/17 assists
Andre Miller (February 12, 2002, vs. Toronto) – 22 points/10 rebounds/17 assists
LeBron James (January 19, 2005, at Portland) – 27 points/11 rebounds/10 assists
LeBron James (Jan. 22, 2005, at Golden State) – 28 points/12 rebounds/10 assists
LeBron James (April 9, 2005, vs. Milwaukee) – 40 points/10 rebounds/10 assists
LeBron James (April 20, 2005, at Toronto) – 27 points/14 rebounds/14 assists
LeBron James (November 19, 2005, at Philadelphia) – 36 points/11 rebounds/10 assists
LeBron James (January 4, 2006, at Milwaukee) – 32 points/11 rebounds/11 assists
LeBron James (February 1, 2006, vs. New Jersey) – 26 points/11 rebounds/10 assists
LeBron James (February 15, 2006, at Boston) – 43 points/12 rebounds/11 assists
LeBron James (March 22, 2006, vs. Charlotte) – 37 points/11 rebounds/12 assists
LeBron James (January 19, 2007, at Denver) – 30 points/10 rebounds/10 assists
LeBron James (November 7, 2007, at Utah) – 32 points/15 rebounds/13 assists
LeBron James (November 14, 2007, vs. Orlando) – 39 points/13 rebounds/14 assists
LeBron James (November 24, 2007, vs. Toronto) – 37 points/12 rebounds/12 assists
LeBron James (November 25, 2007, at Indiana) – 30 points/11 rebounds/10 assists
LeBron James (February 19, 2008, vs. Houston) – 26 points/13 rebounds/11 assists
LeBron James (February 20, 2008, at Indiana) – 31 points/14 rebounds/12 assists
LeBron James (March 10, 2008, vs. Portland) – 24 points/10 rebounds/11 assists
LeBron James (January 2, 2009, vs. Chicago) – 16 points/10 rebounds/11 assists
LeBron James (January 13, 2009, at Memphis) – 30 points/11 rebounds/10 assists
LeBron James (January 27, 2009, vs. Sacramento) – 23 points/15 rebounds/11 assists
LeBron James (March 7, 2009, vs. Miami) – 14 points/10 rebounds/12 assists
LeBron James (March 10, 2009, at L.A. Clippers) – 32 points/13 rebounds/11 assists
LeBron James (March 12, 2009, at Phoenix) – 34 points/10 rebounds/13 assists
LeBron James (March 19, 2009, vs. Portland) – 26 points/11 rebounds/10 assists
LeBron James (October 28, 2009, at Toronto) – 23 points/11 rebounds/12 assists
LeBron James (December 23, 2009, at Sacramento) – 34 points/16 rebounds/10 assists
LeBron James (February 18, 2010, vs. Denver) – 43 points/13 rebounds/15 assists
LeBron James (March 16, 2010, at Detroit) – 29 points/12 rebounds/12 assists

Kyrie Irving (February 28, 2014, vs. Utah) – 21 points/10 rebounds/12 assists
LeBron James (April 5, 2015, vs. Chicago) – 20 points/10 rebounds/12 assists
LeBron James (April 13, 2015, vs. Detroit) – 21 points/10 rebounds/11 assists
LeBron James (February 8, 2016, vs. Sacramento) – 33 points/11 rebounds/11 assists
LeBron James (March 21, 2016, vs. Denver) – 21 points/10 rebounds/10 assists
LeBron James (March 26, 2016, at New York) – 27 points/11 rebounds/11 assists

20-20 CLUB

Walt Wesley (February 21, 1971, at Portland) – 30 points/21 rebounds
Walt Wesley (December 26, 1971, at Baltimore) – 20 points/21 rebounds
Rick Roberson (March 4, 1972, vs. Houston) – 23 points/25 rebounds
Rick Roberson (March 7, 1972, at Golden State) – 23 points/22 rebounds
Elmore Smith (February 2, 1978, vs. Washington) – 32 points/24 rebounds
Elmore Smith (February 7, 1978, vs. New Orleans) – 21 points/20 rebounds
Elmore Smith (March 8, 1978, at Golden State) – 22 points/20 rebounds
Kenny Carr (February 12, 1981, vs. New York) – 27 points/20 rebounds
Cliff Robinson (January 20, 1983, at Washington) – 22 points/23 rebounds
Cliff Robinson (February 16, 1983, vs. Dallas) – 23 points/22 rebounds
Cliff Robinson (January 31, 1984, vs. Detroit) – 32 points/21 rebounds
Cliff Robinson (April 3, 1984, vs. Boston) – 26 points/21 rebounds
Brad Daugherty (March 8, 1991, at Sacramento) – 21 points/24 rebounds
Michael Cage (January 10, 1996, at San Antonio) – 20 points/20 rebounds
Shawn Kemp (January 20, 1998, vs. Portland) – 31 points/20 rebounds
Carlos Boozer (January 20, 2004, vs. Seattle) – 32 points/20 rebounds
Carlos Boozer (March 30, 2004, at Dallas) – 23 points/20 rebounds
Anderson Varejao (January 31, 2012, vs. Boston) – 20 points/20 rebounds

HEAD COACHES' WIN-LOSS RECORDS, BEST TO WORST

1. David Blatt (2014-15 to 2015-16)	83-40 .675
2. Tyronn Lue (2015-16)	27-14.659
3. Mike Brown (2005-06 to 2009-10, 2013-14)	305-187 .620
4. Lenny Wilkens (1986-87 to 1992-93)	316-258 .551
5. Mike Fratello (1993-94 to 1998-99)	248-212 .539
6. Paul Silas (2003-04 to 2004-05)	69-77 .473
7. Stan Albeck (1979-80)	37-45.451
8. Brendan Malone (2004-05)	8-10 .444
9. Bill Fitch (1970-71 to 1978-79)	304-434 .412
10. George Karl (1984-85 to 1985-86)	61-88 .409

11. Byron Scott (2010-11 to 2012-13)	64-166 .386
12. Randy Wittman (1999-2000 to 2000-01)	62-102 .378
13. Tom Nissalke (1982-83 to 1983-84)	51-113 .311
14. John Lucas (2001-02 to 2002-03)	37-87 .298
15. Bill Musselman (1980-81 to 1981-82)	27-67.287
16. Gene Littles (1985-86)	4-11 .267
17. Don Delaney (1980-81 to 1981-82)	7-21 .250
18. Keith Smart (2002-03)	9-31 .225
19. Chuck Daly (1981-82)	9-32 .220
20. Bob Kloppenburg (1981-82)	0-1 .000

Overall – 1,728-1,996 (.464)

POSTSEASON

TOP TENS (CAREER)

SEASONS PLAYED

1. LeBron James	7
2. Mark Price	7
3. Danny Ferry	6
4. Zydrunas Ilgauskas	6
5 John Williams	6
6. Brad Daugherty	5
7. Craig Ehlo	5
8. Larry Nance	5
9. Bobby Phills	5
10. Anderson Varejao	5

GAMES PLAYED

1. LeBron James	112
2. Zydrunas Ilgauskas	71
3. Anderson Varejao	71
4. Daniel Gibson	50
5. Mark Price	47
6. John Williams	45
7. Sasha Pavlovic	42
8. Brad Daugherty	41
9. Larry Nance	41
10. Iman Shumpert	41
11. Tristan Thompson	41

POINTS

1. LeBron James	3,234
2. Mark Price	818
3. Zydrunas Ilgauskas	784
4. Brad Daugherty	782
5. Kyrie Irving	777
6. Larry Nance	693
7. John Williams	559
8. J. R. Smith	473
9. Craig Ehlo	422
10. Anderson Varejao	420

SCORING AVERAGE (MINIMUM 150 POINTS)

1. LeBron James	28.9
2. Kyrie Irving	22.9
3. Brad Daugherty	19.1

4. Ron Harper	18.8
5. Mark Price	17.4
6. Larry Nance	16.9
7. Campy Russell	15.8
8. Mo Williams	15.4
9. Antawn Jamison	15.3
10. Kevin Love	14.6

ASSISTS

1. LeBron James	849
2. Mark Price	327
3. Craig Ehlo	164
4. Kyrie Irving	148
5. Delonte West	141
6. Brad Daugherty	137
7. Mo Williams	120
8. Larry Nance	110
9. Matthew Dellavedova	109
10. John Williams	95

FIELD GOALS

1. LeBron James	1,136
2. Zydrunas Ilgauskas	313
3. Larry Nance	283
4. Kyrie Irving	282
5. Mark Price	280
6. Brad Daugherty	275
7. John Williams	206
8. J. R. Smith	165
9. Craig Ehlo	161
10. Anderson Varejao	160

FIELD GOAL ATTEMPTS

1. LeBron James	2,465
2. Zydrunas Ilgauskas	656
3. Kyrie Irving	608
4. Mark Price	603
5. Larry Nance	537
6. Brad Daugherty	530
7. John Williams	426
8. J. R. Smith	394
9. Craig Ehlo	384
10. Mo Williams	351

FIELD GOAL PERCENTAGE (MINIMUM 50 FIELD GOALS

1. Tristan Thompson	.545
2. Larry Nance	.527
3. Ron Harper	.523
4. Brad Daugherty	.519
5. Drew Gooden	.503
6. Anderson Varejao	.494
7. Timofey Mozgov	.491
8. Mike Sanders	.486
9. John Williams	.484
10. Zydrunas Ilgauskas	.477

STEALS

1. LeBron James	199
2. Anderson Varejao	67
3. Mark Price	64
4. Kyrie Irving	53
5. Craig Ehlo	47
6. Larry Hughes	45
7. John Williams	45
8. J. R. Smith	43
9. Delonte West	43
10. Iman Shumpert	35

FREE THROWS MADE

1. LeBron James	798
2. Brad Daugherty	232

3.	Mark Price	202
4.	Zydrunas Ilgauskas	156
5.	John Williams	147
6.	Kyrie Irving	135
7.	Larry Nance	127
8.	Anderson Varejao	100
9.	Tristan Thompson	90
10.	Delonte West	85

FREE THROW ATTEMPTS

1.	LeBron James	1,091
2.	Brad Daugherty	307
3.	Mark Price	214
4.	Zydrunas Ilgauskas	209
5.	John Williams	198
6.	Larry Nance	162
7.	Anderson Varejao	159
8.	Kyrie Irving	157
9.	Tristan Thompson	155
10.	Delonte West	99

FREE THROW PERCENTAGE (MINIMUM 20 FREE THROWS MADE)

1.	Mark Price	.944
2.	World B. Free	.920
3.	John Battle	.913
4.	Wally Szczerbiak	.897
5.	Bingo Smith	.893
6.	Derek Anderson	.885
7.	Terrell Brandon	.871
8.	Daniel Gibson	.871
9.	Kyrie Irving	.860
10.	Delonte West	.859

BLOCKED SHOTS

1.	LeBron James	116
2.	Larry Nance	93
3.	Zydrunas Ilgauskas	82
4.	John Williams	53
5.	Tristan Thompson	42
6.	Brad Daugherty	40
7.	Timofey Mozgov	39
8.	Anderson Varejao	39
9.	Nate Thurmond	30
10.	Kyrie Irving	24
11.	Tristan Thompson	24

THREE-POINT FIELD GOALS

1.	LeBron James	164
2.	J. R. Smith	116
3.	Kyrie Irving	78
4.	Daniel Gibson	57
5.	Mark Price	56
6.	Kevin Love	55
7.	Mo Williams	55
8.	Iman Shumpert	46
9.	Craig Ehlo	41
10.	Delonte West	33

THREE-POINT FIELD GOAL ATTEMPTS

1.	LeBron James	543
2.	J. R. Smith	293
3.	Kyrie Irving	176
4.	Mark Price	166
5.	Mo Williams	159
6.	J. R. Smith	142
7.	Daniel Gibson	140
8.	Kevin Love	132

9. Iman Shumpert 127
10. Craig Ehlo 113

THREE-POINT FIELD GOAL PERCENTAGE (MINIMUM FIVE THREE-POINT FIELD GOALS)

1. Channing Frye .565
2. Chris Mills .500
3. Jamario Moon .500
4. Anthony Parker .455
5. Kyrie Irving .443
6. Dan Majerle .435
7. Kevin Love .417
8. Daniel Gibson .407
9. J. R. Smith .396
10. Richard Jefferson .393
11. Gerald Wilkins .393

MINUTES

1. LeBron James 4,755
2. Zydrunas Ilgauskas 2,017
3. Mark Price 1,691
4. Brad Daugherty 1,600
5. Anderson Varejao 1,600
6. Larry Nance 1,564
7. John Williams 1,416
8. Tristan Thompson 1,349
9. Delonte West 1,312
10. J. R. Smith 1,290

REBOUNDS

1. LeBron James 1,024
2. Zydrunas Ilgauskas 523
3. Brad Daugherty 419
4. Anderson Varejao 405
5. Tristan Thompson 404
6. Larry Nance 330
7. John Williams 305
8. Drew Gooden 258
9. Kevin Love 203
10. Jim Brewer 176

DEFENSIVE REBOUNDS

1. LeBron James 847
2. Zydrunas Ilgauskas 343
3. Brad Daugherty 330
4. Anderson Varejao 258
5. Tristan Thompson 230
6. Larry Nance 220
7. John Williams 206
8. Drew Gooden 178
9. Kevin Love 163
10. J. R. Smith 136

OFFENSIVE REBOUNDS

1. Zydrunas Ilgauskas 180
2. LeBron James 177
3. Tristan Thompson 174
4. Anderson Varejao 147
5. Larry Nance 110
6. John Williams 99
7. Brad Daugherty 89
8. Drew Gooden 80
9. Timofey Mozgov 62
10. Jim Brewer 51

FOULS

1. LeBron James 282
2. Zydrunas Ilgauskas 220
3. Anderson Varejao 220

4. John Williams	143	8. J. R. Smith	109
5. Larry Nance	134	9. Tristan Thompson	105
6. Brad Daugherty	113	10. Drew Gooden	102
7. Mike Sanders	111		

TRIPLE-DOUBLES

LeBron James (April 22, 2006, vs. Washington) – 32 points/11 rebounds/11 assists
LeBron James (May 13, 2006, vs. Detroit) – 21 points/10 rebounds/10 assists
LeBron James (May 2, 2008, at Washington) – 27 points/13 rebounds/13 assists
LeBron James (May 28, 2009, vs. Orlando) – 37 points/14 rebounds/12 assists
LeBron James (April 25, 2010, at Chicago) – 37 points/12 rebounds/11 assists
LeBron James (May 13, 2010, at Boston) – 27 points/19 rebounds/10 assists
LeBron James (May 24, 2015, vs. Atlanta) – 37 points/18 rebounds/13 assists
LeBron James (June 7, 2015, at Golden State) – 39 points/16 rebounds/11 assists
LeBron James (June 14, 2015, at Golden State) – 40 points/14 rebounds/11 assists
LeBron James (May 19, 2016, vs. Toronto) – 23 points/11 rebounds/11 assists
LeBron James (June 19, 2016, at Golden State) – 27 points/11 rebounds/11 assists

20-20 CLUB

Brad Daugherty (May 9, 1993, vs. New Jersey) – 24 points/20 rebounds

HEAD COACHES' WIN-LOSS RECORDS, BEST TO WORST

1. Tyronn Lue (2015-16)	16-5 .762
2. David Blatt (2014-15 to 2015-16)	14-6 .700
3. Mike Brown (2005-06 to 2009-10, 2013-14)	42-29 .592
4. Lenny Wilkens (1986-87 to 1992-93)	18-23 .439
5. Bill Fitch (1970-71 to 1978-79)	7-11 .389
6. George Karl (1984-85 to 1985-86)	1-3 .250
7. Mike Fratello (1993-94 to 1998-99)	2-12 .143

Overall – 100-89 (.529)

Team Statistics

REGULAR SEASON

Season Win-Loss Records

OVERALL

1970-71 – 15-67 .183
1971-72 – 23-59 .280
1972-73 – 32-50 .390
1973-74 – 29-53 .354
1974-75 – 40-42 .488
1975-76 – 49-33 .598
1976-77 – 43-39 .524
1977-78 – 43-39 .524
1978-79 – 30-52 .366
1979-80 – 37-45 .451
1980-81 – 28-54 .341
1981-82 – 15-67 .183
1982-83 – 23-59 .280
1983-84 – 28-54 .341
1984-85 – 36-46 .439
1985-86 – 29-53 .354
1986-87 – 31-51 .378
1987-88 – 42-40 .512
1988-89 – 57-25 .695
1989-90 – 42-40 .512
1990-91 – 33-49 .402
1991-92 – 57-25 .695
1992-93 – 54-28 .659
1993-94 – 47-35 .573
1994-95 – 43-39 .524
1995-96 – 47-35 .573
1996-97 – 42-40 .512
1997-98 – 47-35 .573
1998-99 – 22-28 .440
1999-2000 – 32-50 .390
2000-01 – 30-52 .366
2001-02 – 29-53 .354
2002-03 – 17-65 .207
2003-04 – 35-47 .427
2004-05 – 42-40 .512
2005-06 – 50-32 .610
2006-07 – 50-32 .610
2007-08 – 45-37 .549
2008-09 – 66-16 .805
2009-10 – 61-21 .744
2010-11 – 19-63 .232
2011-12 – 21-45 .318
2012-13 – 24-58 .293
2013-14 – 33-49 .402
2014-15 – 53-29 .646
2015-16 – 57-25 .695
Overall – 1,728-1,996 (.464)

HOME

1970-71 – 11-30 .268
1971-72 – 13-28 .317
1972-73 – 20-21 .488
1973-74 – 18-23 .439
1974-75 – 29-12 .707
1975-76 – 29-12 .707

1976-77 – 29-12 .707
1977-78 – 27-14 .659
1978-79 – 20-21 .488
1979-80 – 28-13 .683
1980-81 – 20-21 .488
1981-82 – 9-32 .220
1982-83 – 15-26 .366
1983-84 – 23-18 .561
1984-85 – 20-21 .488
1985-86 – 16-25 .390
1986-87 – 25-16 .610
1987-88 – 31-10 .756
1988-89 – 37-4 .902
1989-90 – 27-14 .659
1990-91 – 23-18 .561
1991-92 – 35-6 .854
1992-93 – 35-6 .854
1993-94 – 31-10 .756
1994-95 – 26-15 .634
1995-96 – 26-15 .634
1996-97 – 25-16 .610
1997-98 – 27-14 .659
1998-99 – 15-10 .600
1999-2000 – 22-19 .537
2000-01 – 20-21 .488
2001-02 – 20-21 .488
2002-03 – 14-27 .341
2003-04 – 23-18 .561
2004-05 – 29-12 .707
2005-06 – 31-10 .756
2006-07 – 30-11 .732
2007-08 – 27-14 .659
2008-09 – 39-2 .951
2009-10 – 35-6 .854
2010-11 – 12-29 .293
2011-12 – 11-22 .333
2012-13 – 14-27 .341
2013-14 – 19-22 .463
2014-15 – 31-10 .756
2015-16 – 33-8 .805
Overall – 1,100-762 (.591)

AWAY

1970-71 – 2-37 .051
1971-72 – 8-30 .211
1972-73 – 10-27 .270
1973-74 – 11-28 .282
1974-75 – 11-30 .268
1975-76 – 20-21 .488
1976-77 – 14-27 .341
1977-78 – 16-25 .390
1978-79 – 10-31 .244
1979-80 – 9-32 .220
1980-81 – 8-33 .195
1981-82 – 6-35 .146
1982-83 – 8-33 .195
1983-84 – 5-36 .122
1984-85 – 16-25 .390
1985-86 – 13-28 .317
1986-87 – 6-35 .146
1987-88 – 11-30 .268
1988-89 – 20-21 .488
1989-90 – 15-26 .366
1990-91 – 10-31 .244
1991-92 – 22-19 .537
1992-93 – 19-22 .463
1993-94 – 16-25 .390
1994-95 – 17-24 .415
1995-96 – 21-20 .512
1996-97 – 17-24 .415
1997-98 – 20-21 .488
1998-99 – 7-18 .280
1999-2000 – 10-31 .244
2000-01 – 10-31 .244
2001-02 – 9-32 .220
2002-03 – 3-38 .073
2003-04 – 12-29 .293

2004-05 – 13-28 .317
2005-06 – 19-22 .463
2006-07 – 20-21 .488
2007-08 – 18-23 .439
2008-09 – 27-14 .659
2009-10 – 26-15 .634
2010-11 – 7-34 .171
2011-12 – 10-23 .303
2012-13 – 10-31 .244
2013-14 – 14-27 .341
2014-15 – 22-19 .537
2015-16 – 24-17 .585
Overall – 622-1,229 (.336)

NEUTRAL

1970-71 – 2-0 1.000
1971-72 – 2-1 .667
1972-73 – 2-2 .500
1973-74 – 0-2 .000
Overall – 6-5 (.545)

Season Win-Loss Records By Division

CENTRAL

1970-71 – 1-13 .071
1971-72 – 9-11 .450
1972-73 – 8-14 .364
1973-74 – 8-14 .364
1974-75 – 17-13 .567
1975-76 – 15-11 .577
1976-77 – 8-12 .400
1977-78 – 9-11 .450
1978-79 – 6-14 .300
1979-80 – 16-14 .533
1980-81 – 11-19 .367
1981-82 – 5-25 .167
1982-83 – 8-21 .276
1983-84 – 11-19 .367
1984-85 – 13-16 .448
1985-86 – 10-19 .345
1986-87 – 8-22 .267
1987-88 – 11-19 .367
1988-89 – 19-11 .633
1989-90 – 14-16 .467
1990-91 – 11-19 .367
1991-92 – 21-7 .750
1992-93 – 22-6 .786
1993-94 – 16-12 .571
1994-95 – 17-11 .607
1995-96 – 13-15 .464
1996-97 – 13-15 .464
1997-98 – 14-14 .500
1998-99 – 9-13 .409
1999-2000 – 8-20 .286
2000-01 – 11-17 .393
2001-02 – 12-16 .429
2002-03 – 5-23 .179
2003-04 – 14-14 .500
2004-05 – 7-9 .438
2005-06 – 11-5 .688
2006-07 – 10-6 .625
2007-08 – 7-9 .438
2008-09 – 13-3 .813
2009-10 – 12-4 .750
2010-11 – 3-13 .188
2011-12 – 3-12 .200
2012-13 – 3-13 .188
2013-14 – 7-9 .438
2014-15 – 11-5 .688
2015-16 – 8-8 .500
Overall – 488-612 (.444)

ATLANTIC

1970-71 – 9-15 .375
1971-72 – 6-18 .250
1972-73 – 12-12 .500

1973-74 – 9-15 .375
1974-75 – 6-10 .375
1975-76 – 10-10 .500
1976-77 – 11-9 .550
1977-78 – 13-7 .650
1978-79 – 9-11 .450
1979-80 – 12-18 .400
1980-81 – 8-20 .286
1981-82 – 1-27 .036
1982-83 – 5-24 .172
1983-84 – 9-19 .321
1984-85 – 12-17 .414
1985-86 – 9-20 .310
1986-87 – 14-14 .500
1987-88 – 19-9 .679
1988-89 – 19-7 .731
1989-90 – 16-8 .667
1990-91 – 12-12 .500
1991-92 – 21-7 .750
1992-93 – 15-13 .536
1993-94 – 15-13 .536
1994-95 – 16-12 .571
1995-96 – 16-10 .615
1996-97 – 13-13 .500
1997-98 – 14-12 .538
1998-99 – 9-13 .409
1999-2000 – 12-14 .462
2000-01 – 11-15 .423
2001-02 – 8-18 .308
2002-03 – 4-22 .154
2003-04 – 15-11 .577
2004-05 – 7-11 .389
2005-06 – 12-6 .667
2006-07 – 12-6 .667
2007-08 – 10-8 .556
2008-09 – 15-3 .833
2009-10 – 15-3 .833
2010-11 – 8-10 .444
2011-12 – 6-12 .333
2012-13 – 5-13 .278
2013-14 – 8-10 .444
2014-15 – 12-6 .667
2015-16 – 14-4 .778
Overall – 514-567 (.475)

MIDWEST

1970-71 – 2-14 .125
1971-72 – 1-15 .063
1972-73 – 2-14 .125
1973-74 – 2-14 .125
1974-75 – 7-9 .438
1975-76 – 11-5 .688
1976-77 – 13-10 .565
1977-78 – 13-10 .565
1978-79 – 7-12 .368
1979-80 – 4-6 .400
1980-81 – 5-7 .417
1981-82 – 6-6 .500
1982-83 – 5-7 .417
1983-84 – 3-9 .250
1984-85 – 5-7 .417
1985-86 – 5-7 .417
1986-87 – 3-9 .250
1987-88 – 7-5 .583
1988-89 – 10-2 .833
1989-90 – 4-10 .286
1990-91 – 6-8 .429
1991-92 – 7-5 .583
1992-93 – 8-4 .667
1993-94 – 6-6 .500
1994-95 – 3-9 .250
1995-96 – 8-6 .571
1996-97 – 8-6 .571
1997-98 – 9-5 .643
1998-99 – 1-2 .333
1999-2000 – 8-6 .571
2000-01 – 4-10 .286

2001-02 – 7-7 .500
2002-03 – 3-11 .214
2003-04 – 2-12 .143
Overall – 195-275 (.415)

PACIFIC

1970-71 – 3-25 .107
1971-72 – 7-15 .318
1972-73 – 10-10 .500
1973-74 – 10-10 .500
1974-75 – 10-10 .500
1975-76 – 13-7 .650
1976-77 – 11-8 .579
1977-78 – 8-11 .421
1978-79 – 8-15 .348
1979-80 – 5-7 .417
1980-81 – 4-8 .333
1981-82 – 3-9 .250
1982-83 – 5-7 .417
1983-84 – 5-7 .417
1984-85 – 6-6 .500
1985-86 – 5-7 .417
1986-87 – 6-6 .500
1987-88 – 5-7 .417
1988-89 – 9-5 .643
1989-90 – 8-6 .571
1990-91 – 4-10 .286
1991-92 – 8-6 .571
1992-93 – 9-5 .643
1993-94 – 10-4 .714
1994-95 – 7-7 .500
1995-96 – 10-4 .714
1996-97 – 8-6 .571
1997-98 – 10-4 .714
1998-99 – 3-0 1.000
1999-2000 – 4-10 .286
2000-01 – 4-10 .286
2001-02 – 2-12 .143
2002-03 – 5-9 .357
2003-04 – 4-10 .286
2004-05 – 5-5 .500
2005-06 – 4-6 .400
2006-07 – 8-2 .800
2007-08 – 7-3 .700
2008-09 – 8-2 .800
2009-10 – 10-0 1.000
2010-11 – 3-7 .300
2011-12 – 3-3 .500
2012-13 – 2-8 .200
2013-14 – 5-5 .500
2014-15 – 7-3 .700
2015-16 – 8-2 .800
Overall – 299-329 (.476)

SOUTHEAST

2004-05 – 12-6 .667
2005-06 – 11-7 .611
2006-07 – 9-9 .500
2007-08 – 11-7 .611
2008-09 – 12-6 .667
2009-10 – 11-7 .611
2010-11 – 4-14 .222
2011-12 – 4-11 .267
2012-13 – 10-8 .556
2013-14 – 6-12 .333
2014-15 – 12-6 .667
2015-16 – 13-5 .722
Overall – 115-98 (.540)

NORTHWEST

2004-05 – 6-4 .600
2005-06 – 6-4 .600
2006-07 – 5-5 .500
2007-08 – 6-4 .600

2008-09 – 10-0 1.000
2009-10 – 7-3 .700
2010-11 – 0-10 .000
2011-12 – 3-3 .500
2012-13 – 3-7 .300
2013-14 – 6-4 .600
2014-15 – 6-4 .600
2015-16 – 8-2 .800
Overall – 66-50 (.569)

SOUTHWEST

2004-05 – 5-5 .500
2005-06 – 6-4 .600
2006-07 – 6-4 .600
2007-08 – 4-6 .400
2008-09 – 8-2 .800
2009-10 – 6-4 .600
2010-11 – 1-9 .100
2011-12 – 2-4 .333
2012-13 – 1-9 .100
2013-14 – 1-9 .100
2014-15 – 5-5 .500
2015-16 – 6-4 .600
Overall – 51-65 (.440)

SEASON WIN-LOSS RECORDS BY MONTH

OCTOBER

1970-71 – 0-9 .000
1971-72 – 2-8 .200
1972-73 – 3-8 .273
1973-74 – 2-7 .222
1974-75 – 4-4 .500
1975-76 – 1-2 .333
1976-77 – 5-0 1.000
1977-78 – 3-3 .500
1978-79 – 4-4 .500
1979-80 – 3-8 .273
1980-81 – 4-8 .333
1981-82 – 0-1 .000
1982-83 – 0-2 .000
1983-84 – 0-2 .000
1984-85 – 0-3 .000
1985-86 – 1-3 .250
1997-98 – 0-1 .000
2000-01 – 1-0 1.000
2001-02 – 0-2 .000
2002-03 – 1-1 .500
2003-04 – 0-2 .000
2007-08 – 0-1 .000
2008-09 – 1-1 .500
2009-10 – 2-2 .500
2010-11 – 1-2 .333
2012-13 – 1-0 1.000
2013-14 – 1-0 1.000
2014-15 – 1-1 .500
2015-16 – 2-1 .667
Overall – 43-86 (.333)

NOVEMBER

1970-71 – 1-17 .056
1971-72 – 6-6 .500
1972-73 – 5-8 .385
1973-74 – 7-9 .438
1974-75 – 7-4 .636
1975-76 – 6-9 .400
1976-77 – 10-4 .714
1977-78 – 10-2 .833
1978-79 – 3-11 .214
1979-80 – 8-7 .533
1980-81 – 4-10 .286
1981-82 – 4-10 .286
1982-83 – 2-11 .154

1983-84 – 5-10 .333
1984-85 – 2-10 .167
1985-86 – 6-7 .462
1986-87 – 5-9 .357
1987-88 – 3-8 .273
1988-89 – 8-3 .727
1989-90 – 6-7 .462
1990-91 – 9-7 .563
1991-92 – 9-5 .643
1992-93 – 6-7 .462
1993-94 – 6-6 .500
1994-95 – 8-5 .615
1995-96 – 6-8 .429
1996-97 – 9-5 .643
1997-98 – 9-5 .643
1999-2000 – 7-6 .538
2000-01 – 8-5 .615
2001-02 – 5-9 .357
2002-03 – 1-15 .063
2003-04 – 4-11 .267
2004-05 – 9-5 .643
2005-06 – 10-4 .714
2006-07 – 9-6 .600
2007-08 – 9-7 .563
2008-09 – 13-2 .867
2009-10 – 10-3 .769
2010-11 – 6-8 .429
2012-13 – 3-12 .200
2013-14 – 4-12 .250
2014-15 – 7-6 .538
2015-16 – 11-3 .786
Overall – 286-324 (.469)

DECEMBER

1970-71 – 4-13 .235
1971-72 – 7-10 .412
1972-73 – 2-12 .143
1973-74 – 5-11 .313
1974-75 – 7-6 .538
1975-76 – 11-4 .733
1976-77 – 5-9 .357
1977-78 – 5-10 .333
1978-79 – 7-6 .538
1979-80 – 8-5 .615
1980-81 – 5-9 .357
1981-82 – 2-12 .143
1982-83 – 2-12 .143
1983-84 – 4-10 .286
1984-85 – 4-9 .308
1985-86 – 7-8 .467
1986-87 – 8-7 .533
1987-88 – 9-7 .563
1988-89 – 13-2 .867
1989-90 – 5-9 .357
1990-91 – 2-11 .154
1991-92 – 10-4 .714
1992-93 – 11-5 .688
1993-94 – 6-9 .400
1994-95 – 12-3 .800
1995-96 – 9-4 .692
1996-97 – 10-5 .667
1997-98 – 8-5 .615
1999-2000 – 5-11 .313
2000-01 – 7-7 .500
2001-02 – 7-7 .500
2002-03 – 4-11 .267
2003-04 – 6-9 .400
2004-05 – 8-7 .533
2005-06 – 8-6 .571
2006-07 – 8-6 .571
2007-08 – 5-9 .357
2008-09 – 12-2 .857
2009-10 – 14-3 .824
2010-11 – 1-14 .067
2011-12 – 1-2 .333
2012-13 – 3-13 .188
2013-14 – 5-9 .357

2014-15 – 10-7 .588
2015-16 – 8-5 .615
Overall – 300-345 (.465)

JANUARY

1970-71 – 5-9 .357
1971-72 – 1-13 .071
1972-73 – 9-5 .643
1973-74 – 5-9 .357
1974-75 – 4-12 .250
1975-76 – 9-6 .600
1976-77 – 6-7 .462
1977-78 – 4-9 .308
1978-79 – 6-8 .429
1979-80 – 4-12 .250
1980-81 – 9-5 .643
1981-82 – 2-11 .154
1982-83 – 5-10 .333
1983-84 – 4-8 .333
1984-85 – 7-9 .438
1985-86 – 4-11 .267
1986-87 – 5-11 .313
1987-88 – 9-6 .600
1988-89 – 11-4 .733
1989-90 – 8-7 .533
1990-91 – 3-11 .214
1991-92 – 10-4 .714
1992-93 – 8-6 .571
1993-94 – 9-6 .600
1994-95 – 6-8 .429
1995-96 – 8-8 .500
1996-97 – 5-9 .357
1997-98 – 9-7 .563
1999-2000 – 6-9 .400
2000-01 – 4-11 .267
2001-02 – 2-13 .133
2002-03 – 3-11 .214
2003-04 – 7-7 .500
2004-05 – 9-5 .643
2005-06 – 8-7 .533
2006-07 – 9-7 .563
2007-08 – 11-3 .786
2008-09 – 10-4 .714
2009-10 – 12-3 .800
2010-11 – 0-16 .000
2011-12 – 7-10 .412
2012-13 – 6-8 .429
2013-14 – 6-9 .400
2014-15 – 11-6 .647
2015-16 – 13-3 .813
Overall – 299-363 (.452)

FEBRUARY

1970-71 – 2-12 .143
1971-72 – 4-12 .250
1972-73 – 5-9 .357
1973-74 – 4-11 .267
1974-75 – 10-6 .625
1975-76 – 9-3 .750
1976-77 – 5-7 .417
1977-78 – 8-7 .533
1978-79 – 6-8 .429
1979-80 – 3-10 .231
1980-81 – 3-9 .250
1981-82 – 4-9 .308
1982-83 – 6-7 .462
1983-84 – 9-5 .643
1984-85 – 9-6 .600
1985-86 – 5-7 .417
1986-87 – 5-7 .417
1987-88 – 7-8 .467
1988-89 – 10-3 .769
1989-90 – 6-6 .500
1990-91 – 6-7 .462

1991-92 – 8-5 .615
1992-93 – 12-1 .923
1993-94 – 11-3 .786
1994-95 – 7-6 .538
1995-96 – 10-2 .833
1996-97 – 7-5 .583
1997-98 – 4-9 .308
1998-99 – 5-6 .455
1999-2000 – 4-8 .333
2000-01 – 2-10 .167
2001-02 – 7-5 .583
2002-03 – 2-9 .182
2003-04 – 7-6 .538
2004-05 – 5-7 .417
2005-06 – 6-8 .429
2006-07 – 7-5 .583
2007-08 – 8-6 .571
2008-09 – 9-3 .750
2009-10 – 8-3 .727
2010-11 – 3-8 .273
2011-12 – 5-8 .385
2012-13 – 7-5 .583
2013-14 – 8-6 .571
2014-15 – 8-3 .727
2015-16 – 8-5 .615
Overall – 294-301 (.494)

MARCH

1970-71 – 3-7 .300
1971-72 – 3-10 .231
1972-73 – 8-8 .500
1973-74 – 6-6 .500
1974-75 – 7-9 .438
1975-76 – 9-6 .600
1976-77 – 9-8 .529
1977-78 – 8-8 .500
1978-79 – 3-11 .214
1979-80 – 11-3 .786
1980-81 – 3-13 .188
1981-82 – 3-13 .188
1982-83 – 4-12 .250
1983-84 – 4-13 .235
1984-85 – 9-6 .600
1985-86 – 5-10 .333
1986-87 – 4-12 .250
1987-88 – 5-9 .357
1988-89 – 9-8 .529
1989-90 – 8-8 .500
1990-91 – 5-10 .333
1991-92 – 12-4 .750
1992-93 – 6-6 .500
1993-94 – 8-7 .533
1994-95 – 6-9 .400
1995-96 – 8-9 .471
1996-97 – 6-10 .375
1997-98 – 11-4 .733
1998-99 – 9-8 .529
1999-2000 – 6-9 .400
2000-01 – 4-14 .222
2001-02 – 4-12 .250
2002-03 – 3-12 .200
2003-04 – 8-7 .533
2004-05 – 6-9 .400
2005-06 – 10-4 .714
2006-07 – 11-5 .688
2007-08 – 8-7 .533
2008-09 – 16-1 .941
2009-10 – 13-2 .867
2010-11 – 4-11 .267
2011-12 – 4-13 .235
2012-13 – 2-12 .143
2013-14 – 6-9 .400
2014-15 – 11-4 .733
2015-16 – 11-5 .688
Overall – 319-383 (.454)

APRIL

1974-75 – 1-1 .500
1975-76 – 4-3 .571
1976-77 – 3-4 .429
1977-78 – 5-0 1.000
1978-79 – 1-4 .200
1981-82 – 0-11 .000
1982-83 – 4-5 .444
1983-84 – 2-6 .250
1984-85 – 5-3 .625
1985-86 – 1-7 .125
1986-87 – 4-5 .444
1987-88 – 9-2 .818
1988-89 – 6-5 .545
1989-90 – 9-3 .750
1990-91 – 8-3 .727
1991-92 – 8-3 .727
1992-93 – 11-3 .786
1993-94 – 7-4 .636
1994-95 – 4-8 .333
1995-96 – 6-4 .600
1996-97 – 5-6 .455
1997-98 – 6-4 .600
1998-99 – 8-11 .421
1999-2000 – 4-7 .364
2000-01 – 4-5 .444
2001-02 – 4-5 .444
2002-03 – 3-6 .333
2003-04 – 3-5 .375
2004-05 – 5-7 .417
2005-06 – 8-3 .727
2006-07 – 6-3 .667
2007-08 – 4-4 .500
2008-09 – 5-3 .625
2009-10 – 2-5 .286
2010-11 – 4-4 .500
2011-12 – 4-12 .250
2012-13 – 2-8 .200
2013-14 – 3-4 .429
2014-15 – 5-2 .714
2015-16 – 4-3 .571
Overall – 187-191 (.495)

MAY

1998-99 – 0-3 (.000)

SEASON AVERAGES PER GAME

POINTS

1970-71 – 102.1
1971-72 – 105.8
1972-73 – 102.7
1973-74 – 100.3
1974-75 – 99
1975-76 – 101.7
1976-77 – 102.1
1977-78 – 104.4
1978-79 – 106.5
1979-80 – 114.1
1980-81 – 105.7
1981-82 – 103.2
1982-83 – 97.1
1983-84 – 102.3
1984-85 – 108.6
1985-86 – 107.8
1986-87 – 104.4
1987-88 – 104.5
1988-89 – 108.8
1989-90 – 102.6
1990-91 – 101.7
1991-92 – 108.9
1992-93 – 107.7
1993-94 – 101.2
1994-95 – 90.5

1995-96 – 91.1
1996-97 – 87.5
1997-98 – 92.5
1998-99 – 86.4
1999-2000 – 97
2000-01 – 92.2
2001-02 – 95.3
2002-03 – 91.4
2003-04 – 92.9
2004-05 – 96.5
2005-06 – 97.6
2006-07 – 96.8
2007-08 – 96.4
2008-09 – 100.3
2009-10 – 102.1
2010-11 – 95.5
2011-12 – 93
2012-13 – 96.5
2013-14 – 98.2
2014-15 – 103.1
2015-16 – 104.3
Overall – 100

OPPONENTS POINTS

1970-71 – 113.3
1971-72 – 113.4
1972-73 – 105.3
1973-74 – 104.6
1974-75 – 99.4
1975-76 – 99.2
1976-77 – 101
1977-78 – 103.9
1978-79 – 110.2
1979-80 – 113.8
1980-81 – 110.6
1981-82 – 111.7
1982-83 – 104.6
1983-84 – 106.5
1984-85 – 111.3
1985-86 – 110.6
1986-87 – 108.2
1987-88 – 103.7
1988-89 – 101.2
1989-90 – 102.9
1990-91 – 104.2
1991-92 – 103.4
1992-93 – 101.3
1993-94 – 97.1
1994-95 – 89.8
1995-96 – 88.5
1996-97 – 85.6
1997-98 – 89.8
1998-99 – 88.2
1999-2000 – 100.5
2000-01 – 96.5
2001-02 – 98.6
2002-03 – 101
2003-04 – 95.5
2004-05 – 95.7
2005-06 – 95.4
2006-07 – 92.9
2007-08 – 96.7
2008-09 – 91.4
2009-10 – 95.6
2010-11 – 104.5
2011-12 – 100.2
2012-13 – 101.2
2013-14 – 101.5
2014-15 – 98.7
2015-16 – 98.3
Overall – 101

REBOUNDS

1970-71 – 48.6
1971-72 – 50
1972-73 – 49.5

1973-74 – 45.9
1974-75 – 43.4
1975-76 – 46.1
1976-77 – 47.3
1977-78 – 47.1
1978-79 – 42.5
1979-80 – 45
1980-81 – 42.7
1981-82 – 41
1982-83 – 43.7
1983-84 – 43.9
1984-85 – 44.5
1985-86 – 43.2
1986-87 – 44.8
1987-88 – 40.3
1988-89 – 42.8
1989-90 – 42.8
1990-91 – 40.7
1991-92 – 42.6
1992-93 – 41.8
1993-94 – 42
1994-95 – 40
1995-96 – 35.6
1996-97 – 37.4
1997-98 – 40.1
1998-99 – 35.8
1999-2000 – 42.8
2000-01 – 42.1
2001-02 – 42.1
2002-03 – 44.6
2003-04 – 45.6
2004-05 – 42.3
2005-06 – 42.3
2006-07 – 43.5
2007-08 – 44.6
2008-09 – 42.2
2009-10 – 42.5
2010-11 – 40.3
2011-12 – 42.3
2012-13 – 41
2013-14 – 44.1
2014-15 – 43
2015-16 – 44.5
Overall – 43.1

OPPONENTS REBOUNDS

1970-71 – 50.9
1971-72 – 49.2
1972-73 – 50.2
1973-74 – 48
1974-75 – 47.9
1975-76 – 47.9
1976-77 – 47.7
1977-78 – 48.7
1978-79 – 45.2
1979-80 – 47.2
1980-81 – 44.6
1981-82 – 44.6
1982-83 – 40.9
1983-84 – 41.3
1984-85 – 44.6
1985-86 – 44.2
1986-87 – 44.5
1987-88 – 41.6
1988-89 – 42.6
1989-90 – 43.7
1990-91 – 42.6
1991-92 – 44
1992-93 – 42.6
1993-94 – 41.4
1994-95 – 37.8
1995-96 – 37.1
1996-97 – 37
1997-98 – 38.7
1998-99 – 39.9
1999-2000 – 43.9
2000-01 – 41.3

2001-02 – 40.4
2002-03 – 41.7
2003-04 – 42
2004-05 – 39.8
2005-06 – 39.4
2006-07 – 39.9
2007-08 – 40.4
2008-09 – 38.9
2009-10 – 38.5
2010-11 – 43.5
2011-12 – 42.8
2012-13 – 42.1
2013-14 – 42.5
2014-15 – 41.1
2015-16 – 41
Overall – 43

ASSISTS

1970-71 – 25.2
1971-72 – 25.1
1972-73 – 25.9
1973-74 – 25
1974-75 – 23.2
1975-76 – 22.5
1976-77 – 22.5
1977-78 – 21.2
1978-79 – 21.9
1979-80 – 25.7
1980-81 – 24.5
1981-82 – 22.8
1982-83 – 21.2
1983-84 – 23.5
1984-85 – 25.6
1985-86 – 25.2
1986-87 – 23.3
1987-88 – 25.2
1988-89 – 27.6
1989-90 – 25.7
1990-91 – 27.3
1991-92 – 27.6
1992-93 – 28.6
1993-94 – 25
1994-95 – 20.4
1995-96 – 22.2
1996-97 – 20.9
1997-98 – 23.1
1998-99 – 21.9
1999-2000 – 23.7
2000-01 – 20.8
2001-02 – 23.1
2002-03 – 20.9
2003-04 – 22
2004-05 – 22.6
2005-06 – 19
2006-07 – 20.8
2007-08 – 20
2008-09 – 20.3
2009-10 – 22.4
2010-11 – 21
2011-12 – 19.8
2012-13 – 20.7
2013-14 – 21.2
2014-15 – 22.1
2015-16 – 22.7
Overall – 23.1

OPPONENTS ASSISTS

1970-71 – 28.1
1971-72 – 28.3
1972-73 – 28.2
1973-74 – 25.9
1974-75 – 21.3
1975-76 – 21.1
1976-77 – 21.2
1977-78 – 23.4

1978-79 – 25.1
1979-80 – 26.9
1980-81 – 26.4
1981-82 – 26.5
1982-83 – 24.5
1983-84 – 26.1
1984-85 – 27
1985-86 – 25.9
1986-87 – 25.1
1987-88 – 24.3
1988-89 – 24.9
1989-90 – 26.1
1990-91 – 26.2
1991-92 – 26.3
1992-93 – 25.7
1993-94 – 24.5
1994-95 – 22.1
1995-96 – 22.2
1996-97 – 20.1
1997-98 – 21.8
1998-99 – 21.1
1999-2000 – 23.7
2000-01 – 22.9
2001-02 – 24.3
2002-03 – 24
2003-04 – 21.7
2004-05 – 21.2
2005-06 – 20.3
2006-07 – 20.1
2007-08 – 21
2008-09 – 19.1
2009-10 – 20.3
2010-11 – 24.2
2011-12 – 23.1
2012-13 – 23.9
2013-14 – 24.8
2014-15 – 24.1
2015-16 – 21.4
Overall – 23.8

FOULS

1970-71 – 25.8
1971-72 – 23.6
1972-73 – 23.7
1973-74 – 23.5
1974-75 – 22.9
1975-76 – 22.8
1976-77 – 23.8
1977-78 – 22.3
1978-79 – 24.7
1979-80 – 23.6
1980-81 – 24.3
1981-82 – 26.7
1982-83 – 27.3
1983-84 – 26.9
1984-85 – 26.5
1985-86 – 27.6
1986-87 – 22.6
1987-88 – 22.4
1988-89 – 19.4
1989-90 – 20.3
1990-91 – 20.4
1991-92 – 19
1992-93 – 19.3
1993-94 – 20.7
1994-95 – 20.7
1995-96 – 20.5
1996-97 – 23
1997-98 – 23.6
1998-99 – 24.2
1999-2000 – 27.1
2000-01 – 23.2
2001-02 – 21.4
2002-03 – 22.7
2003-04 – 21.3
2004-05 – 22.6
2005-06 – 21.1
2006-07 – 21.7

2007-08 – 20.9
2008-09 – 20.3
2009-10 – 19.4
2010-11 – 20.1
2011-12 – 20
2012-13 – 21.2
2013-14 – 20
2014-15 – 18.4
2015-16 – 20.3
Overall – 22.5

OPPONENTS FOULS

1970-71 – 23.2
1971-72 – 23.6
1972-73 – 23.6
1973-74 – 22.6
1974-75 – 23.6
1975-76 – 22.7
1976-77 – 23.3
1977-78 – 23.8
1978-79 – 24.4
1979-80 – 24.8
1980-81 – 23.9
1981-82 – 25.3
1982-83 – 22.3
1983-84 – 23.2
1984-85 – 25.6
1985-86 – 23.7
1986-87 – 25.3
1987-88 – 24.6
1988-89 – 24
1989-90 – 23.1
1990-91 – 23.1
1991-92 – 22.9
1992-93 – 22.3
1993-94 – 21.9
1994-95 – 21.6
1995-96 – 20.3
1996-97 – 21.3
1997-98 – 23.2
1998-99 – 24
1999-2000 – 25.1
2000-01 – 22.1
2001-02 – 20
2002-03 – 20.8
2003-04 – 20.2
2004-05 – 21.6
2005-06 – 22.5
2006-07 – 22
2007-08 – 20.3
2008-09 – 20.3
2009-10 – 20.8
2010-11 – 21.3
2011-12 – 20.9
2012-13 – 19.7
2013-14 – 19.5
2014-15 – 20.5
2015-16 – 20.6
Overall – 22.5

DISQUALIFICATIONS

1970-71 – .45
1971-72 – .28
1972-73 – .26
1973-74 – .27
1974-75 – .2
1975-76 – .12
1976-77 – .29
1977-78 – .18
1978-79 – .26
1979-80 – .22
1980-81 – .39
1981-82 – .43
1982-83 – .68
1983-84 – .46
1984-85 – .5

1985-86 – .45
1986-87 – .24
1987-88 – .24
1988-89 – .06
1989-90 – .2
1990-91 – .15
1991-92 – .1
1992-93 – .12
1993-94 – .18
1994-95 – .13
1995-96 – .17
1996-97 – .2
1997-98 – .35
1998-99 – .26
1999-2000 – .41
2000-01 – .07
2001-02 – .29
2002-03 – .28
2003-04 – .1
2004-05 – .17
2005-06 – .2
2006-07 – .16
2007-08 – .15
2008-09 – .12
2009-10 – .07
2010-11 – .1
2011-12 – .09
2012-13 – .16
2013-14 – .07
2014-15 – .05
2015-16 – .05
Overall – .23

OPPONENTS DISQUALIFICATIONS

1970-71 – .18
1971-72 – .29
1972-73 – .3
1973-74 – .33
1974-75 – .32
1975-76 – .21
1976-77 – .28
1977-78 – .2
1978-79 – .26
1979-80 – .37
1980-81 – .26
1981-82 – .21
1982-83 – .17
1983-84 – .26
1984-85 – .28
1985-86 – .28
1986-87 – .28
1987-88 – .32
1988-89 – .23
1989-90 – .23
1990-91 – .24
1991-92 – .11
1992-93 – .23
1993-94 – .15
1994-95 – .17
1995-96 – .11
1996-97 – .2
1997-98 – .26
1998-99 – .28
1999-2000 – .32
2000-01 – .15
2001-02 – .16
2002-03 – .09
2003-04 – .1
2004-05 – .15
2005-06 – .23
2006-07 – .17
2007-08 – .16
2008-09 – .2
2009-10 – .12
2010-11 – .09
2011-12 – .14

2012-13 – .09
2013-14 – .12
2014-15 – .11
2015-16 – .16
Overall – .21

STEALS

1973-74 – 7.3
1974-75 – 7.3
1975-76 – 7.8
1976-77 – 7.1
1977-78 – 8.4
1978-79 – 8.3
1979-80 – 9.3
1980-81 – 7.7
1981-82 – 7.7
1982-83 – 7.5
1983-84 – 7.7
1984-85 – 7.6
1985-86 – 7.6
1986-87 – 8.2
1987-88 – 8.9
1988-89 – 9.6
1989-90 – 7.9
1990-91 – 7.8
1991-92 – 7.5
1992-93 – 7.5
1993-94 – 8.6
1994-95 – 7.7
1995-96 – 8.2
1996-97 – 8
1997-98 – 9.9
1998-99 – 9
1999-2000 – 8.7
2000-01 – 7.8
2001-02 – 7
2002-03 – 7.8
2003-04 – 7.1
2004-05 – 8
2005-06 – 6.9
2006-07 – 7.6
2007-08 – 7.1
2008-09 – 7.2
2009-10 – 6.9
2010-11 – 6.6
2011-12 – 7.1
2012-13 – 7.9
2013-14 – 7.1
2014-15 – 7.4
2015-16 – 6.7
Overall – 8

OPPONENTS STEALS

1973-74 – 7.7
1974-75 – 8.7
1975-76 – 7.4
1976-77 – 8
1977-78 – 8.4
1978-79 – 8
1979-80 – 8.6
1980-81 – 8.3
1981-82 – 8
1982-83 – 7.6
1983-84 – 7.1
1984-85 – 7.5
1985-86 – 8.7
1986-87 – 9.9
1987-88 – 8.4
1988-89 – 8.4
1989-90 – 8.3
1990-91 – 8.7
1991-92 – 7.9
1992-93 – 7.4
1993-94 – 7.7
1994-95 – 6.8
1995-96 – 6.1

1996-97 – 6.7
1997-98 – 8.6
1998-99 – 7.8
1999-2000 – 8
2000-01 – 8.5
2001-02 – 7.3
2002-03 – 9.8
2003-04 – 7.7
2004-05 – 6.7
2005-06 – 6.6
2006-07 – 6.6
2007-08 – 6.8
2008-09 – 6.3
2009-10 – 6.6
2010-11 – 7.5
2011-12 – 7.9
2012-13 – 7.6
2013-14 – 7.2
2014-15 – 7.8
2015-16 – 7.2
Overall – 7.7

BLOCKED SHOTS

1973-74 – 3.6
1974-75 – 4.2
1975-76 – 4.8
1976-77 – 5.8
1977-78 – 5.5
1978-79 – 4.1
1979-80 – 4.2
1980-81 – 3.9
1981-82 – 4.3
1982-83 – 3.5
1983-84 – 4.6
1984-85 – 5.8
1985-86 – 5.3
1986-87 – 6.8
1987-88 – 6.4
1988-89 – 7.1
1989-90 – 6.2
1990-91 – 5.5
1991-92 – 7.6
1992-93 – 6.5
1993-94 – 5.2
1994-95 – 4.3
1995-96 – 4.1
1996-97 – 3.8
1997-98 – 5.1
1998-99 – 4.1
1999-2000 – 4.4
2000-01 – 5.3
2001-02 – 5.7
2002-03 – 6.4
2003-04 – 6.5
2004-05 – 5.6
2005-06 – 4.8
2006-07 – 4.3
2007-08 – 5.2
2008-09 – 5.3
2009-10 – 5.2
2010-11 – 4.2
2011-12 – 4
2012-13 – 4.1
2013-14 – 3.7
2014-15 – 4.1
2015-16 – 3.9
Overall – 5

OPPONENTS BLOCKED SHOTS

1973-74 – 4.2
1974-75 – 3.4
1975-76 – 4
1976-77 – 4.7
1977-78 – 5.4
1978-79 – 6.1

1979-80 – 6
1980-81 – 5.5
1981-82 – 5.9
1982-83 – 5.3
1983-84 – 4.8
1984-85 – 5.2
1985-86 – 4.4
1986-87 – 5.8
1987-88 – 5.5
1988-89 – 4.4
1989-90 – 4.6
1990-91 – 4.8
1991-92 – 5.1
1992-93 – 4.5
1993-94 – 5.6
1994-95 – 5.3
1995-96 – 4.1
1996-97 – 4.3
1997-98 – 5.5
1998-99 – 5.6
1999-2000 – 6.1
2000-01 – 6.6
2001-02 – 5.6
2002-03 – 6
2003-04 – 5.3
2004-05 – 5.1
2005-06 – 4.4
2006-07 – 4.3
2007-08 – 4.7
2008-09 – 4.1
2009-10 – 4
2010-11 – 6
2011-12 – 6.2
2012-13 – 6.8
2013-14 – 5.6
2014-15 – 4.5
2015-16 – 4.4
Overall – 5.1

TURNOVERS

1973-74 – 18.8
1974-75 – 17.8
1975-76 – 16.2
1976-77 – 16.5
1977-78 – 16.9
1978-79 – 16.8
1979-80 – 16.7
1980-81 – 17
1981-82 – 16.1
1982-83 – 18.8
1983-84 – 16.2
1984-85 – 16.9
1985-86 – 17.2
1986-87 – 19.7
1987-88 – 17.5
1988-89 – 16.1
1989-90 – 15.2
1990-91 – 15.6
1991-92 – 13.1
1992-93 – 13.7
1993-94 – 13.9
1994-95 – 14.3
1995-96 – 13.1
1996-97 – 14.5
1997-98 – 17.3
1998-99 – 15.7
1999-2000 – 17.4
2000-01 – 16.5
2001-02 – 14.6
2002-03 – 18.3
2003-04 – 14.8
2004-05 – 13.9
2005-06 – 13.9
2006-07 – 14.4
2007-08 – 14
2008-09 – 12.7
2009-10 – 13.9

2010-11 – 14.2
2011-12 – 15.4
2012-13 – 14
2013-14 – 14.2
2014-15 – 14.3
2015-16 – 13.6
Overall – 15.6

OPPONENTS TURNOVERS

1973-74 – 20.2
1974-75 – 19.7
1975-76 – 19.3
1976-77 – 18.8
1977-78 – 18
1978-79 – 19
1979-80 – 20.3
1980-81 – 18
1981-82 – 17.1
1982-83 – 15.5
1983-84 – 14.9
1984-85 – 16.5
1985-86 – 16.2
1986-87 – 17
1987-88 – 17.5
1988-89 – 17.4
1989-90 – 15.8
1990-91 – 15
1991-92 – 14
1992-93 – 14.7
1993-94 – 15.8
1994-95 – 14.8
1995-96 – 15.6
1996-97 – 16.2
1997-98 – 17.6
1998-99 – 16.4
1999-2000 – 16.9
2000-01 – 15
2001-02 – 13
2002-03 – 14.2
2003-04 – 13.1
2004-05 – 14.8
2005-06 – 13.2
2006-07 – 15.3
2007-08 – 13.3
2008-09 – 13.9
2009-10 – 12.7
2010-11 – 13.5
2011-12 – 13.9
2012-13 – 15.2
2013-14 – 14
2014-15 – 13.3
2015-16 – 13.3
Overall – 15.8

SEASON PERCENTAGES

FIELD GOAL

1970-71 – .424
1971-72 – .428
1972-73 – .435
1973-74 – .439
1974-75 – .462
1975-76 – .454
1976-77 – .449
1977-78 – .454
1978-79 – .468
1979-80 – .474
1980-81 – .467
1981-82 – .464
1982-83 – .465
1983-84 – .465
1984-85 – .471
1985-86 – .480
1986-87 – .470
1987-88 – .490

1988-89 – .502
1989-90 – .461
1990-91 – .475
1991-92 – .488
1992-93 – .497
1993-94 – .465
1994-95 – .441
1995-96 – .460
1996-97 – .453
1997-98 – .454
1998-99 – .439
1999-2000 – .442
2000-01 – .442
2001-02 – .448
2002-03 – .422
2003-04 – .433
2004-05 – .447
2005-06 – .454
2006-07 – .447
2007-08 – .439
2008-09 – .468
2009-10 – .485
2010-11 – .434
2011-12 – .422
2012-13 – .434
2013-14 – .437
2014-15 – .458
2015-16 – .460
Overall – .456

OPPONENTS FIELD GOAL

1970-71 – .465
1971-72 – .485
1972-73 – .452
1973-74 – .469
1974-75 – .451
1975-76 – .454
1976-77 – .449
1977-78 – .456
1978-79 – .503
1979-80 – .501
1980-81 – .503
1981-82 – .512
1982-83 – .489
1983-84 – .487
1984-85 – .478
1985-86 – .475
1986-87 – .478
1987-88 – .476
1988-89 – .461
1989-90 – .479
1990-91 – .486
1991-92 – .470
1992-93 – .466
1993-94 – .464
1994-95 – .461
1995-96 – .462
1996-97 – .441
1997-98 – .433
1998-99 – .436
1999-2000 – .443
2000-01 – .445
2001-02 – .457
2002-03 – .453
2003-04 – .437
2004-05 – .452
2005-06 – .455
2006-07 – .448
2007-08 – .455
2008-09 – .431
2009-10 – .442
2010-11 – .475
2011-12 – .467
2012-13 – .476
2013-14 – .452
2014-15 – .456

2015-16 – .448
Overall – .464

THREE-POINT FIELD GOAL

1979-80 – .193
1980-81 – .289
1981-82 – .182
1982-83 – .250
1983-84 – .262
1984-85 – .287
1985-86 – .338
1986-87 – .240
1987-88 – .378
1988-89 – .359
1989-90 – .407
1990-91 – .334
1991-92 – .357
1992-93 – .381
1993-94 – .362
1994-95 – .385
1995-96 – .377
1996-97 – .376
1997-98 – .372
1998-99 – .341
1999-2000 – .373
2000-01 – .334
2001-02 – .377
2002-03 – .327
2003-04 – .314
2004-05 – .332
2005-06 – .339
2006-07 – .352
2007-08 – .358
2008-09 – .393
2009-10 – .381
2010-11 – .342
2011-12 – .346
2012-13 – .346
2013-14 – .356
2014-15 – .367
2015-16 – .363
Overall – .337

OPPONENTS THREE-POINT FIELD GOAL

1979-80 – .291
1980-81 – .310
1981-82 – .298
1982-83 – .219
1983-84 – .263
1984-85 – .277
1985-86 – .290
1986-87 – .278
1987-88 – .318
1988-89 – .339
1989-90 – .312
1990-91 – .323
1991-92 – .332
1992-93 – .329
1993-94 – .354
1994-95 – .357
1995-96 – .388
1996-97 – .373
1997-98 – .344
1998-99 – .350
1999-2000 – .342
2000-01 – .365
2001-02 – .394
2002-03 – .358
2003-04 – .371
2004-05 – .376
2005-06 – .356
2006-07 – .329
2007-08 – .357
2008-09 – .333
2009-10 – .347

2010-11 – .411
2011-12 – .362
2012-13 – .372
2013-14 – .367
2014-15 – .343
2015-16 – .347
Overall – .337

FREE THROW

1970-71 – .746
1971-72 – .736
1972-73 – .747
1973-74 – .772
1974-75 – .742
1975-76 – .737
1976-77 – .737
1977-78 – .741
1978-79 – .770
1979-80 – .772
1980-81 – .778
1981-82 – .747
1982-83 – .721
1983-84 – .743
1984-85 – .749
1985-86 – .752
1986-87 – .697
1987-88 – .744
1988-89 – .747
1989-90 – .744
1990-91 – .765
1991-92 – .805
1992-93 – .802
1993-94 – .770
1994-95 – .760
1995-96 – .763
1996-97 – .723
1997-98 – .756
1998-99 – .749
1999-2000 – .750
2000-01 – .765
2001-02 – .772
2002-03 – .747
2003-04 – .753
2004-05 – .752
2005-06 – .729
2006-07 – .695
2007-08 – .717
2008-09 – .757
2009-10 – .720
2010-11 – .745
2011-12 – .716
2012-13 – .756
2013-14 – .751
2014-15 – .751
2015-16 – .748
Overall – .749

OPPONENTS FREE THROW

1970-71 – .773
1971-72 – .764
1972-73 – .765
1973-74 – .784
1974-75 – .771
1975-76 – .748
1976-77 – .752
1977-78 – .745
1978-79 – .758
1979-80 – .765
1980-81 – .752
1981-82 – .754
1982-83 – .743
1983-84 – .763
1984-85 – .769
1985-86 – .767
1986-87 – .753
1987-88 – .788

1988-89 – .777
1989-90 – .761
1990-91 – .764
1991-92 – .769
1992-93 – .766
1993-94 – .735
1994-95 – .757
1995-96 – .759
1996-97 – .742
1997-98 – .755
1998-99 – .743
1999-2000 – .776
2000-01 – .768
2001-02 – .748
2002-03 – .772
2003-04 – .749
2004-05 – .750
2005-06 – .742
2006-07 – .734
2007-08 – .748
2008-09 – .770
2009-10 – .757
2010-11 – .759
2011-12 – .748
2012-13 – .739
2013-14 – .757
2014-15 – .745
2015-16 – .743
Overall – .758

SEASON OVERTIME GAMES

1971-72 – 3
1972-73 – 5
1973-74 – 3
1974-75 – 5
1975-76 – 4
1976-77 – 4
1977-78 – 7
1979-80 – 7
1980-81 – 4
1981-82 – 5
1982-83 – 3
1983-84 – 6
1984-85 – 4
1985-86 – 4
1986-87 – 2
1987-88 – 4
1988-89 – 3
1989-90 – 8
1990-91 – 6
1991-92 – 5
1992-93 – 4
1993-94 – 7
1994-95 – 7
1995-96 – 4
1996-97 – 6
1997-98 – 6
1998-99 – 2
1999-2000 – 7
2000-01 – 5
2001-02 – 6
2002-03 – 5
2003-04 – 6
2004-05 – 6
2005-06 – 5
2006-07 – 7
2007-08 – 5
2008-09 – 4
2009-10 – 4
2010-11 – 3
2011-12 – 5
2012-13 – 1
2013-14 – 8
2014-15 – 4
2015-16 – 6
Overall – 4.7

SEASON POINT DIFFERENTIALS

1970-71 – -11.2
1971-72 – -7.6
1972-73 – -2.6
1973-74 – -4.3
1974-75 – -.4
1975-76 – +2.5
1976-77 – +1.1
1977-78 – +.5
1978-79 – -3.7
1979-80 – +.3
1980-81 – -4.9
1981-82 – -8.5
1982-83 – -7.4
1983-84 – -4.3
1984-85 – -2.8
1985-86 – -2.8
1986-87 – -3.8
1987-88 – +.8
1988-89 – +7.6
1989-90 – -.3
1990-91 – -2.5
1991-92 – +5.5
1992-93 – +6.5
1993-94 – +4
1994-95 – +.6
1995-96 – +2.6
1996-97 – +1.8
1997-98 – +2.7
1998-99 – -1.7
1999-2000 – -3.5
2000-01 – -4.2
2001-02 – -3.3
2002-03 – -9.6
2003-04 – -2.6
2004-05 – +.8
2005-06 – +2.2
2006-07 – +3.8
2007-08 – -.4
2008-09 – +8.9
2009-10 – +6.5
2010-11 – -9
2011-12 – -7.2
2012-13 – -4.7
2013-14 – -3.3
2014-15 – +4.5
2015-16 – +6
Overall – -1

SEASON HIGHEST/LOWEST-SCORING GAMES

Highest

1970-71 – 125 (February 19 vs. Cincinnati)
1971-72 – 133 (February 18 vs. Cincinnati)
1972-73 – 136 (February 8 at Atlanta)
1973-74 – 125 (February 10 vs. Buffalo)
1974-75 – 129 (October 18 at Portland)
1975-76 – 132 (January 24 vs. Milwaukee)
1976-77 – 130 (January 22 vs. Milwaukee)

1977-78 – 136 (February 14 vs. New York)
1978-79 – 127 (December 12 vs. Detroit, February 17 at New York)
1979-80 – 154 (January 29 vs. Los Angeles)
1980-81 – 132 (January 3 vs. Washington)
1981-82 – 127 (March 7 at Denver)
1982-83 – 132 (November 10 at Golden State, April 15 at Indiana)
1983-84 – 137 (February 28 at Kansas City)
1984-85 – 135 (March 16 at Dallas)
1985-86 – 135 (February 13 vs. New Jersey)
1986-87 – 129 (February 18 vs. Sacramento)
1987-88 – 128 (January 30 vs. Washington)
1988-89 – 142 (January 23 vs. Golden State)
1989-90 – 131 (November 17 vs. Atlanta, February 14 vs. Indiana)
1990-91 – 125 (January 29 vs. Charlotte)
1991-92 – 148 (December 17 vs. Miami)
1992-93 – 132 (January 15 at Indiana)
1993-94 – 127 (December 28 vs. Charlotte)
1994-95 – 123 (December 26 vs. Boston)
1995-96 – 124 (December 30 vs. Portland)
1996-97 – 125 (April 12 vs. Philadelphia)
1997-98 – 122 (March 4 vs. Toronto)
1998-99 – 116 (March 2 vs. Boston)
1999-2000 – 127 (December 11 vs. Atlanta)
2000-01 – 124 (March 11 vs. Milwaukee)
2001-02 – 123 (April 13 at Atlanta)
2002-03 – 133 (December 9 vs. Milwaukee)
2003-04 – 115 (November 29 vs. Memphis)
2004-05 – 114 (Three times)
2005-06 – 124 (April 4 vs. Philadelphia)
2006-07 – 124 (January 30 vs. Golden State, March 13 vs. Sacramento)
2007-08 – 132 (January 15 at Memphis)
2008-09 – 126 (March 13 at Sacramento)
2009-10 – 126 (February 26 at Toronto)
2010-11 – 126 (February 11 vs. L.A. Clippers)
2011-12 – 118 (March 11 vs. Houston)
2012-13 – 122 (February 6 vs. Charlotte)
2013-14 – 127 (November 9 vs. Philadelphia)
2014-15 – 129 (January 23 vs. Charlotte)
2015-16 – 125 (January 8 at Minnesota)

OPPONENTS HIGHEST

1970-71 – 141 (November 2 at Philadelphia)
1971-72 – 148 (January 2 vs. Philadelphia)
1972-73 – 132 (February 8 at Atlanta)
1973-74 – 130 (December 2 vs. Houston)
1974-75 – 131 (October 18 at Portland)
1975-76 – 125 (December 5 at Buffalo)
1976-77 – 133 (March 15 vs. Philadelphia)
1977-78 – 129 (December 17 at Philadelphia)
1978-79 – 139 (February 28 at Milwaukee, March 24 at New Orleans)
1979-80 – 153 (January 29 vs. Los Angeles)
1980-81 – 140 (March 6 at San Diego, March 13 vs. New Jersey)
1981-82 – 147 (March 7 at Denver)
1982-83 – 132 (March 1 at Denver)
1983-84 – 142 (February 28 at Kansas City)
1984-85 – 144 (January 26 at Denver)
1985-86 – 138 (March 8 at Golden State)
1986-87 – 134 (November 16 at Houston, December 19 vs. Utah)
1987-88 – 128 (November 13 at Boston, November 14 vs. Detroit)
1988-89 – 127 (November 26 at New York)
1989-90 – 145 (March 8 at Golden State)
1990-91 – 128 (January 12 at Denver)
1991-92 – 134 (April 9 vs. Charlotte)
1992-93 – 122 (November 12 at Golden State)
1993-94 – 119 (March 15 vs. Phoenix)
1994-95 – 116 (January 4 vs. Seattle, January 10 vs. Charlotte)
1995-96 – 121 (December 30 vs. Portland)
1996-97 – 118 (April 12 vs. Philadelphia)
1997-98 – 109 (January 8 vs. Seattle)
1998-99 – 113 (March 20 at Washington)
1999-2000 – 136 (December 10 at Indiana)
2000-01 – 120 (February 13 vs. Toronto, March 2 at Orlando)
2001-02 – 128 (April 13 at Atlanta)
2002-03 – 140 (December 9 vs. Milwaukee)
2003-04 – 126 (March 30 at Dallas)
2004-05 – 128 (April 1 vs. Sacramento)
2005-06 – 120 (November 19 at Philadelphia)
2006-07 – 118 (January 24 vs. Philadelphia)

2007-08 – 124 (January 15 at Memphis)
2008-09 – 123 (March 13 at Sacramento)
2009-10 – 118 (February 18 vs. Denver, February 26 at Toronto)
2010-11 – 129 (December 4 at Minnesota)
2011-12 – 125 (April 3 vs. San Antonio)
2012-13 – 124 (January 14 at Sacramento)
2013-14 – 127 (December 26 vs. Atlanta)
2014-15 – 127 (December 17 vs. Atlanta)
2015-16 – 132 (January 18 vs. Golden State)

LOWEST

1970-71 – 73 (January 2 at Milwaukee)
1971-72 – 82 (October 19 at Milwaukee)
1972-73 – 80 (January 3 at Baltimore)
1973-74 – 83 (October 14 vs. Detroit)
1974-75 – 74 (December 21 vs. Chicago)
1975-76 – 78 (April 11 at New York)
1976-77 – 78 (November 17 at Seattle)
1977-78 – 67 (November 19 at Portland)
1978-79 – 79 (January 16 vs. Kansas City)
1979-80 – 95 (October 12 at New Jersey)
1980-81 – 79 (October 17 at Chicago, December 17 at Philadelphia)
1981-82 – 73 (December 18 at Indiana)
1982-83 – 73 (March 18 vs. Atlanta)
1983-84 – 82 (March 15 at New York)
1984-85 – 86 (March 23 vs. Atlanta)
1985-86 – 84 (December 3 vs. Indiana)
1986-87 – 76 (March 21 at Indiana)
1987-88 – 81 (March 2 at Denver)
1988-89 – 80 (January 27 at Detroit)
1989-90 – 74 (December 2 vs. Minnesota)
1990-91 – 79 (March 8 at Sacramento)
1991-92 – 85 (January 16 vs. Chicago)
1992-93 – 78 (March 28 at Detroit)
1993-94 – 77 (March 23 at Indiana)
1994-95 – 67 (February 8 at Boston)
1995-96 – 68 (March 1 at Atlanta)
1996-97 – 59 (March 25 at San Antonio)

1997-98 – 70 (November 15 at Chicago)
1998-99 – 65 (April 26 vs. Miami, May 2 vs. Atlanta)
1999-2000 – 72 (March 12 at Milwaukee)
2000-01 – 71 (December 5 vs. Charlotte)
2001-02 – 64 (November 7 at New York, January 13 at Portland)
2002-03 – 67 (October 29 at Sacramento)
2003-04 – 69 (January 7 at Toronto)
2004-05 – 69 (December 16 at Detroit)
2005-06 – 72 (February 27 vs. Detroit)
2006-07 – 63 (December 2 at Houston)
2007-08 – 70 (December 2 at Boston)
2008-09 – 74 (February 26 at Houston)
2009-10 – 83 (April 14 at Atlanta)
2010-11 – 57 (January 11 at L.A. Lakers)
2011-12 – 75 (Four times)
2012-13 – 73 (December 7 at Minnesota)
2013-14 – 74 (November 2 at Indiana)
2014-15 – 78 (November 21 at Washington, April 12 at Boston)
2015-16 – 76 (December 26 at Portland)

Opponents Lowest

1970-71 – 79 (January 19 vs. Buffalo at Syracuse, NY)
1971-72 – 85 (December 14 at Baltimore)
1972-73 – 88 (November 21 vs. Seattle, January 2 vs. Phoenix)
1973-74 – 75 (December 5 at Philadelphia)
1974-75 – 74 (November 21 vs. Golden State)
1975-76 – 77 (March 13 vs. Phoenix)
1976-77 – 75 (November 1 at N.Y. Nets)
1977-78 – 78 (March 26 vs. Chicago)
1978-79 – 86 (January 16 vs. Kansas City)
1979-80 – 91 (January 22 vs. Washington)
1980-81 – 88 (October 16 vs. Washington)
1981-82 – 87 (February 6 at Atlanta)
1982-83 – 77 (December 21 at Washington)
1983-84 – 76 (February 3 vs. Chicago)
1984-85 – 89 (March 19 vs. Philadelphia)
1985-86 – 90 (November 24 vs. Atlanta, November 30 vs. New Jersey)
1986-87 – 77 (March 21 at Indiana)

1987-88 – 83 (February 1 vs. Detroit)
1988-89 – 79 (January 27 at Detroit)
1989-90 – 82 (February 8 vs. Miami)
1990-91 – 74 (December 19 vs. L.A. Lakers)
1991-92 – 80 (December 17 vs. Miami, March 22 vs. Atlanta)
1992-93 – 81 (April 20 vs. Detroit)
1993-94 – 61 (March 22 vs. Indiana)
1994-95 – 63 (December 19 at Chicago)
1995-96 – 64 (March 30 at Golden State)
1996-97 – 57 (December 4 at Orlando)
1997-98 – 67 (December 3 at Golden State)
1998-99 – 67 (April 10 vs. Atlanta)
1999-2000 – 75 (January 6 vs. Golden State)
2000-01 – 58 (January 22 vs. Portland)
2001-02 – 75 (November 27 vs. Washington)
2002-03 – 70 (November 5 vs. L.A. Lakers)
2003-04 – 74 (December 28 vs. Portland)
2004-05 – 71 (January 15 at Utah)
2005-06 – 66 (January 24 vs. Indiana)
2006-07 – 68 (March 23 vs. New York)
2007-08 – 73 (March 19 vs. Detroit)
2008-09 – 70 (December 17 at Minnesota)
2009-10 – 73 (January 29 at Indiana)
2010-11 – 81 (November 24 vs. Milwaukee)
2011-12 – 80 (April 6 at Toronto)
2012-13 – 82 (December 22 at Milwaukee)
2013-14 – 76 (March 30 vs. Indiana)
2014-15 – 74 (November 24 vs. Orlando)
2015-16 – 76 (October 28 at Memphis, December 11 at Orlando)

Best/Highest Season Performances

Points – 9,360 (1979-80)
Field Goal Attempts – 8,074 (1971-72)
Field Goals – 3,811 (1979-80)
Field Goal Percentage – 50.2 (1988-89)
Free Throw Attempts – 2,554 (1986-87)
Free Throws Made – 1,867 (1984-85)
Free Throw Percentage – 80.5 (1991-92)

Three-Point Field Goal Attempts – 2,427 (2015-16)
Three-Point Field Goals – 880 (2015-16)
Three-Point Field Goal Percentage – 40.7 (1989-90)
Rebounds – 4,098 (1971-72)
Defensive Rebounds – 2,777 (2015-16)
Offensive Rebounds – 1,312 (1976-77)
Assists – 2,349 (1992-93)
Steals – 814 (1997-98)
Blocked Shots – 621 (1991-92)
Fouls – 2,267 (1985-86)
Disqualifications – 56 (1982-83)
Turnovers – 1,590 (1986-87)
Fewest Turnovers Per Game – 12.7 (2008-09)
Scoring Average – 114.1 (1979-80)
Opponents Scoring Average – 85.6 (1996-97)

Composite Win-Loss Records Vs. Other Teams, Best To Worst

1. Minnesota	33-18 .647	16. Atlanta	99-117 .458
2. Memphis	25-14 .641	17. Denver	37-45 .451
3. L.A. Clippers	73-49 .598	18. New York	89-109 .449
4. Charlotte	58-41 .586	19. Portland	51-66 .436
5. Brooklyn	95-74 .562	20. L.A. Lakers	47-61 .435
6. Toronto	43-36 .544	21. Oklahoma City	46-61 .430
7. Dallas	37-32 .536	22. Milwaukee	87-116 .429
8. Orlando	51-48 .515	23. Chicago	85-118 .419
9. Sacramento	57-56 .504	24. Miami	42-59 .416
10. Philadelphia	97-102 .487	25. Detroit	85-121 .413
11. Indiana	88-93 .486	26. Phoenix	43-64 .402
12. New Orleans	15-16 .484	27. Boston	75-123 .379
13. Washington	99-108 .478	28. San Antonio	31-58 .348
14. Golden State	51-56 .477	29. Houston	43-82 .344
15. Utah	46-53 .465	Overall – 1,728-1,996 (.464)	

OPENERS

Buffalo 107, Cleveland 92 (October 14, 1970, at Buf.)
Buffalo 111, Cleveland 109 (OT) (October 15, 1971, at Cle.)
Baltimore 102, Cleveland 90 (October 10, 1972, at Cle.)

Houston 106, Cleveland 99 (October 12, 1973, at Cle.)
Portland 131, Cleveland 129 (4OT) (October 18, 1974, at Por.)
Golden State 89, Cleveland 83 (October 23, 1975, at Cle.)
Cleveland 106, Chicago 95 (October 22, 1976, at Cle.)
Chicago 91, Cleveland 88 (October 18, 1977, at Cle.)
Cleveland 115, Boston 101 (October 13, 1978, at Bos.)
New Jersey 102, Cleveland 95 (October 12, 1979, at N.J.)
Boston 130, Cleveland 103 (October 10, 1980, at Bos.)
Philadelphia 128, Cleveland 104 (October 30, 1981, at Phi.)
Boston 104, Cleveland 93 (October 29, 1982, at Cle.)
New York 113, Cleveland 106 (October 28, 1983, at Cle.)
Philadelphia 111, Cleveland 101 (October 26, 1984, at Phi.)
Chicago 116, Cleveland 115 (OT) (October 25, 1985, at Chi.)
Cleveland 113, Washington 106 (November 1, 1986, at Cle.)
Cleveland 114, New Jersey 108 (November 6, 1987, at N.J.)
Cleveland 133, Charlotte 93 (November 4, 1988, at Cha.)
Chicago 124, Cleveland 119 (OT) (November 3, 1989, at Chi.)
Boston 125, Cleveland 101 (November 2, 1990, at Bos.)
Portland 117, Cleveland 106 (November 1, 1991, at Por.)
Chicago 101, Cleveland 96 (November 6, 1992, at Cle.)
Milwaukee 94, Cleveland 91 (November 5, 1993, at Cle.)
Cleveland 115, Charlotte 107 (November 5, 1994, at Cha.)
Orlando 99, Cleveland 88 (November 3, 1995, at Orl.)
Cleveland 90, New Jersey 77 (November 1, 1996, at N.J.)
Houston 94, Cleveland 86 (October 31, 1997, at Hou.)
Atlanta 100, Cleveland 83 (February 5, 1999, at Atl.)
New York 92, Cleveland 84 (November 2, 1999, at N.Y.)
Cleveland 86, New Jersey 82 (October 31, 2000, at N.J.)
Boston 108, Cleveland 89 (October 30, 2001, at Cle.)
Sacramento 94, Cleveland 67 (October 29, 2002, at Sac.)
Sacramento 106, Cleveland 92 (October 29, 2003, at Sac.)
Indiana 109, Cleveland 104 (2OT) (November 3, 2004, at Cle.)
Cleveland 109, New Orleans/Oklahoma City 87 (November 2, 2005, at Cle.)
Cleveland 97, Washington 94 (November 1, 2006, at Cle.)
Dallas 92, Cleveland 74 (October 31, 2007, at Cle.)
Boston 90, Cleveland 85 (October 28, 2008, at Bos.)
Boston 95, Cleveland 89 (October 27, 2009, at Cle.)
Cleveland 95, Boston 87 (October 27, 2010, at Cle.)
Toronto 104, Cleveland 96 (December 26, 2011, at Cle.)

Cleveland 94, Washington 84 (October 30, 2012, at Cle.)
Cleveland 98, Brooklyn 94 (October 30, 2013, at Cle.)
New York 95, Cleveland 90 (October 30, 2014, at Cle.)
Chicago 97, Cleveland 95 (October 27, 2015, at Chi.)
Overall Record – 13-33 (.283)

OVERTIME GAMES

Buffalo 111, Cleveland 109 (October 15, 1971, at Cle.)
New York 121, Cleveland 120 (October 17, 1971, at Cle.)
Cleveland 127, Baltimore 118 (March 14, 1972, at Bal.)
Cleveland 105, Seattle 103 (December 3, 1972, at Cle.)
Cleveland 113, Philadelphia 109 (2OT) (January 12, 1973, at Pittsburgh)
Cleveland 136, Atlanta 132 (February 8, 1973, at Atl.)
Baltimore 120, Cleveland 116 (March 24, 1973, at Bal.)
Detroit 131, Cleveland 119 (March 28, 1973, at Cle.)
Cleveland 101, Los Angeles 100 (December 11, 1973, at Cle.)
Cleveland 117, Detroit 112 (January 12, 1974, at Det.)
Cleveland 111, Los Angeles 110 (January 22, 1974, at L.A.)
Portland 131, Cleveland 129 (4OT) (October 18, 1974, at Por.)
Atlanta 113, Cleveland 112 (January 7, 1975, at Atl.)
Cleveland 112, Atlanta 109 (February 1, 1975, at Cle.)
Cleveland 92, Kansas City-Omaha 91 (February 8, 1975, at Cle.)
Cleveland 111, Atlanta 105 (February 23, 1975, at Cle.)
Seattle 100, Cleveland 97 (November 14, 1975, at Sea.)
Buffalo 118, Cleveland 115 (November 20, 1975, at Cle.)
Cleveland 128, Phoenix 124 (2OT) (December 19, 1975, at Pho.)
Detroit 119, Cleveland 118 (January 7, 1976, at Det.)
Cleveland 98, Kansas City 91 (December 1, 1976, at K.C.)
N.Y. Knicks 115, Cleveland 113 (December 18, 1976, at N.Y.)
Los Angeles 101, Cleveland 99 (January 11, 1977, at Cle.)
Washington 119, Cleveland 113 (April 5, 1977, at Cle.)
Cleveland 117, New York 112 (October 25, 1977, at N.Y.)
Cleveland 102, Los Angeles 95 (November 15, 1977, at L.A.)
New Jersey 116, Cleveland 106 (December 16, 1977, at N.J.)
San Antonio 109, Cleveland 107 (January 7, 1978, at Cle.)
Detroit 120, Cleveland 116 (January 29, 1978, at Det.)
Milwaukee 108, Cleveland 98 (February 10, 1978, at Mil.)
Cleveland 136, New York 127 (2OT) (February 14, 1978, at Cle.)

Houston 113, Cleveland 111 (November 28, 1979, at Hou.)
Washington 115, Cleveland 113 (December 13, 1979, at Cle.)
Cleveland 128, Golden State 125 (December 19, 1979, at G.S.)
Houston 118, Cleveland 115 (January 8, 1980, at Cle.)
Cleveland 154, Los Angeles 153 (4OT) (January 29, 1980, at Cle.)
Atlanta 111, Cleveland 103 (February 29, 1980, at Atl.)
Cleveland 108, Detroit 107 (March 18, 1980, at Det.)
New York 119, Cleveland 113 (November 26, 1980, at Cle.)
Cleveland 108, Atlanta 107 (January 9, 1981, at Atl.)
Philadelphia 122, Cleveland 120 (February 11, 1981, at Phi.)
Cleveland 112, Atlanta 110 (March 14, 1981, at Atl.)
Atlanta 94, Cleveland 92 (November 24, 1981, at Atl.)
Cleveland 112, Atlanta 108 (December 9, 1981, at Cle.)
New York 110, Cleveland 108 (December 30, 1981, at Cle.)
Cleveland 113, San Diego 107 (March 17, 1982, at Cle.)
Detroit 116, Cleveland 113 (April 18, 1982, at Cle.)
Cleveland 132, Golden State 120 (November 10, 1982, at G.S.)
Washington 95, Cleveland 92 (March 15, 1983, at Was.)
Cleveland 132, Indiana 124 (April 15, 1983, at Ind.)
Detroit 132, Cleveland 131 (January 14, 1984, at Cle.)
Cleveland 114, Detroit 112 (January 31, 1984, at Cle.)
Cleveland 116, Philadelphia 109 (February 23, 1984, at Cle.)
Kansas City 142, Cleveland 137 (2OT) (February 28, 1984, at K.C.)
Chicago 108, Cleveland 104 (March 20, 1984, at Chi.)
Indiana 120, Cleveland 119 (March 31, 1984, at Cle.)
Cleveland 123, Chicago 118 (February 26, 1985, at Chi.)
Cleveland 135, Dallas 128 (March 16, 1985, at Dal.)
Atlanta 91, Cleveland 86 (March 23, 1985, at Cle.)
Cleveland 109, New York 108 (April 12, 1985, at N.Y.)
Chicago 116, Cleveland 115 (October 25, 1985, at Chi.)
Cleveland 132, Chicago 128 (November 16, 1985, at Chi.)
Milwaukee 114, Cleveland 112 (December 28, 1985, at Cle.)
Philadelphia 118, Cleveland 112 (March 17, 1986, at Cle.)
Utah 134, Cleveland 128 (2OT) (December 19, 1986, at Cle.)
Boston 133, Cleveland 128 (January 16, 1987, at Bos.)
Cleveland 91, Chicago 88 (January 14, 1988, at Cle.)
Cleveland 128, Washington 126 (January 30, 1988, at Cle.)
Golden State 96, Cleveland 90 (February 4, 1988, at Cle.)
Chicago 111, Cleveland 110 (March 25, 1988, at Cle.)

Cleveland 119, Seattle 107 (December 23, 1988, at Cle.)
Washington 122, Cleveland 117 (January 29, 1989, at Baltimore)
Milwaukee 113, Cleveland 105 (March 25, 1989, at Mil.)
Chicago 124, Cleveland 119 (November 3, 1989, at Chi.)
Orlando 117, Cleveland 110 (November 8, 1989, at Cle.)
Cleveland 131, Atlanta 125 (November 17, 1989, at Cle.)
Cleveland 113, Utah 110 (December 11, 1989, at Utah)
Dallas 105, Cleveland 96 (January 20, 1990, at Dal.)
Indiana 133, Cleveland 131 (February 14, 1990, at Cle.)
New York 119, Cleveland 108 (February 17, 1990, at N.Y.)
Chicago 117, Cleveland 113 (March 28, 1990, at Cle.)
Milwaukee 113, Cleveland 109 (December 5, 1990, at Mil.)
San Antonio 116, Cleveland 106 (December 14, 1990, at Cle.)
Utah 106, Cleveland 99 (January 18, 1991, at Cle.)
Cleveland 113, Minnesota 110 (February 2, 1991, at Cle.)
Cleveland 113, Seattle 111 (March 5, 1991, at Sea.)
Cleveland 124, Boston 117 (April 19, 1991, at Cle.)
San Antonio 107, Cleveland 101 (November 8, 1991, at S.A.)
Cleveland 115, Seattle 109 (November 14, 1991, at Cle.)
Cleveland 119, Indiana 115 (January 22, 1992, at Cle.)
Cleveland 110, Philadelphia 108 (February 5, 1992, at Phi.)
Cleveland 109, L.A. Lakers 107 (March 13, 1992, at Cle.)
Cleveland 126, Golden State 122 (2OT) (November 12, 1992, at G.S.)
Cleveland 111, Washington 107 (December 21, 1992, at Was.)
Seattle 108, Cleveland 105 (March 2, 1993, at Sea.)
Cleveland 112, Atlanta 109 (2OT) (April 13, 1993, at Atl.)
New York 115, Cleveland 107 (November 7, 1993, at Cle.)
Detroit 98, Cleveland 92 (December 18, 1993, at Det.)
Cleveland 107, Indiana 103 (December 26, 1993, at Cle.)
Cleveland 127, Charlotte 115 (December 28, 1993, at Cle.)
Cleveland 119, Sacramento 109 (January 22, 1994, at Sac.)
Cleveland 105, Charlotte 101 (February 20, 1994, at Cha.)
New York 97, Cleveland 94 (April 7, 1994, at N.Y.)
Cleveland 89, Charlotte 86 (November 15, 1994, at Cle.)
Cleveland 95, New Jersey 88 (2OT) (December 14, 1994, at N.J.)
Charlotte 116, Cleveland 108 (January 10, 1995, at Cle.)
Cleveland 103, Golden State 97 (January 14, 1995, at G.S.)
Cleveland 101, Denver 100 (2OT) (January 21, 1995, at Den.)
Cleveland 100, Orlando 99 (February 15, 1995, at Cle.)

Dallas 102, Cleveland 100 (2OT) (March 20, 1995, at Cle.)
Cleveland 108, Dallas 107 (December 3, 1995, at Cle.)
Cleveland 124, Portland 121 (2OT) (December 30, 1995, at Cle.)
Seattle 107, Cleveland 101 (2OT) (March 5, 1996, at Cle.)
Sacramento 105, Cleveland 100 (March 31, 1996, at Sac.)
Cleveland 98, Washington 96 (November 2, 1996, at Was.)
Denver 88, Cleveland 87 (January 16, 1997, at Den.)
Cleveland 107, L.A. Clippers 102 (2OT) (January 19, 1997, at L.A.)
Golden State 101, Cleveland 95 (March 13, 1997, at G.S.)
Charlotte 110, Cleveland 105 (April 7, 1997, at Cle.)
Boston 103, Cleveland 101 (April 11, 1997, at Bos.)
Atlanta 99, Cleveland 97 (November 8, 1997, at Cle.)
Orlando 96, Cleveland 93 (November 19, 1997, at Cle.)
Dallas 84, Cleveland 77 (January 27, 1998, at Dal.)
Orlando 91, Cleveland 89 (March 6, 1998, at Orl.)
Cleveland 88, New York 85 (March 14, 1998, at Cle.)
Cleveland 88, Detroit 87 (March 27, 1998, at Cle.)
Cleveland 89, Chicago 85 (March 15, 1999, at Chi.)
Cleveland 91, Toronto 90 (April 16, 1999, at Tor.)
Philadelphia 102, Cleveland 100 (December 3, 1999, at Cle.)
Cleveland 116, Detroit 107 (January 25, 2000, at Cle.)
Cleveland 109, Vancouver 108 (February 21, 2000, at Cle.)
Cleveland 114, Chicago 110 (March 2, 2000, at Chi.)
Philadelphia 98, Cleveland 97 (March 14, 2000, at Cle.)
Miami 92, Cleveland 90 (March 18, 2000, at Cle.)
Minnesota 111, Cleveland 107 (March 21, 2000, at Minn.)
Cleveland 102, Sacramento 100 (2OT) (November 1, 2000, at Cle.)
Charlotte 115, Cleveland 110 (December 26, 2000, at Cha.)
Detroit 88, Cleveland 81 (February 3, 2001, at Cle.)
Seattle 101, Cleveland 99 (March 1, 2001, at Cle.)
Indiana 105, Cleveland 101 (April 18, 2001, at Cle.)
Cleveland 100, Miami 96 (November 24, 2001, at Cle.)
Cleveland 86, Miami 81 (December 21, 2001, at Mia.)
Miami 95, Cleveland 93 (January 21, 2002, at Cle.)
Cleveland 114, San Antonio 107 (February 28, 2002, at Cle.)
Cleveland 115, Milwaukee 109 (March 8, 2002, at Mil.)
Atlanta 128, Cleveland 123 (2OT) (April 13, 2002, at Atl.)
Milwaukee 140, Cleveland 133 (2OT) (December 9, 2002, at Cle.)
Detroit 111, Cleveland 106 (December 18, 2002, at Cle.)

Detroit 109, Cleveland 107 (December 20, 2002, at Det.)
Atlanta 102, Cleveland 101 (January 25, 2003, at Cle.)
Cleveland 104, New York 99 (April 12, 2003, at Cle.)
Cleveland 91, Philadelphia 88 (November 15, 2003, at Cle.)
Memphis 122, Cleveland 115 (2OT) (November 29, 2003, at Cle.)
Orlando 113, Cleveland 101 (December 25, 2003, at Orl.)
Cleveland 102, Utah 96 (January 17, 2004, at Utah)
L.A. Lakers 111, Cleveland 106 (February 4, 2004, at Cle.)
Cleveland 112, Orlando 107 (February 27, 2004, at Orl.)
Indiana 109, Cleveland 104 (2OT) (November 3, 2004, at Cle.)
Cleveland 114, Phoenix 109 (November 10, 2004, at Cle.)
Boston 114, Cleveland 107 (December 18, 2004, at Cle.)
Cleveland 100, Charlotte 98 (January 11, 2005, at Cle.)
Cleveland 109, New Orleans 108 (March 28, 2005, at N.O.)
Chicago 102, Cleveland 90 (March 31, 2005, at Chi.)
Cleveland 108, Orlando 100 (November 13, 2005, at Orl.)
Cleveland 112, L.A. Clippers 105 (November 30, 2005, at Cle.)
Cleveland 113, Boston 109 (2OT) (February 15, 2006, at Bos.)
Cleveland 120, Charlotte 118 (March 22, 2006, at Cle.)
Cleveland 104, Houston 102 (March 26, 2006, at Hou.)
Atlanta 104, Cleveland 95 (November 7, 2006, at Cle.)
Cleveland 106, Golden State 104 (January 20, 2007, at G.S.)
Philadelphia 118, Cleveland 115 (2OT) (January 24, 2007, at Cle.)
Cleveland 101, Detroit 97 (March 7, 2007, at Det.)
Charlotte 108, Cleveland 100 (March 20, 2007, at Cha.)
Cleveland 112, Chicago 108 (March 31, 2007, at Chi.)
Miami 94, Cleveland 90 (April 5, 2007, at Cle.)
Orlando 117, Cleveland 116 (November 14, 2007, at Cle.)
Cleveland 109, Boston 104 (November 27, 2007, at Cle.)
Cleveland 104, Milwaukee 99 (2OT) (December 17, 2007, at Cle.)
Cleveland 113, Charlotte 106 (2OT) (January 11, 2008, at Cle.)
Cleveland 132, Memphis 124 (January 15, 2008, at Mem.)
Chicago 102, Cleveland 93 (January 15, 2009, at Chi.)
Cleveland 126, Sacramento 123 (March 13, 2009, at Sac.)
Cleveland 97, Portland 92 (March 19, 2009, at Cle.)
Philadelphia 111, Cleveland 110 (April 15, 2009, at Cle.)
Memphis 111, Cleveland 109 (December 8, 2009, at Mem.)
Cleveland 117, Sacramento 104 (December 23, 2009, at Sac.)
Denver 118, Cleveland 116 (February 18, 2010, at Cle.)

Cleveland 126, Toronto 118 (February 26, 2010, at Tor.)
Cleveland 109, New York 102 (December 18, 2010, at Cle.)
Cleveland 126, L.A. Clippers 119 (February 11, 2011, at Cle.)
New Jersey 98, Cleveland 94 (March 23, 2011, at Cle.)
Indiana 98, Cleveland 91 (December 30, 2011, at Ind.)
Milwaukee 113, Cleveland 112 (February 10, 2012, at Cle.)
Atlanta 103, Cleveland 102 (March 21, 2012, at Atl.)
New Jersey 122, Cleveland 117 (April 8, 2012, at N.J.)
Indiana 104, Cleveland 98 (April 11, 2012, at Cle.)
Portland 118, Cleveland 117 (2OT) (December 1, 2012, at Cle.)
Cleveland 127, Philadelphia 125 (2OT) (November 9, 2013, at Cle.)
Cleveland 103, Washington 96 (November 16, 2013, at Was.)
Cleveland 114, Milwaukee 111 (December 20, 2013, at Cle.)
Atlanta 127, Cleveland 125 (2OT) (December 26, 2013, at Cle.)
Golden State 108, Cleveland 104 (December 29, 2013, at Cle.)
Cleveland 87, Orlando 81 (January 2, 2014, at Cle.)
Cleveland 91, Memphis 83 (February 9, 2014, at Cle.)
Charlotte 96, Cleveland 94 (April 5, 2014, at Cle.)
Cleveland 114, Chicago 108 (October 31, 2014, at Chi.)
Houston 105, Cleveland 103 (March 1, 2015, at Hou.)
Cleveland 128, San Antonio 125 (March 12, 2015, at S.A.)
Cleveland 113, Washington 108 (April 15, 2015, at Cle.)
Milwaukee 108, Cleveland 105 (2OT) (November 14, 2015, at Mil.)
New Orleans 114, Cleveland 108 (December 4, 2015, at N.O.)
Cleveland 110, Dallas 107 (January 12, 2016, at Dal.)
Cleveland 111, Indiana 106 (February 1, 2016, at Ind.)
Cleveland 110, Atlanta 108 (April 1, 2016, at Atl.)
Detroit 112, Cleveland 110 (April 13, 2016, at Cle.)
Overall Record – 106-109 (.493)

NEUTRAL-SITE GAMES

Cleveland 111, Buffalo 79 (January 19, 1971, at Syracuse, NY)
Cleveland 101, Buffalo 91 (February 2, 1971, at Rochester, NY)
Cleveland 109, Baltimore 101 (October 23, 1971, at College Park, MD)
Cleveland 103, Philadelphia 102 (December 29, 1971, at Hershey, PA)
Cincinnati 128, Cleveland 108 (January 16, 1972, at Las Cruces, NM)
Baltimore 108, Cleveland 98 (November 4, 1972, at College Park, MD)

Cleveland 113, Philadelphia 109 (2OT) (January 12, 1973, at Pittsburgh)
Milwaukee 118, Cleveland 100 (February 20, 1973, at Madison, WI)
Cleveland 118, Houston 100 (March 7, 1973, at San Antonio)
Buffalo 104, Cleveland 97 (October 26, 1973, at Toronto)
Boston 111, Cleveland 92 (December 29, 1973, at Providence, RI)
Overall Record – 6-5 (.545)

CAVS ON CHRISTMAS

Cincinnati 117, Cleveland 100 (1970 at Cin.)
Washington 117, Cleveland 99 (1976 at Was.)
Cleveland 111, Buffalo 105 (1977 at Cle.)
Cleveland 111, Detroit 101 (1979 at Cle.)
Cleveland 109, Atlanta 106 (1984 at Cle.)
Atlanta 115, Cleveland 104 (1989 at Atl.)
Orlando 113, Cleveland 101 (OT) (2003 at Orl.)
Cleveland 96, Miami 82 (2007 at Cle.)
Cleveland 93, Washington 89 (2008 at Cle.)
Cleveland 102, L.A. Lakers 87 (2009 at L.A.)
Miami 101, Cleveland 91 (2014 at Mia.)
Golden State 89, Cleveland 83 (2015 at G.S.)
Overall – 6-6 (.500)

TEN HIGHEST/LOWEST-SCORING GAMES

Highest

1. 154 – Cleveland 154, Los Angeles 153 (4OT) (January 29, 1980, at Cle.)
2. 148 – Cleveland 148, Miami 80 (December 17, 1991, at Cle.)
3. 142 – Cleveland 142, Golden State 109 (January 23, 1989, at Cle.)
4. 141 – Cleveland 141, San Antonio 134 (October 18, 1979, at Cle.)
   Cleveland 141, Charlotte 134 (April 9, 1992, at Cle.)
6. 137 – Cleveland 137, Detroit 117 (October 16, 1979, at Cle.)
   Kansas City 142, Cleveland 137 (2OT) (February 28, 1984, at K.C.)
8. 136 – Cleveland 136, Atlanta 132 (OT) (February 8, 1973, at Atl.)
   Cleveland 136, New York 127 (2OT) (February 14, 1978, at Cle.)
10. 135 – Cleveland 135, Dallas 128 (OT) (March 16, 1985, at Dal.)
    Cleveland 135, New Jersey 117 (February 13, 1986, at Cle.)

OPPONENTS HIGHEST

1. 153 – Cleveland 154, Los Angeles 153 (4OT) (January 29, 1980, at Cle.)
2. 148 – Philadelphia 148, Cleveland 119 (January 2, 1972, at Cle.)
3. 147 – Denver 147, Cleveland 127 (March 7, 1982, at Den.)
4. 145 – Golden State 145, Cleveland 105 (March 8, 1990, at G.S.)
5. 144 – Denver 144, Cleveland 127 (January 26, 1985, at Den.)
6. 142 – Kansas City 142, Cleveland 137 (2OT) (February 28, 1984, at K.C.)
7. 141 – Philadelphia 141, Cleveland 87 (November 2, 1970, at Phi.)
8. 140 – San Diego 140, Cleveland 110 (October 22, 1970, at S.D.)
   Los Angeles 140, Cleveland 126 (November 11, 1979, at L.A.)
   San Diego 140, Cleveland 125 (March 6, 1981, at S.D.)
   New Jersey 140, Cleveland 125 (March 13, 1981, at Cle.)
   Milwaukee 140, Cleveland 133 (2OT) (December 9, 2002, at Cle.)

LOWEST

1. 57 – L.A. Lakers 112, Cleveland 57 (January 11, 2011, at L.A.)
2. 59 – San Antonio 64, Cleveland 59 (March 25, 1997, at S.A.)
3. 63 – Houston 81, Cleveland 63 (December 2, 2006, at Hou.)
4. 64 – New York 82, Cleveland 64 (November 7, 2001, at N.Y.)
   Portland 96, Cleveland 64 (January 13, 2002, at Por.)
6. 65 – New York 75, Cleveland 65 (January 29, 1997, at Cle.)
   Miami 90, Cleveland 65 (April 26, 1999, at Cle.)
   Atlanta 76, Cleveland 65 (May 2, 1999, at Cle.)
9. 66 – Miami 71, Cleveland 66 (February 1, 1997, at Cle.)
   Seattle 72, Cleveland 66 (February 25, 1997, at Cle.)

OPPONENTS LOWEST

1. 57 – Cleveland 84, Orlando 57 (December 4, 1996, at Orl.)
2. 58 – Cleveland 84, Portland 58 (January 22, 2001, at Cle.)
3. 61 – Cleveland 93, Indiana 61 (March 22, 1994, at Cle.)
4. 62 – Cleveland 84, New Jersey 62 (January 28, 1997, at N.J.)
5. 63 – Cleveland 77, Chicago 63 (December 19, 1994, at Chi.)
   Cleveland 73, Atlanta 63 (November 19, 1996, at Cle.)
   Cleveland 78, Orlando 63 (April 16, 1997, at Cle.)
8. 64 – Cleveland 90, Golden State 64 (March 30, 1996, at G.S.)
   San Antonio 64, Cleveland 59 (March 25, 1997, at S.A.)

10. 66 – Cleveland 71, Charlotte 66 (December 5, 2000, at Cle.)
Cleveland 96, Indiana 66 (January 24, 2006, at Cle.)

Highest Between Both Teams

1. 307 – Cleveland 154, Los Angeles 153 (4OT) (January 29, 1980, at Cle.)
2. 279 – Kansas City 142, Cleveland 137 (2OT) (February 28, 1984, at K.C.)
3. 275 – Cleveland 141, San Antonio 134 (October 18, 1979, at Cle.)
Cleveland 141, Charlotte 134 (April 9, 1992, at Cle.)
5. 274 – Denver 147, Cleveland 127 (March 7, 1982, at Den.)
6. 273 – Milwaukee 140, Cleveland 133 (2OT) (December 9, 2002, at Cle.)
7. 271 – Denver 144, Cleveland 127 (January 26, 1985, at Den.)
8. 268 – Cleveland 136, Atlanta 132 (OT) (February 8, 1973, at Atl.)
9. 267 – Philadelphia 148, Cleveland 119 (January 2, 1972, at Cle.)
10. 266 – Los Angeles 140, Cleveland 126 (November 11, 1979, at L.A.)
Golden State 138, Cleveland 128 (March 8, 1986, at G.S.)

Lowest Between Both Teams

1. 123 – San Antonio 64, Cleveland 59 (March 25, 1997, at S.A.)
2. 136 – Cleveland 73, Atlanta 63 (November 19, 1996, at Cle.)
3. 137 – Miami 71, Cleveland 66 (February 1, 1997, at Cle.)
Cleveland 71, Charlotte 66 (December 5, 2000, at Cle.)
5. 138 – Seattle 72, Cleveland 66 (February 25, 1997, at Cle.)
6. 140 – Cleveland 77, Chicago 63 (December 19, 1994, at Chi.)
New York 75, Cleveland 65 (January 29, 1997, at Cle.)
8. 141 – Cleveland 84, Orlando 57 (December 4, 1996, at Orl.)
Cleveland 78, Orlando 63 (April 16, 1997, at Cle.)
Atlanta 76, Cleveland 65 (May 2, 1999, at Cle.)

TEN MOST ONE-SIDED GAMES

Victories

1. 68 – Cleveland 148, Miami 80 (December 17, 1991, at Cle.)
2. 43 – Cleveland 132, Milwaukee 89 (January 24, 1976, at Cle.)
Cleveland 123, Atlanta 80 (March 22, 1992, at Cle.)
Cleveland 110, Philadelphia 67 (January 15, 1994, at Cle.)

5. 40 – Cleveland 133, Charlotte 93 (November 4, 1988, at Cha.)
6. 39 – Cleveland 131, Washington 92 (November 10, 1992, at Cle.)
Cleveland 129, Charlotte 90 (January 23, 2015, at Cle.)
8. 38 – Cleveland 117, L.A. Lakers 79 (November 30, 1994, at Cle.)
Cleveland 127, Washington 89 (February 20, 2015, at Was.)
10. 37 – Cleveland 128, Portland 91 (February 24, 1989, at Cle.)
Cleveland 127, San Antonio 90 (March 23, 1993, at Cle.)

DEFEATS

1. 55 – L.A. Lakers 112, Cleveland 57 (January 11, 2011, at L.A.)
2. 54 – Philadelphia 141, Cleveland 87 (November 2, 1970, at Phi.)
3. 50 – Portland 129, Cleveland 79 (November 21, 1982, at Por.)
4. 48 – Indiana 136, Cleveland 88 (December 10, 1999, at Ind.)
5. 45 – Milwaukee 118, Cleveland 73 (January 2, 1971, at Mil.)
6. 44 – Sacramento 124, Cleveland 80 (January 12, 2014, at Sac.)
7. 43 – Los Angeles 127, Cleveland 84 (March 4, 1973, at L.A.)
8. 42 – Milwaukee 134, Cleveland 92 (December 11, 1970, at Mil.)
Portland 109, Cleveland 67 (November 19, 1977, at Por.)
10. 41 – Chicago 121, Cleveland 80 (December 22, 1970, at Chi.)
New Jersey 120, Cleveland 79 (November 22, 2002, at N.J.)
Portland 111, Cleveland 70 (March 17, 2011, at Por.)

STREAKS

FIVE LONGEST WINNING IN A SEASON

1. 13 games – March 7–31, 2009 (48-13 to 61-13)
January 16–February 11, 2010 (30-11 to 43-11)
3. 12 games – January 15–February 5, 2015 (19-20 to 31-20)
4. 11 games – December 15, 1988–January 7, 1989 (13-5 to 24-5)
December 20, 1991–January 11, 1992 (13-9 to 24-9)
February 18–March 8, 1994 (25-24 to 36-24)
December 9–30, 1994 (9-8 to 20-8)
November 22–December 12, 2008 (9-3 to 20-3)

FIVE LONGEST WINNING TO START A SEASON

1. 8 games – October 22–November 6, 1976
2. 4 games – October 13–24, 1978

November 4–12, 1988
October 31–November 8, 2000
5. 2 games – November 1–2, 1996
November 1–3, 2006

Five Longest Winning To End A Season

1. 6 games – March 31–April 9, 1978 (37-39 to 43-39)
April 12–22, 1990 (36-40 to 42-40)
3. 4 games – April 15–23, 1988 (38-40 to 42-40)
April 13–21, 1991 (29-49 to 33-49)
April 12–18, 2007 (46-32 to 50-32)

Five Longest Losing In A Season

1. 26 games – December 20, 2010–February 9, 2011 (8-19 to 8-45)
2. 19 games – March 19–April 18, 1982 (15-48 to 15-67)
3. 15 games – October 14–November 10, 1970 (0-0 to 0-15)
November 6–December 2, 2002 (2-2 to 2-17)
5. 12 games – November 13–December 4, 1970 (1-15 to 1-27)
January 4–26, 2002 (13-18 to 13-30)

Five Longest Losing To Start A Season

1. 15 games – October 14–November 10, 1970
2. 9 games – October 26–November 13, 1984
3. 7 games – October 10–24, 1972
November 3–15, 1995
5. 5 games – October 29–November 5, 1982
October 29–November 7, 2003

Five Longest Losing To End A Season

1. 19 games – March 19–April 18, 1982 (15-48 to 15-67)
2. 7 games – March 19–29, 1981 (28-47 to 28-54)
3. 6 games – April 9–17, 2013 (24-52 to 24-58)
4. 4 games – April 3–8, 1979 (30-48 to 30-52)
April 12–17, 2002 (29-49 to 29-53)
April 8–14, 2010 (61-17 to 61-21)
April 22–26, 2012 (21-41 to 21-45)

POSTSEASON

RESULTS

1975-76

EASTERN CONFERENCE SEMIFINALS, CLEVELAND DEFEATED WASHINGTON, 4–3

Washington 100, Cleveland 95 (April 13 at Cle.)
Cleveland 80, Washington 79 (April 15 at Was.)
Cleveland 88, Washington 76 (April 17 at Cle.)
Washington 109, Cleveland 98 (April 21 at Was.)
Cleveland 92, Washington 91 (April 22 at Cle.)
Washington 102, Cleveland 98 (OT) (April 26 at Was.)
Cleveland 87, Washington 85 (April 29 at Cle.)

EASTERN CONFERENCE FINALS, BOSTON DEFEATED CLEVELAND, 4–2

Boston 111, Cleveland 99 (May 6 at Bos.)
Boston 94, Cleveland 89 (May 9 at Bos.)
Cleveland 83, Boston 78 (May 11 at Cle.)
Cleveland 106, Boston 87 (May 14 at Cle.)
Boston 99, Cleveland 94 (May 16 at Bos.)
Boston 94, Cleveland 87 (May 18 at Cle.)

1976-77

EASTERN CONFERENCE FIRST ROUND, WASHINGTON DEFEATED CLEVELAND, 2–1

Washington 109, Cleveland 100 (April 13 at Was.)
Cleveland 91, Washington 83 (April 15 at Cle.)
Washington 104, Cleveland 98 (April 17 at Was.)

1977-78

EASTERN CONFERENCE FIRST ROUND, NEW YORK DEFEATED CLEVELAND, 2–0

New York 132, Cleveland 114 (April 12 at Cle.)
New York 109, Cleveland 107 (April 14 at N.Y.)

1984-85

EASTERN CONFERENCE FIRST ROUND, BOSTON DEFEATED CLEVELAND, 3–1

Boston 126, Cleveland 123 (April 18 at Bos.)
Boston 108, Cleveland 106 (April 20 at Bos.)
Cleveland 105, Boston 98 (April 23 at Cle.)
Boston 117, Cleveland 115 (April 25 at Cle.)

1987-88

EASTERN CONFERENCE FIRST ROUND, CHICAGO DEFEATED CLEVELAND, 3–2

Chicago 104, Cleveland 93 (April 28 at Chi.)
Chicago 106, Cleveland 101 (May 1 at Chi.)
Cleveland 110, Chicago 102 (May 3 at Cle.)
Cleveland 97, Chicago 91 (May 5 at Cle.)
Chicago 107, Cleveland 101 (May 8 at Chi.)

1988-89

EASTERN CONFERENCE FIRST ROUND, CHICAGO DEFEATED CLEVELAND, 3–2

Chicago 95, Cleveland 88 (April 28 at Cle.)
Cleveland 96, Chicago 88 (April 30 at Cle.)
Chicago 101, Cleveland 94 (May 3 at Chi.)
Cleveland 108, Chicago 105 (OT) (May 5 at Chi.)
Chicago 101, Cleveland 100 (May 7 at Cle.)

1989-90

EASTERN CONFERENCE FIRST ROUND, PHILADELPHIA DEFEATED CLEVELAND, 3–2

Philadelphia 111, Cleveland 106 (April 26 at Phi.)
Philadelphia 107, Cleveland 101 (April 28 at Phi.)
Cleveland 122, Philadelphia 95 (May 1 at Cle.)
Cleveland 108, Philadelphia 96 (May 3 at Cle.)
Philadelphia 113, Cleveland 97 (May 5 at Phi.)

1991-92

EASTERN CONFERENCE FIRST ROUND, CLEVELAND DEFEATED NEW JERSEY, 3–1

Cleveland 120, New Jersey 113 (April 23 at Cle.)
Cleveland 118, New Jersey 96 (April 25 at Cle.)
New Jersey 109, Cleveland 104 (April 28 at N.J.)
Cleveland 98, New Jersey 89 (April 30 at N.J.)

EASTERN CONFERENCE SEMIFINALS, CLEVELAND DEFEATED BOSTON, 4–3

Cleveland 101, Boston 76 (May 2 at Cle.)
Boston 104, Cleveland 98 (May 4 at Cle.)
Boston 110, Cleveland 107 (May 8 at Bos.)
Cleveland 114, Boston 112 (OT) (May 10 at Bos.)
Cleveland 114, Boston 98 (May 13 at Cle.)
Boston 122, Cleveland 91 (May 15 at Bos.)
Cleveland 122, Boston 104 (May 17 at Cle.)

EASTERN CONFERENCE FINALS, CHICAGO DEFEATED CLEVELAND, 4–2

Chicago 103, Cleveland 89 (May 19 at Chi.)
Cleveland 107, Chicago 81 (May 21 at Chi.)
Chicago 105, Cleveland 96 (May 23 at Cle.)
Cleveland 99, Chicago 85 (May 25 at Chi.)
Chicago 112, Cleveland 89 (May 27 at Chi.)
Chicago 99, Cleveland 94 (May 29 at Cle.)

1992-93

EASTERN CONFERENCE FIRST ROUND, CLEVELAND DEFEATED NEW JERSEY, 3–2

Cleveland 114, New Jersey 98 (April 29 at Cle.)
New Jersey 101, Cleveland 99 (May 1 at Cle.)
Cleveland 93, New Jersey 84 (May 5 at N.J.)
New Jersey 96, Cleveland 79 (May 7 at N.J.)
Cleveland 99, New Jersey 89 (May 9 at Cle.)

EASTERN CONFERENCE SEMIFINALS, CHICAGO DEFEATED CLEVELAND, 4–0

Chicago 91, Cleveland 84 (May 11 at Chi.)
Chicago 104, Cleveland 85 (May 13 at Chi.)
Chicago 96, Cleveland 90 (May 15 at Cle.)
Chicago 103, Cleveland 101 (May 17 at Cle.)

1993-94

EASTERN CONFERENCE FIRST ROUND, CHICAGO DEFEATED CLEVELAND, 3–0

Chicago 104, Cleveland 96 (April 29 at Chi.)
Chicago 105, Cleveland 96 (May 1 at Chi.)
Chicago 95, Cleveland 92 (OT) (May 3 at Cle.)

1994-95

EASTERN CONFERENCE FIRST ROUND, NEW YORK DEFEATED CLEVELAND, 3–1

New York 103, Cleveland 79 (April 27 at N.Y.)
Cleveland 90, New York 84 (April 29 at N.Y.)
New York 83, Cleveland 81 (May 1 at Cle.)
New York 93, Cleveland 80 (May 4 at Cle.)

1995-96

EASTERN CONFERENCE FIRST ROUND, NEW YORK DEFEATED CLEVELAND, 3–0

New York 106, Cleveland 83 (April 25 at Cle.)
New York 84, Cleveland 80 (April 27 at Cle.)
New York 81, Cleveland 76 (May 1 at N.Y.)

1997-98

EASTERN CONFERENCE FIRST ROUND, INDIANA DEFEATED CLEVELAND, 3–1

Indiana 106, Cleveland 77 (April 23 at Ind.)
Indiana 92, Cleveland 86 (April 25 at Ind.)
Cleveland 86, Indiana 77 (April 27 at Cle.)
Indiana 80, Cleveland 74 (April 30 at Cle.)

2005-06

EASTERN CONFERENCE FIRST ROUND, CLEVELAND DEFEATED WASHINGTON, 4–2

Cleveland 97, Washington 86 (April 22 at Cle.)
Washington 89, Cleveland 84 (April 25 at Cle.)
Cleveland 97, Washington 96 (April 28 at Was.)
Washington 106, Cleveland 96 (April 30 at Was.)
Cleveland 121, Washington 120 (OT) (May 3 at Cle.)
Cleveland 114, Washington 113 (OT) (May 5 at Was.)

EASTERN CONFERENCE SEMIFINALS, DETROIT DEFEATED CLEVELAND, 4–3

Detroit 113, Cleveland 86 (May 7 at Det.)
Detroit 97, Cleveland 91 (May 9 at Det.)
Cleveland 86, Detroit 77 (May 13 at Cle.)
Cleveland 74, Detroit 72 (May 15 at Cle.)
Cleveland 86, Detroit 84 (May 17 at Det.)
Detroit 84, Cleveland 82 (May 19 at Cle.)
Detroit 79, Cleveland 61 (May 21 at Det.)

2006-07

EASTERN CONFERENCE FIRST ROUND, CLEVELAND DEFEATED WASHINGTON, 4–0

Cleveland 97, Washington 82 (April 22 at Cle.)
Cleveland 109, Washington 102 (April 25 at Cle.)
Cleveland 98, Washington 92 (April 28 at Was.)
Cleveland 97, Washington 90 (April 30 at Was.)

EASTERN CONFERENCE SEMIFINALS, CLEVELAND DEFEATED NEW JERSEY, 4–2

Cleveland 81, New Jersey 77 (May 6 at Cle.)
Cleveland 102, New Jersey 92 (May 8 at Cle.)
New Jersey 96, Cleveland 85 (May 12 at N.J.)
Cleveland 87, New Jersey 85 (May 14 at N.J.)
New Jersey 83, Cleveland 72 (May 16 at Cle.)
Cleveland 88, New Jersey 72 (May 18 at N.J.)

EASTERN CONFERENCE FINALS, CLEVELAND DEFEATED DETROIT, 4–2

Detroit 79, Cleveland 76 (May 21 at Det.)
Detroit 79, Cleveland 76 (May 24 at Det.)
Cleveland 88, Detroit 82 (May 27 at Cle.)
Cleveland 91, Detroit 87 (May 29 at Cle.)
Cleveland 109, Detroit 107 (2OT) (May 31 at Det.)
Cleveland 98, Detroit 82 (June 2 at Cle.)

NBA FINALS, SAN ANTONIO DEFEATED CLEVELAND, 4–0

San Antonio 85, Cleveland 76 (June 7 at S.A.)
San Antonio 103, Cleveland 92 (June 10 at S.A.)
San Antonio 75, Cleveland 72 (June 12 at Cle.)
San Antonio 83, Cleveland 82 (June 14 at Cle.)

2007-08

EASTERN CONFERENCE FIRST ROUND, CLEVELAND DEFEATED WASHINGTON, 4–2

Cleveland 93, Washington 86 (April 19 at Cle.)
Cleveland 116, Washington 86 (April 21 at Cle.)
Washington 108, Cleveland 72 (April 24 at Was.)
Cleveland 100, Washington 97 (April 27 at Was.)
Washington 88, Cleveland 87 (April 30 at Cle.)
Cleveland 105, Washington 88 (May 2 at Was.)

EASTERN CONFERENCE SEMIFINALS, BOSTON DEFEATED CLEVELAND, 4–3

Boston 76, Cleveland 72 (May 6 at Bos.)
Boston 89, Cleveland 73 (May 8 at Bos.)
Cleveland 108, Boston 84 (May 10 at Cle.)
Cleveland 88, Boston 77 (May 12 at Cle.)
Boston 96, Cleveland 89 (May 14 at Bos.)
Cleveland 74, Boston 69 (May 16 at Cle.)
Boston 97, Cleveland 92 (May 18 at Bos.)

2008-09

EASTERN CONFERENCE FIRST ROUND, CLEVELAND DEFEATED DETROIT, 4–0

Cleveland 102, Detroit 84 (April 18 at Cle.)
Cleveland 94, Detroit 82 (April 21 at Cle.)
Cleveland 79, Detroit 68 (April 24 at Det.)
Cleveland 99, Detroit 78 (April 26 at Det.)

EASTERN CONFERENCE SEMIFINALS, CLEVELAND DEFEATED ATLANTA, 4–0

Cleveland 99, Atlanta 72 (May 5 at Cle.)
Cleveland 105, Atlanta 85 (May 7 at Cle.)
Cleveland 97, Atlanta 82 (May 9 at Atl.)
Cleveland 84, Atlanta 74 (May 11 at Atl.)

EASTERN CONFERENCE FINALS, ORLANDO DEFEATED CLEVELAND, 4–2

Orlando 107, Cleveland 106 (May 20 at Cle.)
Cleveland 96, Orlando 95 (May 22 at Cle.)
Orlando 99, Cleveland 89 (May 24 at Orl.)
Orlando 116, Cleveland 114 (OT) (May 26 at Orl.)
Cleveland 112, Orlando 102 (May 28 at Cle.)
Orlando 103, Cleveland 90 (May 30 at Orl.)

2009-10

EASTERN CONFERENCE FIRST ROUND, CLEVELAND DEFEATED CHICAGO, 4–1

Cleveland 96, Chicago 83 (April 17 at Cle.)
Cleveland 112, Chicago 102 (April 19 at Cle.)
Chicago 108, Cleveland 106 (April 22 at Chi.)
Cleveland 121, Chicago 98 (April 25 at Chi.)
Cleveland 96, Chicago 94 (April 27 at Cle.)

EASTERN CONFERENCE SEMIFINALS, BOSTON DEFEATED CLEVELAND, 4–2

Cleveland 101, Boston 93 (May 1 at Cle.)
Boston 104, Cleveland 86 (May 3 at Cle.)

Cleveland 124, Boston 95 (May 7 at Bos.)
Boston 97, Cleveland 87 (May 9 at Bos.)
Boston 120, Cleveland 88 (May 11 at Cle.)
Boston 94, Cleveland 85 (May 13 at Bos.)

2014-15

Eastern Conference First Round, Cleveland Defeated Boston, 4–0

Cleveland 113, Boston 100 (April 19 at Cle.)
Cleveland 99, Boston 91 (April 21 at Cle.)
Cleveland 103, Boston 95 (April 23 at Bos.)
Cleveland 101, Boston 93 (April 26 at Bos.)

Eastern Conference Semifinals, Cleveland Defeated Chicago, 4–2

Chicago 99, Cleveland 92 (May 4 at Cle.)
Cleveland 106, Chicago 91 (May 6 at Cle.)
Chicago 99, Cleveland 96 (May 8 at Chi.)
Cleveland 86, Chicago 84 (May 10 at Chi.)
Cleveland 106, Chicago 101 (May 12 at Cle.)
Cleveland 94, Chicago 73 (May 14 at Chi.)

Eastern Conference Finals, Cleveland Defeated Atlanta, 4–0

Cleveland 97, Atlanta 89 (May 20 at Atl.)
Cleveland 94, Atlanta 82 (May 22 at Atl.)
Cleveland 114, Atlanta 111 (OT) (May 24 at Cle.)
Cleveland 118, Atlanta 88 (May 26 at Cle.)

NBA Finals, Golden State Defeated Cleveland, 4–2

Golden State 108, Cleveland 100 (OT) (June 4 at G.S.)
Cleveland 95, Golden State 93 (OT) (June 7 at G.S.)
Cleveland 96, Golden State 91 (June 9 at Cle.)
Golden State 103, Cleveland 82 (June 11 at Cle.)

Golden State 104, Cleveland 91 (June 14 at G.S.)
Golden State 105, Cleveland 97 (June 16 at Cle.)

2015-16

EASTERN CONFERENCE FIRST ROUND, CLEVELAND DEFEATED DETROIT, 4–0

Cleveland 106, Detroit 101 (April 17 at Cle.)
Cleveland 107, Detroit 90 (April 20 at Cle.)
Cleveland 101, Detroit 91 (April 22 at Det.)
Cleveland 100, Detroit 98 (April 24 at Det.)

EASTERN CONFERENCE SEMIFINALS, CLEVELAND DEFEATED ATLANTA, 4–0

Cleveland 104, Atlanta 93 (May 2 at Cle.)
Cleveland 123, Atlanta 98 (May 4 at Cle.)
Cleveland 121, Atlanta 108 (May 6 at Atl.)
Cleveland 100, Atlanta 99 (May 8 at Atl.)

EASTERN CONFERENCE FINALS, CLEVELAND DEFEATED TORONTO, 4–2

Cleveland 115, Toronto 84 (May 17 at Cle.)
Cleveland 108, Toronto 89 (May 19 at Cle.)
Toronto 99, Cleveland 84 (May 21 at Tor.)
Toronto 105, Cleveland 99 (May 23 at Tor.)
Cleveland 116, Toronto 78 (May 25 at Cle.)
Cleveland 113, Toronto 87 (May 27 at Tor.)

NBA FINALS, CLEVELAND DEFEATED GOLDEN STATE, 4–3

Golden State 104, Cleveland 89 (June 2 at G.S.)
Golden State 110, Cleveland 77 (June 5 at G.S.)
Cleveland 120, Golden State 90 (June 8 at Cle.)
Golden State 108, Cleveland 97 (June 10 at Cle.)
Cleveland 112, Golden State 97 (June 13 at G.S.)
Cleveland 115, Golden State 101 (June 16 at Cle.)
Cleveland 93, Golden State 89 (June 19 at G.S.)

SEASON WIN-LOSS RECORDS

OVERALL

1975-76 – 6-7 .462
1976-77 – 1-2 .333
1977-78 – 0-2 .000
1984-85 – 1-3 .250
1987-88 – 2-3 .400
1988-89 – 2-3 .400
1989-90 – 2-3 .400
1991-92 – 9-8 .529
1992-93 – 3-6 .333
1993-94 – 0-3 .000
1994-95 – 1-3 .250
1995-96 – 0-3 .000
1997-98 – 1-3 .250
2005-06 – 7-6 .538
2006-07 – 12-8 .600
2007-08 – 7-6 .538
2008-09 – 10-4 .714
2009-10 – 6-5 .545
2014-15 – 14-6 .700
2015-16 – 16-5 .762
Overall – 100-89 (.529)

HOME

1975-76 – 5-2 .714
1976-77 – 1-0 1.000
1977-78 – 0-1 .000
1984-85 – 1-1 .500
1987-88 – 2-0 1.000
1988-89 – 1-2 .333
1989-90 – 2-0 1.000
1991-92 – 6-3 .667
1992-93 – 2-3 .400
1993-94 – 0-1 .000
1994-95 – 0-2 .000
1995-96 – 0-2 .000
1997-98 – 1-1 .500
2005-06 – 4-2 .667
2006-07 – 7-3 .700
2007-08 – 5-1 .833
2008-09 – 6-1 .857
2009-10 – 4-2 .667
2014-15 – 7-3 .700
2015-16 – 9-1 .900
Overall – 63-31 (.670)

AWAY

1975-76 – 1-5 .167
1976-77 – 0-2 .000
1977-78 – 0-1 .000
1984-85 – 0-2 .000
1987-88 – 0-3 .000
1988-89 – 1-1 .500
1989-90 – 0-3 .000
1991-92 – 3-5 .375
1992-93 – 1-3 .250
1993-94 – 0-2 .000
1994-95 – 1-1 .500
1995-96 – 0-1 .000
1997-98 – 0-2 .000
2005-06 – 3-4 .429
2006-07 – 5-5 .500
2007-08 – 2-5 .286
2008-09 – 4-3 .571
2009-10 – 2-3 .400
2014-15 – 7-3 .700
2015-16 – 7-4 .636
Overall – 37-58 (.389)

COMPOSITE WIN-LOSS RECORDS VS. OTHER TEAMS, BEST TO WORST

SERIES

1. Atlanta	3-0	1.000
2. New Jersey	3-0	1.000
3. Toronto	1-0	1.000
4. Washington	4-1	.800
5. Detroit	3-1	.750
6. Golden State	1-1	.500
7. Boston	2-4	.333
8. Chicago	2-5	.286
9. Indiana	0-1	.000
10. Orlando	0-1	.000
11. Philadelphia	0-1	.000
12. San Antonio	0-1	.000
13. New York	0-3	.000

Overall – 19-19 (.500)

GAMES

1. Atlanta	12-0	1.000
2. Detroit	15-6	.714
3. New Jersey	10-5	.667
4. Toronto	4-2	.667
5. Washington	17-9	.654
6. Boston	16-18	.471
7. Golden State	6-7	.462
8. Chicago	14-20	.412
9. Philadelphia	2-3	.400
10. Orlando	2-4	.333
11. Indiana	1-3	.250
12. New York	1-8	.111
13. San Antonio	0-4	.000

Overall – 100-89 (.529)

OVERTIME GAMES

Washington 102, Cleveland 98 (Eastern Conference Semifinals, Game 6, April 26, 1976, at Was.)
Cleveland 108, Chicago 105 (Eastern Conference First Round, Game 4, May 5, 1989, at Chi.)
Cleveland 114, Boston 112 (Eastern Conference Semifinals, Game 4, May 10, 1992, at Bos.)
Chicago 95, Cleveland 92 (Eastern Conference First Round, Game 3, May 3, 1994, at Cle.)
Cleveland 121, Washington 120 (Eastern Conference First Round, Game 5, May 3, 2006, at Cle.)
Cleveland 114, Washington 113 (Eastern Conference First Round, Game 6, May 5, 2006, at Was.)
Cleveland 109, Detroit 107 (2OT) (Eastern Conference Finals, Game 5, May 31, 2007, at Det.)
Orlando 116, Cleveland 114 (Eastern Conference Finals, Game 4, May 26, 2009, at Orl.)

Cleveland 114, Atlanta 111 (Eastern Conference Finals, Game 3, May 24, 2015, at Cle.)
Golden State 108, Cleveland 100 (NBA Finals, Game 1, June 4, 2015, at G.S.)
Cleveland 95, Golden State 93 (NBA Finals, Game 2, June 7, 2015, at G.S.)
Overall Record – 7-4 (.636)

FIVE HIGHEST/LOWEST-SCORING GAMES

HIGHEST

1. 124 – Cleveland 124, Boston 95 (Eastern Conference Semifinals, Game 3, May 7, 2010, at Bos.)
2. 123 – Boston 126, Cleveland 123 (Eastern Conference First Round, Game 1, April 18, 1985, at Bos.)
3. Cleveland 123, Atlanta 98 (Eastern Conference Semifinals, Game 2, May 4, 2016, at Cle.)
4. 122 – Cleveland 122, Philadelphia 95 (Eastern Conference First Round, Game 3, May 1, 1990, at Cle.)
5. Cleveland 122, Boston 104 (Eastern Conference Semifinals, Game 7, May 17, 1992, at Cle.)

OPPONENTS HIGHEST

1. 132 – New York 132, Cleveland 114 (Eastern Conference First Round, Game 1, April 12, 1978, at Cle.)
2. 126 – Boston 126, Cleveland 123 (Eastern Conference First Round, Game 1, April 18, 1985, at Bos.)
3. 122 – Boston 122, Cleveland 91 (Eastern Conference Semifinals, Game 6, May 15, 1992, at Bos.)
4. 120 – Cleveland 121, Washington 120 (OT) (Eastern Conference First Round, Game 5, May 3, 2006, at Cle.)
5. Boston 120, Cleveland 88 (Eastern Conference Semifinals, Game 5, May 11, 2010, at Cle.)

LOWEST

1. 61 – Detroit 79, Cleveland 61 (Eastern Conference Semifinals, Game 7, May 21, 2006, at Det.)

2. 72 – New Jersey 83, Cleveland 72 (Eastern Conference Semifinals, Game 5, May 16, 2007, at Cle.)
3. San Antonio 75, Cleveland 72 (NBA Finals, Game 3, June 12, 2007, at Cle.)
4. Washington 108, Cleveland 72 (Eastern Conference First Round, Game 3, April 24, 2008, at Was.)
5. Boston 76, Cleveland 72 (Eastern Conference Semifinals, Game 1, May 6, 2008, at Bos.)

OPPONENTS LOWEST

1. 68 – Cleveland 79, Detroit 68 (Eastern Conference First Round, Game 3, April 24, 2009, at Det.)
2. 69 – Cleveland 74, Boston 69 (Eastern Conference Semifinals, Game 6, May 16, 2008, at Cle.)
3. 72 – Cleveland 74, Detroit 72 (Eastern Conference Semifinals, Game 4, May 15, 2006, at Cle.)
4. Cleveland 99, Atlanta 72 (Eastern Conference Semifinals, Game 1, May 5, 2009, at Cle.)
5. 73 – Cleveland 94, Chicago 73 (Eastern Conference Semifinals, Game 6, May 14, 2015, at Chi.)

HIGHEST BETWEEN BOTH TEAMS

1. 249 – Boston 126, Cleveland 123 (Eastern Conference First Round, Game 1, April 18, 1985, at Bos.)
2. 246 – New York 132, Cleveland 114 (Eastern Conference First Round, Game 1, April 12, 1978, at Cle.)
3. 241 – Cleveland 121, Washington 120 (OT) (Eastern Conference First Round, Game 5, May 3, 2006, at Cle.)
4. 233 – Cleveland 120, New Jersey 113 (Eastern Conference First Round, Game 1, April 23, 1992, at Cle.)
5. 232 – Boston 117, Cleveland 115 (Eastern Conference First Round, Game 4, April 25, 1985, at Cle.)

LOWEST BETWEEN BOTH TEAMS

1. 140 – Detroit 79, Cleveland 61 (Eastern Conference Semifinals, Game 7, May 21, 2006, at Det.)

2. 143 – Cleveland 74, Boston 69 (Eastern Conference Semifinals, Game 6, May 16, 2008, at Cle.)
3. 146 – Cleveland 74, Detroit 72 (Eastern Conference Semifinals, Game 4, May 15, 2006, at Cle.)
4. 147 – San Antonio 75, Cleveland 72 (NBA Finals, Game 3, June 12, 2007, at Cle.)
5. Cleveland 79, Detroit 68 (Eastern Conference First Round, Game 3, April 24, 2009, at Det.)

FIVE MOST ONE-SIDED GAMES

VICTORIES

1. 38 – Cleveland 116, Toronto 78 (Eastern Conference Finals, Game 5, May 25, 2016, at Cle.)
2. 31 – Cleveland 115, Toronto 84 (Eastern Conference Finals, Game 1, May 17, 2016, at Cle.)
3. 30 – Cleveland 116, Washington 86 (Eastern Conference First Round, Game 2, April 21, 2008, at Cle.)
4. Cleveland 118, Atlanta 88 (Eastern Conference Finals, Game 4, May 26, 2015, at Cle.)
5. Cleveland 120, Golden State 90 (NBA Finals, Game 3, June 8, 2016, at Cle.)

DEFEATS

1. 36 – Washington 108, Cleveland 72 (Eastern Conference First Round, Game 3, April 24, 2008, at Was.)
2. 33 – Golden State 110, Cleveland 77 (NBA Finals, Game 2, June 5, 2016, at G.S.)
3. 32 – Boston 120, Cleveland 88 (Eastern Conference Semifinals, Game 5, May 11, 2010, at Cle.)
4. 31 – Boston 122, Cleveland 91 (Eastern Conference Semifinals, Game 6, May 15, 1992, at Bos.)
5. 27 – Detroit 113, Cleveland 86 (Eastern Conference Semifinals, Game 1, May 7, 2006, at Det.)

ATTENDANCE STATISTICS

ARENA CAPACITIES

Cleveland Arena (1970-71 to 1973-74) – 11,000
The Coliseum (1974-75 to 1993-94) – 20,900 (1974-75 to 1987-88), 20,273 (1988-89 to 1993-94)
Gund Arena/Quicken Loans Arena (1994-95 to present) – 20,562

REGULAR SEASON

AVERAGE SEASON CROWDS, LARGEST TO SMALLEST

HOME

1. 20,562 (2009-10)
   (2014-15)
   (2015-16)
4. 20,512 (2008-09)
5. 20,465 (2007-08)
6. 20,436 (2006-07)
7. 20,338 (1994-95)
8. 20,112 (2010-11)
9. 19,327 (2005-06)
10. 19,128 (2004-05)
11. 18,383 (1993-94)
12. 18,329 (1992-93)
13. 18,288 (2003-04)
14. 17,827 (1988-89)
15. 17,807 (1995-96)
16. 17,330 (2013-14)
17. 16,969 (1989-90)
18. 16,942 (1997-98)
19. 16,895 (1996-97)
20. 16,522 (1991-92)
21. 16,192 (2012-13)
22. 15,927 (2011-12)
23. 15,873 (2000-01)
24. 15,217 (1990-91)
25. 14,724 (1999-2000)
26. 14,539 (2001-02)
27. 14,120 (1998-99)
28. 13,913 (1976-77)
29. 12,659 (1975-76)
30. 12,313 (1987-88)
31. 11,497 (2002-03)
32. 11,097 (1977-78)
33. 10,905 (1986-87)
34. 9,533 (1985-86)
35. 8,161 (1974-75)
36. 7,942 (1978-79)
37. 7,902 (1984-85)
38. 7,873 (1979-80)

39. 5,769 (1981-82)
40. 5,475 (1980-81)
41. 5,222 (1971-72)
42. 5,075 (1983-84)
43. 4,548 (1972-73)
44. 4,013 (1973-74)
45. 3,916 (1982-83)
46. 3,518 (1970-71)
Overall – 13,809

AWAY

1. 19,201 (2009-10)
2. 18,941 (2006-07)
3. 18,916 (2014-15)
4. 18,910 (2015-16)
5. 18,899 (2008-09)
6. 18,801 (2005-06)
7. 18,755 (2003-04)
8. 18,276 (2004-05)
9. 17,992 (2007-08)
10. 17,927 (1998-99)
11. 17,379 (2013-14)
12. 16,892 (1997-98)
13. 16,781 (2012-13)
14. 16,723 (2011-12)
15. 16,642 (1999-2000)
16. 16,620 (1995-96)
17. 16,455 (1996-97)
18. 16,200 (2010-11)
19. 16,088 (2002-03)
20. 16,064 (2000-01)
21. 15,975 (1988-89)
22. 15,809 (2001-02)
23. 15,688 (1993-94)
24. 15,683 (1994-95)
25. 15,496 (1991-92)
26. 15,485 (1992-93)
27. 15,288 (1989-90)
28. 14,788 (1990-91)
29. 12,893 (1987-88)
30. 11,631 (1986-87)
31. 11,562 (1976-77)
32. 10,821 (1985-86)
33. 10,560 (1977-78)
34. 10,059 (1978-79)
35. 9,633 (1984-85)
36. 9,587 (1979-80)
37. 9,557 (1975-76)
38. 9,057 (1980-81)
39. 8,873 (1983-84)
40. 8,611 (1981-82)
41. 8,411 (1982-83)
42. 7,703 (1973-74)
43. 7,660 (1974-75)
44. 7,431 (1972-73)
45. 6,849 (1971-72)
46. 5,905 (1970-71)
Overall – 13,989

LARGEST HOME CROWDS FOR EACH SEASON, HIGHEST TO LOWEST

1. 21,130 (1975-76 – February 8 vs. Washington)
2. 20,900 (1984-85 – March 15 vs. Boston)
(1985-86 – October 26 vs. Boston, December 20 vs. L.A. Lakers)
(1987-88 – January 23 vs. Boston)

5. 20,562 (1994-95 – 31 times)
(1995-96 – Nine times)
(1996-97 – Three times)
(1997-98 – Six times)
(1998-99 – March 18 vs. L.A. Lakers)
(1999-2000 – Six times)
(2000-01 – Four times)
(2001-02 – Three times)
(2002-03 – November 9 vs. Washington, April 8 vs. Washington)
(2003-04 – 16 times)
(2004-05 – 18 times)
(2005-06 – 17 times)
(2006-07 – 32 times)
(2007-08 – 33 times)
(2008-09 – 38 times)
(2009-10 – 41 times)
(2010-11 – 25 times)
(2011-12 – Three times)
(2012-13 – Six times)
(2013-14 – Five times)
(2014-15 – 41 times)
(2015-16 – 41 times)

27. 20,273 (1988-89 – April 18 vs. Detroit)
(1989-90 – Four times)
(1990-91 – Three times)
(1991-92 – Six times)
(1992-93 – 15 times)
(1993-94 – 12 times)

33. 20,239 (1974-75 – April 3 vs. New York)
34. 20,175 (1980-81 – March 27 vs. Philadelphia)
35. 20,103 (1986-87 – January 24 vs. Chicago)
36. 19,912 (1979-80 – March 22 vs. Boston)
37. 19,783 (1976-77 – October 22 vs. Chicago)
38. 19,548 (1977-78 – December 27 vs. New Orleans)
39. 15,209 (1978-79 – March 17 vs. Washington)
40. 14,517 (1983-84 – February 23 vs. Philadelphia)
41. 13,457 (1981-82 – January 2 vs. Boston)
42. 11,270 (1982-83 – January 6 vs. Los Angeles)
43. 11,178 (1971-72 – January 5 vs. Los Angeles)

44. 11,044 (1972-73 – February 4 vs. New York)
45. 9,149 (1973-74 – November 9 vs. Houston)
46. 8,429 (1970-71 – February 17 vs. Chicago)

FIVE LARGEST HOME CROWDS

CLEVELAND ARENA

1. 11,178	Los Angeles 113, Cleveland 103 (January 5, 1972)
2. 11,044	New York 114, Cleveland 97 (February 4, 1973)
3. 10,819	Cleveland 124, Los Angeles 120 (March 22, 1972)
4. 10,409	Boston 105, Cleveland 92 (February 25, 1973)
5. 10,289	Cincinnati 135, Cleveland 122 (March 26, 1972)

THE COLISEUM

1. 21,130	Cleveland 83, Washington 78 (February 8, 1976)
2. 20,900	Boston 119, Cleveland 96 (March 15, 1985)
	Boston 105, Cleveland 100 (October 26, 1985)
	L.A. Lakers 128, Cleveland 116 (December 20, 1985)
	Cleveland 119, Boston 100 (January 23, 1988)

GUND ARENA/QUICKEN LOANS ARENA

20,562	381 times

NEUTRAL-SITE CROWDS, LARGEST TO SMALLEST

1. 7,820	Baltimore 108, Cleveland 98 (November 4, 1972, at College Park, MD)
2. 7,391	Cleveland 103, Philadelphia 102 (December 29, 1971, at Hershey, PA)
3. 7,187	Buffalo 104, Cleveland 97 (October 26, 1973, at Toronto)
4. 6,487	Milwaukee 118, Cleveland 100 (February 20, 1973, at Madison, WI)
5. 6,321	Boston 111, Cleveland 92 (December 29, 1973, at Providence, RI)
6. 4,682	Cleveland 113, Philadelphia 109 (2OT) (January 12, 1973, at Pittsburgh)

7. 4,523	Cleveland 118, Houston 100 (March 7, 1973, at San Antonio)
8. 3,980	Cincinnati 128, Cleveland 108 (January 16, 1972, at Las Cruces, NM)
9. 3,027	Cleveland 109, Baltimore 101 (October 23, 1971, at College Park, MD)
10. 1,471	Cleveland 111, Buffalo 79 (January 19, 1971, at Syracuse, NY)
11. 1,373	Cleveland 101, Buffalo 91 (February 2, 1971, at Rochester, NY)

POSTSEASON

CROWDS, LARGEST TO SMALLEST

HOME

1. 21,564	Cleveland 87, Washington 85 (Eastern Conference Semifinals, Game 7, April 29, 1976)
	Cleveland 83, Boston 78 (Eastern Conference Finals, Game 3, May 11, 1976)
	Cleveland 106, Boston 87 (Eastern Conference Finals, Game 4, May 14, 1976)
	Boston 94, Cleveland 87 (Eastern Conference Finals, Game 6, May 18, 1976)
5. 21,312	Cleveland 92, Washington 91 (Eastern Conference Semifinals, Game 5, April 22, 1976)
6. 21,061	Cleveland 88, Washington 76 (Eastern Conference Semifinals, Game 3, April 17, 1976)
7. 20,900	Cleveland 105, Boston 98 (Eastern Conference First Round, Game 3, April 23, 1985)
	Boston 117, Cleveland 115 (Eastern Conference First Round, Game 4, April 25, 1985)
9. 20,562	Cleveland 97, Washington 86 (Eastern Conference First Round, Game 1, April 22, 2006)
	Washington 89, Cleveland 84 (Eastern Conference First Round, Game 2, April 25, 2006)
	Cleveland 121, Washington 120 (OT) (Eastern Conference First Round, Game 5, May 3, 2006)

Cleveland 86, Detroit 77 (Eastern Conference Semifinals, Game 3, May 13, 2006)
Cleveland 74, Detroit 72 (Eastern Conference Semifinals, Game 4, May 15, 2006)
Detroit 84, Cleveland 82 (Eastern Conference Semifinals, Game 6, May 19, 2006)
Cleveland 97, Washington 82 (Eastern Conference First Round, Game 1, April 22, 2007)
Cleveland 109, Washington 102 (Eastern Conference First Round, Game 2, April 25, 2007)
Cleveland 81, New Jersey 77 (Eastern Conference Semifinals, Game 1, May 6, 2007)
Cleveland 102, New Jersey 92 (Eastern Conference Semifinals, Game 2, May 8, 2007)
New Jersey 83, Cleveland 72 (Eastern Conference Semifinals, Game 5, May 16, 2007)
Cleveland 88, Detroit 82 (Eastern Conference Finals, Game 3, May 27, 2007)
Cleveland 91, Detroit 87 (Eastern Conference Finals, Game 4, May 29, 2007)
Cleveland 98, Detroit 82 (Eastern Conference Finals, Game 6, June 2, 2007)
San Antonio 75, Cleveland 72 (NBA Finals, Game 3, June 12, 2007)
San Antonio 83, Cleveland 82 (NBA Finals, Game 4, June 14, 2007)
Cleveland 93, Washington 86 (Eastern Conference First Round, Game 1, April 19, 2008)
Cleveland 116, Washington 86 (Eastern Conference First Round, Game 2, April 21, 2008)
Washington 88, Cleveland 87 (Eastern Conference First Round, Game 5, April 30, 2008)
Cleveland 108, Boston 84 (Eastern Conference Semifinals, Game 3, May 10, 2008)
Cleveland 88, Boston 77 (Eastern Conference Semifinals, Game 4, May 12, 2008)
Cleveland 74, Boston 69 (Eastern Conference Semifinals, Game 6, May 16, 2008)

Cleveland 102, Detroit 84 (Eastern Conference First Round, Game 1, April 18, 2009)
Cleveland 94, Detroit 82 (Eastern Conference First Round, Game 2, April 21, 2009)
Cleveland 99, Atlanta 72 (Eastern Conference Semifinals, Game 1, May 5, 2009)
Cleveland 105, Atlanta 85 (Eastern Conference Semifinals, Game 2, May 7, 2009)
Orlando 107, Cleveland 106 (Eastern Conference Finals, Game 1, May 20, 2009)
Cleveland 96, Orlando 95 (Eastern Conference Finals, Game 2, May 22, 2009)
Cleveland 112, Orlando 102 (Eastern Conference Finals, Game 5, May 28, 2009)
Cleveland 96, Chicago 83 (Eastern Conference First Round, Game 1, April 17, 2010)
Cleveland 112, Chicago 102 (Eastern Conference First Round, Game 2, April 19, 2010)
Cleveland 96, Chicago 94 (Eastern Conference First Round, Game 5, April 27, 2010)
Cleveland 101, Boston 93 (Eastern Conference Semifinals, Game 1, May 1, 2010)
Boston 104, Cleveland 86 (Eastern Conference Semifinals, Game 2, May 3, 2010)
Boston 120, Cleveland 88 (Eastern Conference Semifinals, Game 5, May 11, 2010)
Cleveland 113, Boston 100 (Eastern Conference First Round, Game 1, April 19, 2015)
Cleveland 99, Boston 91 (Eastern Conference First Round, Game 2, April 21, 2015)
Chicago 99, Cleveland 92 (Eastern Conference Semifinals, Game 1, May 4, 2015)
Cleveland 106, Chicago 91 (Eastern Conference Semifinals, Game 2, May 6, 2015)
Cleveland 106, Chicago 101 (Eastern Conference Semifinals, Game 5, May 12, 2015)
Cleveland 114, Atlanta 111 (OT) (Eastern Conference Finals, Game 3, May 24, 2015)

Cleveland 118, Atlanta 88 (Eastern Conference Finals, Game 4, May 26, 2015)
Cleveland 96, Golden State 91 (NBA Finals, Game 3, June 9, 2015)
Golden State 103, Cleveland 82 (NBA Finals, Game 4, June 11, 2015)
Golden State 105, Cleveland 97 (NBA Finals, Game 6, June 16, 2015)
Cleveland 106, Detroit 101 (Eastern Conference First Round, Game 1, April 17, 2016)
Cleveland 107, Detroit 90 (Eastern Conference First Round, Game 2, April 20, 2016)
Cleveland 104, Atlanta 93 (Eastern Conference Semifinals, Game 1, May 2, 2016)
Cleveland 123, Atlanta 98 (Eastern Conference Semifinals, Game 2, May 4, 2016)
Cleveland 115, Toronto 84 (Eastern Conference Finals, Game 1, May 17, 2016)
Cleveland 108, Toronto 89 (Eastern Conference Finals, Game 2, May 19, 2016)
Cleveland 116, Toronto 78 (Eastern Conference Finals, Game 5, May 25, 2016)
Cleveland 120, Golden State 90 (NBA Finals, Game 3, June 8, 2016)
Golden State 108, Cleveland 97 (NBA Finals, Game 4, June 10, 2016)
Cleveland 115, Golden State 101 (NBA Finals, Game 6, June 16, 2016)

64. 20,273 Cleveland 96, Chicago 88 (Eastern Conference First Round, Game 2, April 30, 1989)
Chicago 101, Cleveland 100 (Eastern Conference First Round, Game 5, May 7, 1989)
Cleveland 118, New Jersey 96 (Eastern Conference First Round, Game 2, April 25, 1992)
Boston 104, Cleveland 98 (Eastern Conference Semifinals, Game 2, May 4, 1992)
Cleveland 114, Boston 98 (Eastern Conference Semifinals, Game 5, May 13, 1992)

	Cleveland 122, Boston 104 (Eastern Conference Semifinals, Game 7, May 17, 1992)
	Chicago 105, Cleveland 96 (Eastern Conference Finals, Game 3, May 23, 1992)
	Cleveland 99, Chicago 85 (Eastern Conference Finals, Game 4, May 25, 1992)
	Chicago 99, Cleveland 94 (Eastern Conference Finals, Game 6, May 29, 1992)
	New Jersey 101, Cleveland 99 (Eastern Conference First Round, Game 2, May 1, 1993)
	Chicago 96, Cleveland 90 (Eastern Conference Semifinals, Game 3, May 15, 1993)
	Chicago 103, Cleveland 101 (Eastern Conference Semifinals, Game 4, May 17, 1993)
76. 20,068	Cleveland 110, Chicago 102 (Eastern Conference First Round, Game 3, May 3, 1988)
77. 20,026	Cleveland 97, Chicago 91 (Eastern Conference First Round, Game 4, May 5, 1988)
78. 19,974	Washington 100, Cleveland 95 (Eastern Conference Semifinals, Game 1, April 13, 1976)
79. 19,739	New York 132, Cleveland 114 (Eastern Conference First Round, Game 1, April 12, 1978)
80. 19,545	Cleveland 91, Washington 83 (Eastern Conference First Round, Game 2, April 15, 1977)
81. 19,352	New York 83, Cleveland 81 (Eastern Conference First Round, Game 3, May 1, 1995)
82. 19,312	Chicago 95, Cleveland 88 (Eastern Conference First Round, Game 1, April 28, 1989)
83. 18,575	New York 93, Cleveland 80 (Eastern Conference First Round, Game 4, May 4, 1995)
84. 18,339	Cleveland 114, New Jersey 98 (Eastern Conference First Round, Game 1, April 29, 1993)
85. 18,188	Indiana 80, Cleveland 74 (Eastern Conference First Round, Game 4, April 30, 1998)
86. 17,778	Chicago 95, Cleveland 92 (OT) (Eastern Conference First Round, Game 3, May 3, 1994)
87. 17,496	Cleveland 101, Boston 76 (Eastern Conference Semifinals, Game 1, May 2, 1992)

88. 17,495	Cleveland 86, Indiana 77 (Eastern Conference First Round, Game 3, April 27, 1998)
89. 17,388	Cleveland 99, New Jersey 89 (Eastern Conference First Round, Game 5, May 9, 1993)
90. 17,232	New York 84, Cleveland 80 (Eastern Conference First Round, Game 2, April 27, 1996)
91. 17,106	Cleveland 108, Philadelphia 96 (Eastern Conference First Round, Game 4, May 3, 1990)
92. 16,512	Cleveland 120, New Jersey 113 (Eastern Conference First Round, Game 1, April 23, 1992)
93. 16,419	New York 106, Cleveland 83 (Eastern Conference First Round, Game 1, April 25, 1996)
94. 16,317	Cleveland 122, Philadelphia 95 (Eastern Conference First Round, Game 3, May 1, 1990)

AWAY

1. 23,058	Cleveland 121, Chicago 98 (Eastern Conference First Round, Game 4, April 25, 2010)
2. 22,991	Chicago 108, Cleveland 106 (Eastern Conference First Round, Game 3, April 22, 2010)
3. 22,695	Cleveland 94, Chicago 73 (Eastern Conference Semifinals, Game 6, May 14, 2015)
4. 22,256	Cleveland 86, Chicago 84 (Eastern Conference Semifinals, Game 4, May 10, 2015)
5. 22,246	Chicago 99, Cleveland 96 (Eastern Conference Semifinals, Game 3, May 8, 2015)
6. 22,076	Detroit 113, Cleveland 86 (Eastern Conference Semifinals, Game 1, May 7, 2006)
	Detroit 97, Cleveland 91 (Eastern Conference Semifinals, Game 2, May 9, 2006)
	Cleveland 86, Detroit 84 (Eastern Conference Semifinals, Game 5, May 17, 2006)
	Detroit 79, Cleveland 61 (Eastern Conference Semifinals, Game 7, May 21, 2006)
	Detroit 79, Cleveland 76 (Eastern Conference Finals, Game 1, May 21, 2007)

	Detroit 79, Cleveland 76 (Eastern Conference Finals, Game 2, May 24, 2007)
	Cleveland 109, Detroit 107 (2OT) (Eastern Conference Finals, Game 5, May 31, 2007)
	Cleveland 79, Detroit 68 (Eastern Conference First Round, Game 3, April 24, 2009)
	Cleveland 99, Detroit 78 (Eastern Conference First Round, Game 4, April 26, 2009)
15. 21,584	Cleveland 101, Detroit 91 (Eastern Conference First Round, Game 3, April 22, 2016)
	Cleveland 100, Detroit 98 (Eastern Conference First Round, Game 4, April 24, 2016)
17. 20,605	Cleveland 113, Toronto 87 (Eastern Conference Finals, Game 6, May 27, 2016)
18. 20,367	Toronto 105, Cleveland 99 (Eastern Conference Finals, Game 4, May 23, 2016)
19. 20,207	Toronto 99, Cleveland 84 (Eastern Conference Finals, Game 3, May 21, 2016)
20. 20,173	Cleveland 97, Washington 96 (Eastern Conference First Round, Game 3, April 28, 2006)
	Washington 106, Cleveland 96 (Eastern Conference First Round, Game 4, April 30, 2006)
	Cleveland 114, Washington 113 (OT) (Eastern Conference First Round, Game 6, May 5, 2006)
	Cleveland 98, Washington 92 (Eastern Conference First Round, Game 3, April 28, 2007)
	Cleveland 97, Washington 90 (Eastern Conference First Round, Game 4, April 30, 2007)
	Washington 108, Cleveland 72 (Eastern Conference First Round, Game 3, April 24, 2008)
	Cleveland 100, Washington 97 (Eastern Conference First Round, Game 4, April 27, 2008)
	Cleveland 105, Washington 88 (Eastern Conference First Round, Game 6, May 2, 2008)
28. 20,143	Cleveland 97, Atlanta 82 (Eastern Conference Semifinals, Game 3, May 9, 2009)
29. 20,032	New Jersey 96, Cleveland 85 (Eastern Conference Semifinals, Game 3, May 12, 2007)

	Cleveland 87, New Jersey 85 (Eastern Conference Semifinals, Game 4, May 14, 2007)
	Cleveland 88, New Jersey 72 (Eastern Conference Semifinals, Game 6, May 18, 2007)
32. 19,763	New York 103, Cleveland 79 (Eastern Conference First Round, Game 1, April 27, 1995)
	Cleveland 90, New York 84 (Eastern Conference First Round, Game 2, April 29, 1995)
	New York 81, Cleveland 76 (Eastern Conference First Round, Game 3, May 1, 1996)
35. 19,596	Golden State 108, Cleveland 100 (OT) (NBA Finals, Game 1, June 4, 2015)
	Cleveland 95, Golden State 93 (OT) (NBA Finals, Game 2, June 7, 2015)
	Golden State 104, Cleveland 91 (NBA Finals, Game 5, June 14, 2015)
	Golden State 104, Cleveland 89 (NBA Finals, Game 1, June 2, 2016)
	Golden State 110, Cleveland 77 (NBA Finals, Game 2, June 5, 2016)
	Cleveland 112, Golden State 97 (NBA Finals, Game 5, June 13, 2016)
	Cleveland 93, Golden State 89 (NBA Finals, Game 7, June 19, 2016)
42. 19,241	Cleveland 84, Atlanta 74 (Eastern Conference Semifinals, Game 4, May 11, 2009)
43. 19,089	Cleveland 121, Atlanta 108 (Eastern Conference Semifinals, Game 3, May 6, 2016)
44. 19,035	Washington 102, Cleveland 98 (OT) (Eastern Conference Semifinals, Game 6, April 26, 1976)
45. 19,031	Cleveland 100, Atlanta 99 (Eastern Conference Semifinals, Game 4, May 8, 2016)
46. 18,965	New York 109, Cleveland 107 (Eastern Conference First Round, Game 2, April 14, 1978)
47. 18,797	San Antonio 85, Cleveland 76 (NBA Finals, Game 1, June 7, 2007)
	San Antonio 103, Cleveland 92 (NBA Finals, Game 2, June 10, 2007)

49. 18,676	Chicago 104, Cleveland 93 (Eastern Conference First Round, Game 1, April 28, 1988)
	Chicago 103, Cleveland 89 (Eastern Conference Finals, Game 1, May 19, 1992)
	Cleveland 107, Chicago 81 (Eastern Conference Finals, Game 2, May 21, 1992)
	Chicago 112, Cleveland 89 (Eastern Conference Finals, Game 5, May 27, 1992)
	Chicago 91, Cleveland 84 (Eastern Conference Semifinals, Game 1, May 11, 1993)
	Chicago 104, Cleveland 85 (Eastern Conference Semifinals, Game 2, May 13, 1993)
	Chicago 104, Cleveland 96 (Eastern Conference First Round, Game 1, April 29, 1994)
	Chicago 105, Cleveland 96 (Eastern Conference First Round, Game 2, May 1, 1994)
57. 18,670	Cleveland 94, Atlanta 82 (Eastern Conference Finals, Game 2, May 22, 2015)
58. 18,645	Chicago 106, Cleveland 101 (Eastern Conference First Round, Game 2, May 1, 1988)
59. 18,624	Boston 76, Cleveland 72 (Eastern Conference Semifinals, Game 1, May 6, 2008)
	Boston 89, Cleveland 73 (Eastern Conference Semifinals, Game 2, May 8, 2008)
	Boston 96, Cleveland 89 (Eastern Conference Semifinals, Game 5, May 14, 2008)
	Boston 97, Cleveland 92 (Eastern Conference Semifinals, Game 7, May 18, 2008)
	Cleveland 124, Boston 95 (Eastern Conference Semifinals, Game 3, May 7, 2010)
	Boston 97, Cleveland 87 (Eastern Conference Semifinals, Game 4, May 9, 2010)
	Boston 94, Cleveland 85 (Eastern Conference Semifinals, Game 6, May 13, 2010)
	Cleveland 103, Boston 95 (Eastern Conference First Round, Game 3, April 23, 2015)
	Cleveland 101, Boston 93 (Eastern Conference First Round, Game 4, April 26, 2015)

68. 18,489	Cleveland 97, Atlanta 89 (Eastern Conference Finals, Game 1, May 20, 2015)
69. 18,264	Cleveland 108, Chicago 105 (OT) (Eastern Conference First Round, Game 4, May 5, 1989)
70. 18,168	Philadelphia 107, Cleveland 101 (Eastern Conference First Round, Game 2, April 28, 1990)
	Philadelphia 113, Cleveland 97 (Eastern Conference First Round, Game 5, May 5, 1990)
72. 18,008	Chicago 107, Cleveland 101 (Eastern Conference First Round, Game 5, May 8, 1988)
73. 17,988	Cleveland 80, Washington 79 (Eastern Conference Semifinals, Game 2, April 15, 1976)
74. 17,721	Chicago 101, Cleveland 94 (Eastern Conference First Round, Game 3, May 3, 1989)
75. 17,542	Washington 109, Cleveland 98 (Eastern Conference Semifinals, Game 4, April 21, 1976)
76. 17,461	Orlando 99, Cleveland 89 (Eastern Conference Finals, Game 3, May 24, 2009)
	Orlando 116, Cleveland 114 (OT) (Eastern Conference Finals, Game 4, May 26, 2009)
	Orlando 103, Cleveland 90 (Eastern Conference Finals, Game 6, May 30, 2009)
79. 16,644	Indiana 106, Cleveland 77 (Eastern Conference First Round, Game 1, April 23, 1998)
80. 16,617	Indiana 92, Cleveland 86 (Eastern Conference First Round, Game 2, April 25, 1998)
81. 16,453	Cleveland 93, New Jersey 84 (Eastern Conference First Round, Game 3, May 5, 1993)
82. 15,319	Philadelphia 111, Cleveland 106 (Eastern Conference First Round, Game 1, April 26, 1990)
83. 15,258	New Jersey 109, Cleveland 104 (Eastern Conference First Round, Game 3, April 28, 1992)
84. 15,238	New Jersey 96, Cleveland 79 (Eastern Conference First Round, Game 4, May 7, 1993)
85. 14,890	Boston 126, Cleveland 123 (Eastern Conference First Round, Game 1, April 18, 1985)
	Boston 108, Cleveland 106 (Eastern Conference First Round, Game 2, April 20, 1985)

	Boston 110, Cleveland 107 (Eastern Conference Semifinals, Game 3, May 8, 1992)
	Cleveland 114, Boston 112 (OT) (Eastern Conference Semifinals, Game 4, May 10, 1992)
	Boston 122, Cleveland 91 (Eastern Conference Semifinals, Game 6, May 15, 1992)
90. 14,264	Boston 111, Cleveland 99 (Eastern Conference Finals, Game 1, May 6, 1976)
91. 13,071	Cleveland 98, New Jersey 89 (Eastern Conference First Round, Game 4, April 30, 1992)
92. 12,951	Boston 99, Cleveland 94 (Eastern Conference Finals, Game 5, May 16, 1976)
93. 12,098	Boston 94, Cleveland 89 (Eastern Conference Finals, Game 2, May 9, 1976)
94. 11,240	Washington 109, Cleveland 100 (Eastern Conference First Round, Game 1, April 13, 1977)
95. 10,488	Washington 104, Cleveland 98 (Eastern Conference First Round, Game 3, April 17, 1977)

ACKNOWLEDGMENTS

I would like to thank Niels Aaboe of Skyhorse Publishing for giving me the opportunity to write this book, and everyone else there for their assistance. I would also like to thank AndersonsClevelandDesign.com and The Cleveland Press Collection in the Michael Schwartz Library at Cleveland State University for providing photos. Special thanks to World B. Free for writing the foreword.